ATLAS OF WORLD INTERIORS

DESIGN MEDIA PUBLISHING LIMITED

Preface

In the past five years, the globalised trend of interior design has seemingly been led by the five cities renowned as the cities of design, including Tokyo, Paris, Milan, London and New York. At the same time, it has become a common realisation of designers around the world to explore and employ the local features for each project with the advancement of economy and culture.

The book, *Atlas of world Interiors*, with 500 projects selected, is a detailed and comprehensive portrayal of the best and latest interior projects from six continents of more than fifty countries. In detail, the projects are of different styles, such as the pragmatism of North America, the naturalism of South America, the regionalism of Asia, the minimalism of North Europe and the luxurism of the Mediterranean area. In countries such as Iran, United Arab Emirates, South Africa, Morocco, and Tunisia, the history and culture of a particular location was subtly integrated into the interior design through innovative approaches. Moreover, designers can also be inspired a lot by this book to search a balance between the overwhelmingly globalised trend and the increasingly personalised feature.

This book offers readers a visual feast with the collection of world's most classic interior projects and is categorised into ten parts, including Culture and Leisure, Restaurants and Bars, Shops and Showrooms, Sport and Spa, Hotels, Research and Teaching, Office and Administration, Hospitals and Clinics, Houses, Traffic and Industrial. Each project is illustrated with photos, plans and a text. In addition, each geographic region is distinguished by a different colour-code. We firmly believe and hope it will serve as a source of pleasure and inspiration to all its readers.

As one of the series books *Atlas of world Interiors*, this book is featured with its timeliness, globalisation, regionalisation, and professionalisation to help readers from all over the world to find inspiration, and approach new materials and the cultural heritage.

Locations of the selected projects of *Atlas of World Interiors*

1. Canada
2. USA
3. Mexico
4. Peru
5. Chile
6. Brazil
7. Iceland
8. Norway
9. Sweden

10. Finland
11. Russia
12. UK
13. Denmark
14. Germany
15. Poland
16. Portugal
17. Spain
18. France

19. The Netherlands
20. Belgium
21. Switzerland
22. Italy
23. Czech Republic
24. Austria
25. Croatia
26. Slovakia
27. Hungary

Contents

Ten categories: Culture and Leisure, Restaurants and Bars, Shops and Showrooms, Sport and Spa, Hotels, Research and Teaching, Office and Administration, Hospitals and Clinics, Houses, Traffic and Industrial

Six continents: Europe/Asia/North America/South America/Oceania/Africa

Oceania

AGF Management Head Office

This renewal project included department space's reorganisation, creating distinctive identities for each division of their business, improving work flow, enhancing teaming opportunities, better utilisation of common facilities, and rationalisation of circulation. The challenge in this project was to meet the aggressive schedule and achieve a minimum amount of disruption to the work environment. The 3 floors of AGF were occupied during the entire renovation and only some departments were relocated off-site during construction. A 14-phase move strategy was implemented to allow this to happen seamlessly.

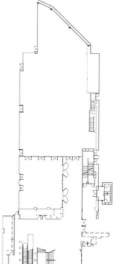

Flow

This former tired outpost of a European restaurant chain was remarkably transformed for a new tenant. Pale stone, rich woods, custom glass and a signature striped fabric and wall covering created an uncluttered, approachable ambience. The new restaurant/lounge quickly became the preferred destination in its upscale shopping neighbourhood.

Pacific Shores Resort & Spa

The spa was designed to create the perfect place, which escapes from the ordinary with the exotic mystique of the Far East. Stone floors mixed with Bamboo flooring works in perfect harmony. World renowned Bronze Artist was commissioned for the Feature Wall which displays a slate and granite water wall with Patina bronzed kelp sculpture. The lobby is the introduction to the Zen-inspired decoration. The furnishings chosen have clean lines so as not to conflict with the artful features and to provide a feeling of openness. A double-sided fireplace in the lounge with granite top tables and bar, custom leather seating greets the guests.

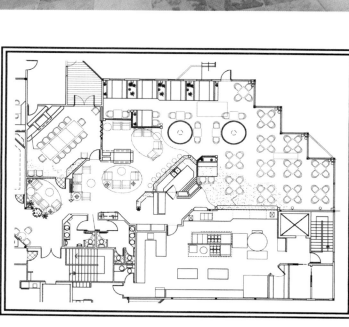

Agnico Eagle Mines Offices

Agnico-Eagle Mines (AEM) is an international company focused on gold, with operations in Canada, Mexico, Finland and the USA. Their LaRonde Mine in Quebec is Canada's largest gold deposit. The design makes subtle references to AEM's core business. At the reception area, the back wall is composed of smooth slabs of horizontally grained travertine that abstractly evoke the geological strata of a mine. Embedded into the wall are random strips of gold coloured bars. A glass display case is also contained within the wall to showcase chunks of the raw mining material. This wall rises up two floors where the slab was cut open to accommodate an open stair that leads to the main boardroom.

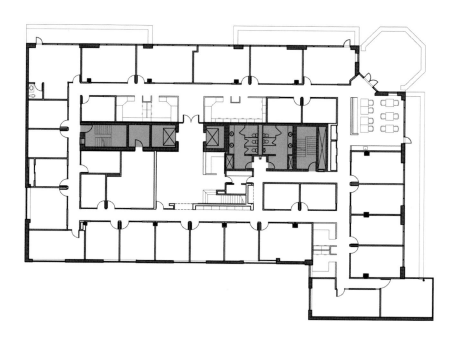

Photo: Ben Rahn/A-Frame

Michael Taylor (Partner-in-Charge), Brian Harmer (Project Manager), Pochi Lu (Team Member) and Joanne Pukier (Team Member)

11

Science Complex, University of Guelph

Providing an architectonic representation of science in a harmonious relationship with the existing campus was always a prime goal, as was the integration of the project within the fabric of the University. The existing architecture on campus is of an eclectic nature, and the Science Complex responds with a similar massing to fit into the campus' long-range development plan, first established in 1964. Using traditional materials and providing a balanced blend of stone, brick, metal, glass, and articulated fenestration, the scale of the complex also relates to that of its neighbours.

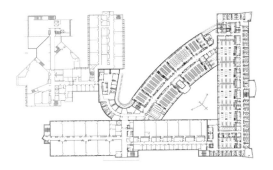

Photo: Philip Castleton

Robbie Young + Wright / IBI Group Architects

Photo: Steven Evans

Robbie Young + Wright / IBI Group Architects

Schulich School of Business and Executive Learning Centre

From the indoor entrance to the building, there is a glimpse into the main space of a spectacular three-storey space typified by concrete walls, parapets and columns. This space has a grand stair connecting the floors, promoting a sense of community and allowing for access to all parts of the building. Circulation is routed through this space. The architecture of the space is sufficiently strong to allow for a variety of informal flexible arrangements of chairs and tables.

Rain

The first challenge was to solve the planning issues, especially, to create an appropriate entrance. The original opening to the leased space was at the corner of the building, quite distant from the building's striking stone-arched main entrance. The designers won Historical Board approval to close the secondary doorway and modify the primary entrance and lobby area. Inside the traditional Victorian oak doors, the designers created a new divided vestibule with a security to the office building and a stunning new passageway leading to Rain itself. To the right, a glossy pebble-finished wall rises above a steel trough of river rocks and bears simple acrylic cut-outs of the restaurant's logo elements.

Bohemian Embassy Bedroom Model Suite

This generously proportioned model suite was designed in a sophisticated urban style, with a serene palette of warm greys and driftwood providing an elegant backdrop for artwork. Stylish modern fittings and furnishings are balanced with unexpected traditional details and accessories that suggest a creative spirit and artistic lifestyle that inform this new component of a distinctively creative urban community. The main living and dining groups of classic contemporary furnishings are defined by a dense, grey plush wool area rug and lit by a sparkling pendant fixture of small mirrored discs. The combination of modern and traditional continues into the white marble clad master bath.

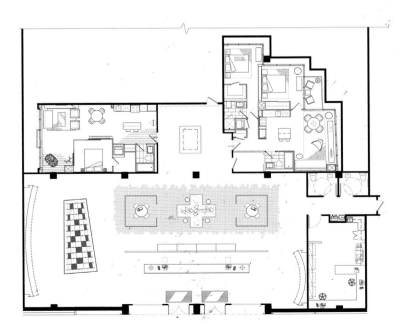

ZONE AD – CJM

The objectives of the room, to be used by children and their parents, were to be exciting, playful, ergonomic, and of course colourful. Based on a conceptual jungle, the room comes to life and the users are transported in a new world, as they are observed through the looking glass. The various storage facilities were to be an integral part of the concept design as well as being functional for daily activities. The lighting design had to be variable, to accommodate the age group using the room. Furthermore, the design accessories, such as the wall mounted leafs were to enhance the concept and define the various zones.

Photo: Jasmin Frechette

Jasmin Frechette, Chantal McDuff

Lab Oratoire

A two-storey fit-out of a base-building, this project consists in designing an administration section on the ground floor and a medical/dental facility on the second floor. The second floor, the lab area, is composed of 30 work stations, ergonomically designed for each user, all divided by colourful fabric walls, a reception area and some technical rooms. The lighting for the entire project had to respect the demanding client's specifications, especially for the second floor lab area, and also had to be energy effective and low maintenance. Within the special lab areas, such as the plaster room, once again, an ergonomic approach was created, as well as being hi-tech.

Culture Centre

The expansion of The Nelson Atkins Museum of Art fuses architecture with landscape to create an experiential building. The new addition, named the Bloch Building, engages the existing sculpture garden, transforming the entire Museum site into the precinct of the visitor's experience. The new addition extends along the eastern edge of the campus, traversing from the existing building through the Sculpture Park to form new spaces and angles of vision. The integrative design concept combines architecture, interior design, graphic design and landscape architecture into a complex aesthetic entity.

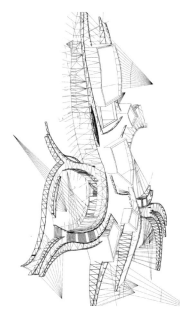

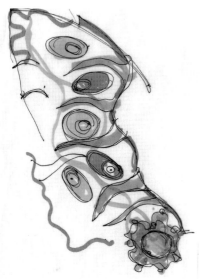

The Georgia Aquarium

Due to the landlocked location and lack of a body of water in Atlanta, the design team was challenged to create an uncommon water experience in Atlanta. Blue terrazzo flooring with Mother of Pearl aggregate catches the light and creates an underwater "sparkling" experience. A water feature at the rotunda provides a feeling of movement. Elevated seating areas or "lily pads" act as a place of rest and also connect the plaza space to the "shore line" where the Georgia, River and Coldwater exhibits are located. The Plaza is a dynamic space all on its own. The concept of the Plaza is similar to that of a mall in a sense that the exhibit galleries feed off this large, central area.

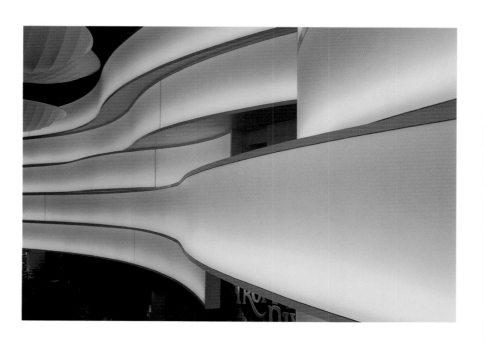

Temple

Facing the street there are few little apertures that provide low light and a subtle union with the exterior. Two big steel covers keep the main interior spaces detached from the street and they are the expressive elements of the façades. This new form takes with freedom the urban landscape in function of the programme. Simple concrete walls and steel columns are the main house structure, and over this structure steel joists hold the foils of the cover. The access is marked by cross of a curve solid concrete wall and a white wall beard by the first in a perfect balance.

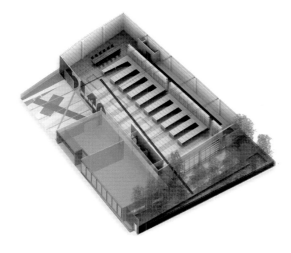

Lehrer Architects LA

The project included succinct interventions, such as blowing out the southern wall, creating 1220mmx2440mm work surfaces of white-painted solid core doors, finishing floors with epoxy, installing off-the-shelf storage systems, painting a dramatic red line along the floor to resolve the trapezoidal shape of the space, and creating a strategic landscape design. The office would specifically house architects and they designed a multipurpose working space that simply and clearly honours the rudiments of work: vast work surfaces, massive natural light, seamless connections to the landscape and fresh air, generous storage, and clearly individuated workstations add up to a coherent, palpable group.

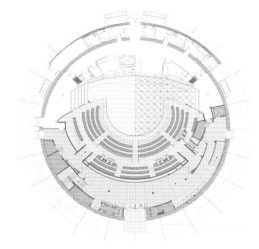

Mark Taper Forum

The architects fully enhanced the interior spaces with modern amenities for patrons and expanded the backstage areas for the actors and production teams. While maintaining the footprint of the original 1967 building, the architects cleverly carved out "found space" within the facility to better serve patrons and crew. From the newly configured entrance into the lobby that showcases an original Tony Duquette mural, to the auditorium with all-new seating, and the expansive lower-level lounge addition that provides patrons with larger restroom facilities, the architects successfully upgraded the space and added accommodations for disabled patrons. The multidisciplinary firm worked closely with the client to design new environmental graphics, including donor recognition walls and plaques, and all interior and exterior wayfinding signage to seamlessly complement the design of the theatre.

Kenny Schachter's Contemporary Gallery

The gallery is part of the gallery-dealers' home: a steel wall passes from outside to inside, which hinges to make a door, and splits & warps into window-shutters & reception desk. Since the gallery is only temporary, the walls aren't renovated but only "screened": they're expanded metal; you don't have to make holes in the walls since they are all holes. They fold into seats & sculpture stands -- twist into ceilings that carry fluorescent light across the room. The wall of the children's play-room twists to make a video screen inside the gallery, and the sounds of screaming children drift over the wall...

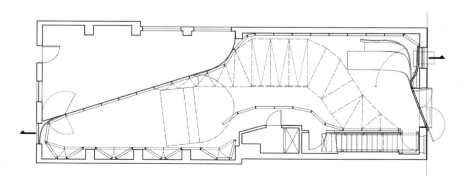

2101 Wilshire Offices

The design reflects the nature of spiritual learning in its symbolic evocation of light descending, in the way it embraces the creative tension that moves one to learn and grow, and in the way it reflects the qualities of balance, peace, and harmony. Furthermore, the solution strives for a clear expression of each part, such that each part is a whole unto itself, yet simultaneously a part of the greater whole. Illuminated translucent planes make their way to the interior where translucent panels are used as artificial or natural light diffusers. Inside, a new, expanded lobby becomes the central hub of circulation.

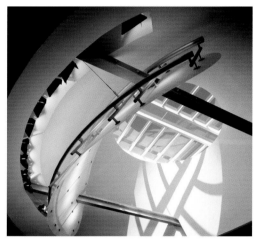

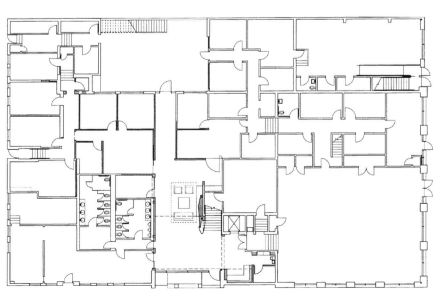

Chelsea Gallery

The project was to transform a derelict 3,500-square-foot space into a gallery that could accommodate the growing business and hold art openings in the evenings. The gallery believes that contemporary art should be affordable and a part of everyone's life. Instead of the usual white walls, the architect and designer decided to use white as the core of the space but use different variations of green for the interiors of the space. Thus the inside of the bathroom, the office and even the interiors of the closet are all different shades of green. The office is grape green; the art wrapping room is celery.

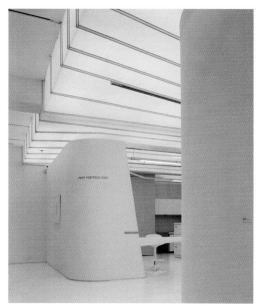

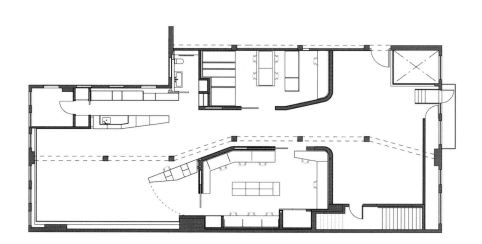

In Heat

J.Mayer H. stems from Friedrich Kieslers design for the 1947 "Blood Flames" exhibition at the Hugo Gallery, New York. His radical new concept proposed merging art, architecture and the viewer into a continuation of painted walls and floors which hosts and interconnects the artwork. "In Heat" develops this confusion of art, viewer and space into an even more radical way by introducing thermosensitive coating as interactive paintings where the viewer, creating a temperature shadow by touching, melts into the overall exhibition design. Everything gets flattened into an architectural surface with depth in time.

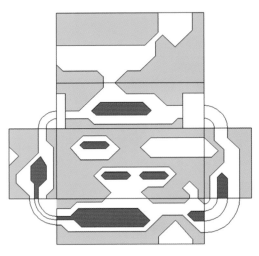

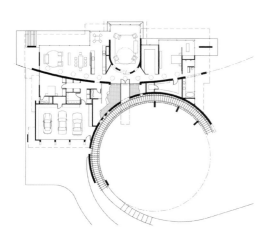

River House

The concept for the design is best described as a journey: from the man-made of the street to the nature of the river, from the public space to the private living quarters, from the screened and enclosed to the transparent and open. The sight and sound of the babbling water are used to signify the transition from public to private, from man-made to the realm of nature. The entrance doors allow passage through the main ordering element of the entire plan: a curved wall that continues through the whole house. The house was designed to allow the owners to enjoy this natural setting whilst providing a nurtural and private realm for family life.

Photo: Robert Shimer, Hedrich Blessing

Elliott + Associates Architects

Chesapeake Boathouse

The interiors of the programme include a multi-purpose facility with the focus on training and rowing events; where possible, the designers create spaces that support events and provide space for activities ranging from weddings to corporate retreats; this income further supports rowing activities; there is a public lobby capable of supporting 100 guests in addition to a multi-purpose conference/event/board room seating 56 modular tables. Locker room space is available for men and women with lockers for 20 each. There is also storage space for 124 boats ranging from single sculls to 8-person shells in addition to a boat repair space.

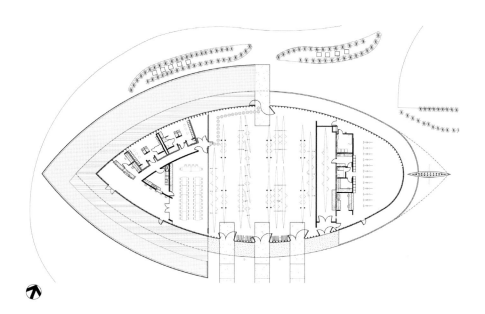

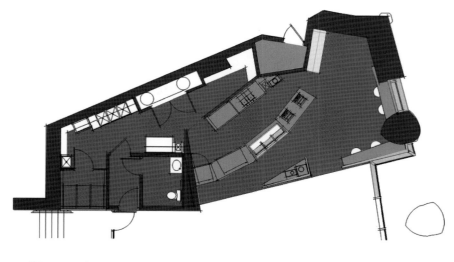

Koffies Café

The lobby café would be one of the amenities of a new Boston office tower. The challenge was to deal with a small 92-square-metre space with a 6-metre-high ceiling. A sail-like form was designed that reduced the height of the space at the place where customers ordered and rose to meet the very high windows at the street. Large lamps were used to fill the ceiling volumes. Very high quality materials were used to match the quality of the lobby finishes in colours that were neutral enough to house any vendor they might get in the future to operate the café. When a vendor was identified, designers created the menu boards and signage.

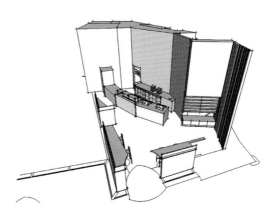

Photo: Anton Grassl

Katy Flammia, Kristin Nakagawa, Kate Swasey, Aishah Farooki

Museum Residences

The Museum Residences make an inspiring contribution to the cultural nexus of the city and complement the neighbouring extension. The soft qualities of the translucent glass skin, combined with the metal-clad geometric forms, provide an elegant partner to the titanium-clad Museum. Out of the seven floors, the top six are residential. The Museum Residences are a joint venture with Davis Partnership Architects, working with Milender White Construction Company.

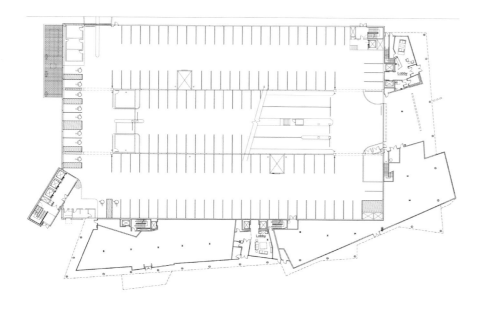

Hangar One

The interior spaces are comfortable and classically modern in design, with rich materials such as macassar ebony, mahogany, wenge, and onyx. The visitor enters the double-height Lobby on a gleaming terrazzo floor with onyx inlay. The oval-shaped Quiet Lounge with mahogany paneled walls was designed specifically for the rest and relaxation of its travel-weary guests and is lit with internally illuminated bamboo and a backlit antique map. Custom-designed carpets in earth tones swathe the floors in a subtle hatched pattern. It features an open kitchen with spectacular views and seats 4 to 40 people in the dining room.

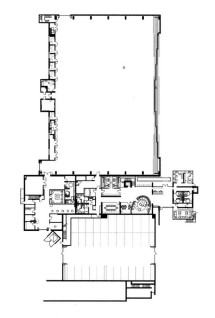

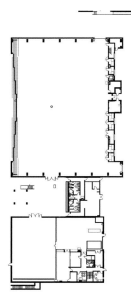

Contiental Vision

Continental Vision is a modern eyeglass boutique located in New York. In order to create a welcoming space, a combination of vivid tangerine orange was used in the furniture and stools along with cool white floors and wood veneer furniture. The entrance faces a busy street so as to attract customers; glass-fronted product displays were recessed and elongated for easy outside viewing. The innovative lighting used helps open up the space as well as adding a warm atmosphere. To save the space, built-in couches were created as well as a continuous service counter that includes the cash area.

Northern Ques Casino Resort

The resort has a striking angularity on the skyline, articulated by sheer reflective glass corners and deeply-expressed and angled roof edges in multi-toned bronze panels. Large exterior casino walls are somewhat dematerialised in size through the use of a subtle exterior palette; tones of pale grey and beige criss-cross over the exterior, creating a varied architectural landscape that complements the warm brown and slate grey building stone. The landscape design creates the perfect counterpoint to the building's striking angularity by creating a softly rolling, richly varied, planting experience that emphasises native species.

210 North

The designers like the term "ebullient" to describe their approach. Joyously unrestrained, 210 North had a previous life as a casino, so designers had inherited a large dark staircase entrance that they transformed into a stunning entry with chain curtain and saturated coloured lighting for the two sidewalls. Overhead floated a canopy of over 200 huge shade pendants that housed programmable LED lights. The physical effect of that much intensely saturated coloured lighting was visceral, and a bit disorienting in a psychedelic kind of way. In that sense, designers had achieved the design objective here.

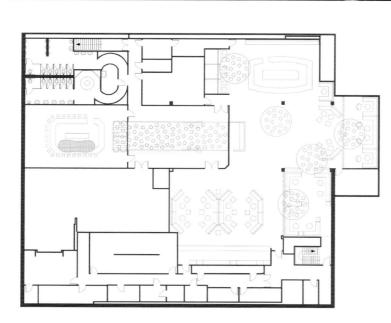

Social Hollywood

A 27,000-square-foot space that includes a restaurant, a bar and a private membership area is housed in the former Hollywood Athletic Club. Social Hollywood has a Moroccan motif and a sense of playfulness that flows through the restaurant. Zeff set the tone with furnishings and objects purchased on trips to Marrakech, Tangier and Fez. Stunning juxtapositions in the dining room include intricately carved and whitewashed Moroccan wood chairs set against a background that features shifting moving projected animations. Social Hollywood has the aura of the Art Deco golden age feel, updated with a modern sexy vibe.

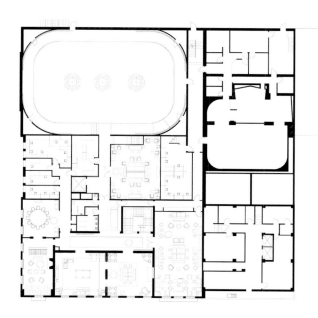

Marsh

The central part of the building is built with trusses, and is column free. The wall separating the low building from the high building has arches leading into the small shops, signs above the arches and windows above the signs. The interior of the supermarket is illuminated with natural light. This area houses produce and kiosks for drinks and snacks. In the centre is an espresso bar located near magazines and the pharmacy. There is a child-care area and some very flexible seasonal displays. It is the soul of the shop and the place where we begin to introduce the idea of lifestyle. The light is much more attractive compared to the light thrown by normal fluorescent lights.

Peace Theological Seminary Dining Hall

The new dining hall is an expression of modernity in contrast to the earlier neo-classical architecture. At the same time, it is an extension of that earlier sensibility. One flows into the other. Each type of architecture maintains its own identity while harmonising with the other. This has been achieved through clarity of plan and utilisation of material. For example, the beautiful figured white oak walls of the original villa segue in the generous use of walnut, teak, alder, and hemlock in the new room. Around a large existing stairwell a series of new spaces were created: a large common booth under the stair, the main dining room, and an adjacent exterior, trellis-covered terrace.

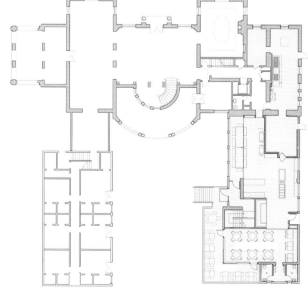

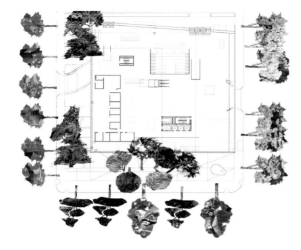

Seattle Public Library

The most characteristic part of the design for the Central Library is the way in which the landscape infiltrates and folds into the interior. The transparent façade of the building is surrounded by native tree species that are inter-planted with grass and perennial fields, which slope, fold and overlap as planes of various greens. Inside, these green fields transform into carpets, printed with large-scale plant patterns, the so called "garden carpets".

In the auditorium, Inside Outside designed a white-and-green finned curtain with a PVC imprinted "bearskin" lining, which connects to the field of green chairs designed by Maarten van Severen and the brown polyurethane floor surface, creating another garden-like space in the heart of the building. During the project's development, Inside Outside also acted as advisor on the interior finishes and colour scope, especially focussing on all horizontal planes, the floor and ceiling surfaces.

Wolfgang Puck Bar & Grill

The design combines the energetic feel of the beach lifestyle and the cool beauty of a California garden. The entry to the restaurant will instantly bring customers to the first dining "layer", the U-shaped Puck Bar, a place for friends to congregate and a centre of great activity. Adjacent to the Bar is the café, a place for casual dining and for a happy hour cocktail or nightcap. The façade of the café section features curly willow twigs intertwined to form nine giant wreaths and the overall dining experience is avant garde. In the second "layer", there is patio dining, a casual and fun atmosphere and a great place to meet friends.

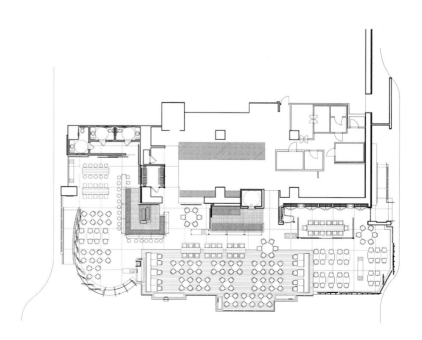

Millennium Tower Loft

Combine wide open spaces for entertainment with enough privacy for a small family with a child and a comfortable place for guests to stay. The main floor layout is designed to transform from single volume entertainment space to distinct kitchen, dining, entry, and guest mini apartment with discreetly built in closets. The extra deep sofa combines with the ottoman to create a full bed, and the powder room contains a hidden shower tucked away behind angled privacy glass panels. The second level has flexible office space that can be used for different family activities and can, in the future, be transformed into a third bedroom if the need arises.

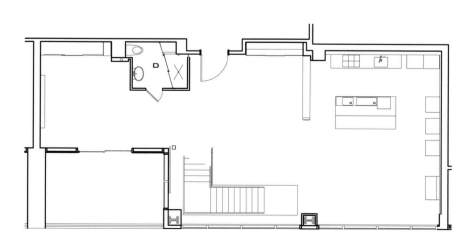

Club Sugar

Thinking about materials and mood more than form, the designers initiated the design of this project by selecting a number of new plastic materials. They wished to exploit their inherently contradictory qualities of transparency and reflectivity, as well as varying degrees of translucency, distortion, and colour. But recognising the hardness of many of these materials, they continuously juxtaposed them against softer and warmer materials such as drapery, the exposed brick of the existing walls, and the exposed wood ceiling structure. This dichotomy appealed to designers as they began to insert programmatic elements into the space.

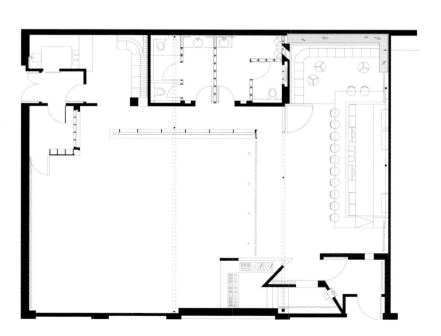

Fresco

Studio GAIA designed the first prototype of Fresco on the go by Scotto family. Fresco on the go is a new take on the New York Fast food frenzy in downtown New York. Granted with a 4000-square-foot space, the Fresco on the go is divided into 3 areas by different height of platforms, welcoming station, ordering station and the seating station. It's a fine Italian deli with crisp and fresh atmosphere motivated from the old Tuscany region in Italy. The sunflower graphic images both on the ceiling and inside of hanging lamp, the dotted mural of Tuscany landscape and the overall colour schemes are the evident of this theme.

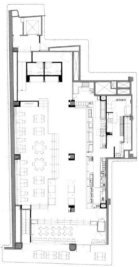

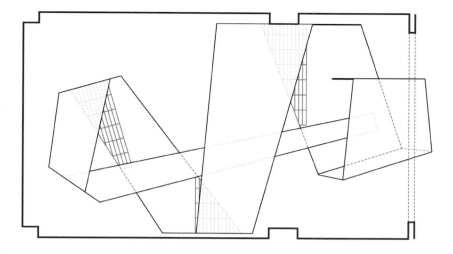

(Wide) Band

(Wide) Band is a portable project; it was moved to the A + D Museum in Los Angeles where it functioned as a café by day and as a bar/lounge space at night. The primary material, 3/4" polycarbonate core panels was chosen for its structural capacity to span large spaces and for its translucency. Walls, floor, and ceiling are shaped by wrapping the panels in a continuous loop. The table bisects the space and becomes a nexus for engagement, promoting the interaction of users with each other as they negotiate. The surface, lit from varying distances, glows in colours ranging from yellow to orange to red and ruby. Even in daylight, the translucent material yields different shades of orange.

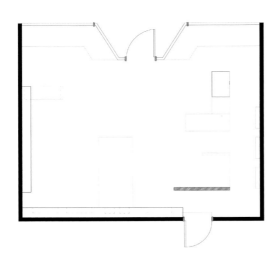

Far4 Shop

The space needed to reflect the luxury of the goods and maintain a relationship with the small scale of the ceramic products, with a focus on product itself. The goal was to build a warm, open environment, where shoppers could meander around various displays, closely inspecting each finely crafted piece. To achieve a feel of intimacy in the shop, and to remain true to the building's history and the Northwest's aesthetics, wood was used extensively throughout the space. Wide-plank Dutch Oak flooring was used as the material for both floor and the display areas. Doing so allowed introducing fewer materials into the space, so as not to compete with the ceramics.

Vintages Wine Shop

The owners of Vintages Wine Shop wanted a shop that expressed their knowledge and understanding about wine. The designers carefully selected materials that express the connection of the vine and earth. Rich slates, cork and oak, in a contemporary composition express the elements of the wine process. The design forms — columns and arches suggest a cellar, the stage-like tasting table and create drama and a sense of discovery to the experience of tasting and purchasing wine. The contemporary design using traditional materials communicates the shop owner's belief that wine has a past but was made for and experienced in the present.

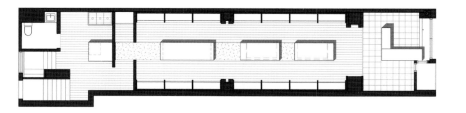

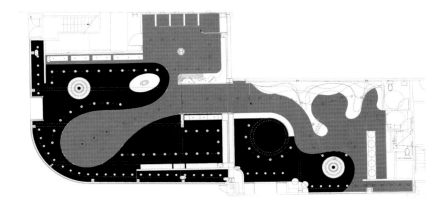

La Miss Sixty

Besides being a part of the Miss Sixty retail design concept, this shop is homage to the city of Los Angeles, the city of cinema and especially the science fiction movies from the 1960s such as "Barbarella" or "Blob". This Melrose Ave. shop was invaded by a big yellow drop pouring down from the ceiling flooding the space, washing floor and counters in bright shiny yellow. Two shiny silvery "UFO" are parked silently at two corners of the shop, watching your every moving or waiting. Although the concept is of a chain shop, every shop has its own characteristics related to the structure of the space and the location of the shop.

Paradies Shops

Located at the end of the fifth gallery, the first and largest shop, the 6,000-square-foot "Beyond the Reef" welcomes visitors to a darkened deep-sea environment that was completed with glimmering jellies and large tendrils of green kelp which climb and twist to form passageways. Internally illuminated fabric forms weave rhythmically through the space while obscuring the irregular column placement. The sparkling terrazzo floor replicates the ambience of a Technicolor ocean bottom glittering with shells and rock fragments. At the point of sale, a stylised coral wall creates the illusion of an underwater reef, complete with cracks and crevices — an illusion heightened through the imaginative use of theatrical lighting and plasma screens featuring oceanographic video.

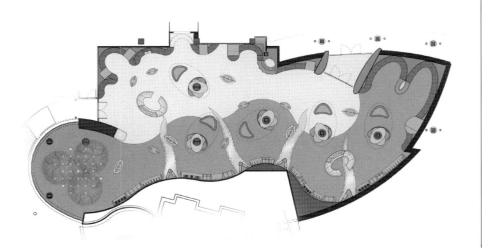

Gokaldas Showroom

The floors, walls, screens and furniture of the showroom are poured in a continuous flow of white epoxy resin in order to create the sensation of buoyancy while viewing the garments. Despite the quantity and diversity of garments presented, the purity of this liquid environment allows the clothes to be seen clearly. A simple system of suspended stainless steel rods on sliding tracks allows the display to be easily reconfigured in minutes. The desire for levitation was inspired by the exhilarating views of the city from the showroom's continuous band of wraparound windows high above Times Square and face-to-face with some of New York's greatest skyscrapers.

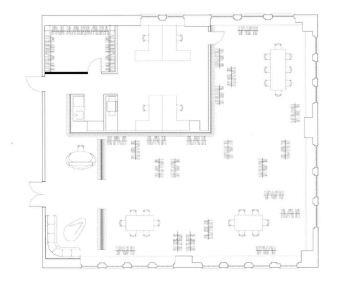

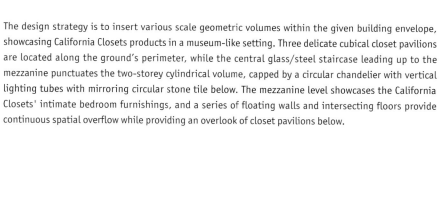

The California Closets Showroom

The design strategy is to insert various scale geometric volumes within the given building envelope, showcasing California Closets products in a museum-like setting. Three delicate cubical closet pavilions are located along the ground's perimeter, while the central glass/steel staircase leading up to the mezzanine punctuates the two-storey cylindrical volume, capped by a circular chandelier with vertical lighting tubes with mirroring circular stone tile below. The mezzanine level showcases the California Closets' intimate bedroom furnishings, and a series of floating walls and intersecting floors provide continuous spatial overflow while providing an overlook of closet pavilions below.

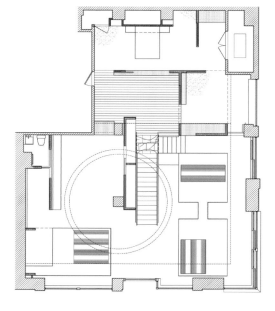

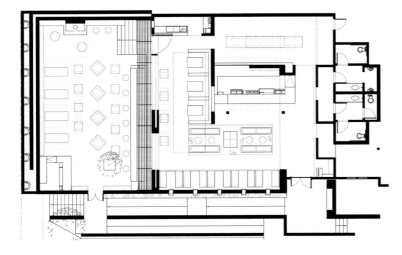

Falcon

The creation of Falcon involved the transformation of a dilapidated craftsman house into a high-end eatery and hangout space for a Hollywood clientele. Organisationally, the restaurant is composed of a series of related but distinct spaces, much as in a film. The sequence is a long ramp. The ramp leads to the indoor dining and bar area, which functions as a lounge much of the evening and takes the theatre as its primary design metaphor: From raised seating areas, diners can view and be viewed by the action in the lounge. Dark and earthy materials combine with low ceilings to create an intimate, cave-like atmosphere.

Open-Book Shop

Two transparent horizontal planes intersect as being in opposite directions: walkways bring you into the middle of books, around islands of books-books float at your ankles, waist, head... Walkways cut through one plane under the other: you walk through the middle of books, around islands of books. Planes cut out of planes fold and tilt and step to make a bookshop for the body: you look over books, pick up books, at your ankles, at your waist, at your head. From under an overhead plane, you look at products (art-prints, special editions) you are not meant to touch; transparency breeds desire. The ribs inside the transparent panels are extruded to make book-stops; surplus books are stored on the plane below a plane. A curved cut around the art-fair booth makes a place for shopkeepers, and storage cuts radiating in from the edges bring customers up to the counter.

Photo: Acconci Studio

Acconci Studio (Vito Acconci, Ezio Blasetti, Nathan DeGraaf, Eduardo Marques, Dario Nunez)

Miyake Madison

This project for the Japanese fashion designer Issey Miyake on Manhattan's Madison Avenue consisted of an interior renovation and a new façade on this historic shopping street. The design breaks the threshold between the sidewalk and the world of Issey Miyake. The flush clear glass façade creates a seamless barrier from which the volume of the shop is extruded. The 2,600-square-foot volume which terminates in a mirrored wall extends without end. In effect, the entire shop becomes a giant shopping window with mannequins dispersed throughout the entire depth of the space. A stretched checkerboard pattern of light boxes in the ceiling meanders around these columns adding a figural element to the volume.

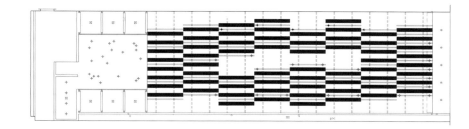

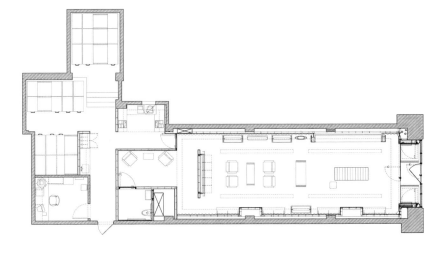

Sergio Rossi

Sergio Rossi is a high-end designer shoe boutique that combines the warmth of Italian luxury with the cool of modern form. The main space is enclosed by a cascading metal chain curtain that ripples like a waterfall as light softly flows down it. Suspended from this curtain wall is a high-gloss white display case which serves as a focal point for the space and highlights its modern viewpoint. A long horizontal niche is cut into this lacquered wood rectangle, serving as display space for the shoes. The free-standing teak displays positioned in front of the curtain wall provide a sense of warmth and, while grounded, give the appearance of furniture that can be moved around the space.

Photo: Jody Kivort

212box Architecture

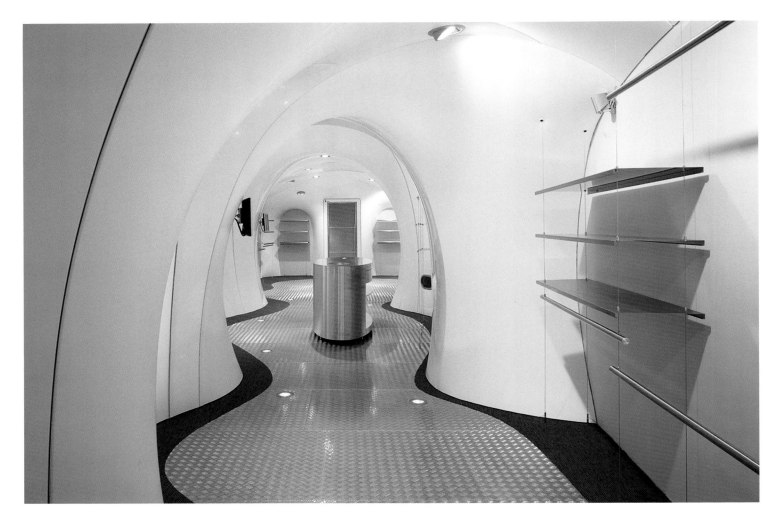

Scott

The space is the pilot showroom for the firm Scott USA. The concept of the presented interior is based on the newly vested space, by locating it in a historical environment with chaotic arches intersecting at the meeting point of two houses. The basic idea was to respect the space's character and the distinct curves of the arches, but in a shifted aesthetical meaning. The floor is made of dual plate and a carpet with a clearly visible continuous structure. The presently remaining walls are only given a surface treatment and painted. The interior is supplemented by a subtle stainless steel shelving system and a stainless steel counter with a display case.

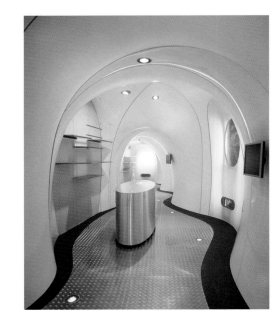

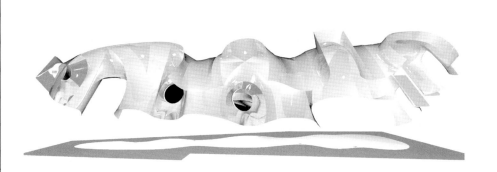

Dermataloge

Architecturally, the existing space had a lot to offer with high ceilings and a floor plan that did not require any walls to be relocated. However, the finishes and lighting needed a complete overhaul to eliminate the corporate atmosphere. Slatted wood screens were used throughout, while exterior landscaping provided the necessary privacy in treatment rooms. Several floor transitions helped distinguish zones, but the long hallway leading to the treatment rooms posed a difficult problem. Ignoring the low dropped ceiling, the designer turned the 25-foot-long wall expanse into a sculptural art piece.

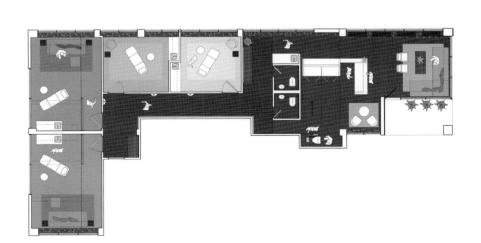

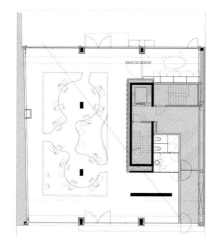

Ritz-Carlto Fitness Centre

In the midst of the spa's treatment rooms, salon, fitness centre, and spacious locker rooms and lounges, space planning became the design team's biggest challenge. A 14,000-squre-foot spa typically has 14 treatment rooms. In this case, however, the client sought 16 rooms for the same size facility. The design team underwent numerous creative space planning exercises in order to produce appropriate adjacencies, minimise circulation and capture a good flow within the space. Additionally, because the space was located above a parking garage, the team was challenged to position whirlpools in places that could accommodate their depth.

Westin Hilton Head Spa

A sense of calmness and renewal is felt immediately upon entering the spa from either the lobby or the porte cochere. A portico of quarter-cut walnut on the walls and ceiling with dropped crystal lights signifies your entry into the spa and leads you to the reception desk of honed black limestone with a white back-painted glass top. A water wall with lacquered glass tiles and stacked white river rocks provides a calming backdrop and is the feature of the reception lobby. The nine treatment rooms are appointed with walnut floors, wenge wood cabinetry, plantation shutters on the windows, and a soft white sheer drapery panel that is lit from above and acts as the light source in the room.

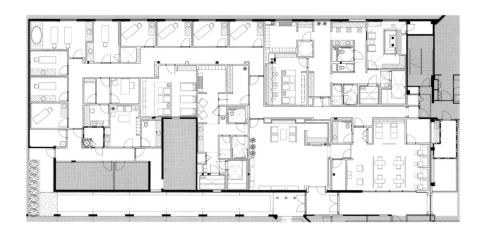

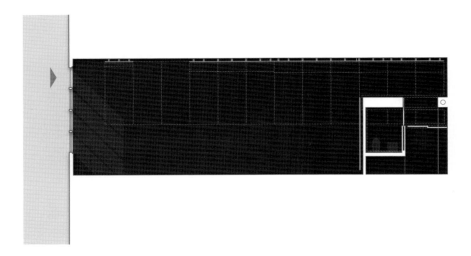

Pilates Studio

The Pilates Studio required a workout area able to accommodate large machines, shelving for various paraphernalia, a work area for scheduling and paperwork, a changing room, and a restroom. The designers employ a single sculptural element that runs the length of the space, and "peels"up to become shelves, bench, and desk, leaving the better part of the space free. Materials used are formaldehyde-free plywood with a tung-oil finish, "elephant bark" recycled rubber flooring adhered with no-VOC adhesive, cold rolled steel, mirrors, T-8 florescent strip lighting w/ 2700° Kelvin bulbs, and no-VOC paint.

Strengthened Parking Garage Supports High-Rise Ice Rinks

A seven-storey parking garage at a shopping mall provided the base on which to construct a pair of rooftop ice skating rinks' Locker rooms, a snack bar, ticket sales space, and various offices. At the eastern end of the new addition is a 1,860-square-metre space on the eighth level that houses a training centre with weights and fitness equipment; a similarly sized space above the training centre. These two sections feature a slanting glass façade that cantilevers out approximately 4.3 metres in a design that resembles the blade of an ice skate. Its eighth-floor location "approximately 24 metres above grade" makes the Iceplex one of the highest elevated ice rinks in the world.

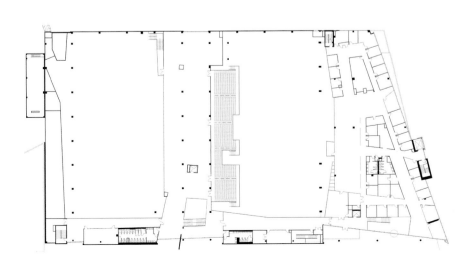

Deutsch NY

The project was required to provide a serene and welcoming environment for company guests, provide office and meeting space for the company employees and integrate the owner's extensive collection of Asian art. The design pursued a sustainable strategy of natural renewable materials and recycled materials throughout to complement the art collection. Bamboo floors and ceilings define the main guest area with live bamboo; a new skylight is cut into the existing roof to allow daylight into the space and reduce the need for artificial lighting. A textured wall of crosscut bamboo terminates the space, and bamboo-veneered niches randomly dot the office areas to provide space for art.

IBM Centres for E-Business Innovation

The architecture is designed to create conditions of possibility, not just in space but also in TIME. The environment is FLEXIBLE and changes over time; everything from network architecture to physical architecture is scalable and upgradeable. The space is OPEN in every sense, creating an environment of accessibility and approachability. Walls and partitions elegantly slide and rotate into place for situations that require more or less privacy and custom materials reinforce continuity and spatial extension through transparency and layering.

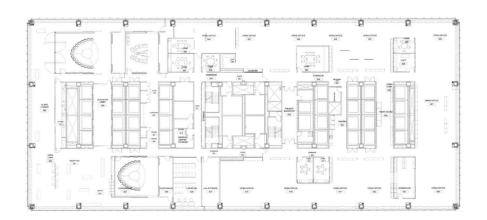

Theory NYC

The space brings Theory's offices, showrooms and retail all under one roof. The interiors are completely custom-tailored to the clients' specifications. Zeff played with colours, finishes and furnishings, while attempting to differentiate and unify the floors at the same time. Rows of desks and workstations are surrounded by executive and private offices. The lounges are furnished with sofas, daybeds, and ottomans — a mix of contemporary, vintage and Zeff designs. The corporate lobby and the four levels above are connected by a staircase of concrete, glass and polished stainless steel, along with the stainless steel mesh curtain.

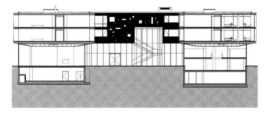

Swiss Army Brands Corporate Headquarters

Inspiration for the selection of materials and finishes was derived from Swiss Army's product line and retail stores, including glass, aluminum, stainless steel, dark wood finishes, stone, felted wool upholstery and the Swiss Army "red". Swiss Army requested that any colour used in the space have a meaning. The one lively colour in the otherwise monochromatic interior is Swiss Army red, which can be seen throughout the building in nearly every room. The new headquarters has two distinct areas with 44,000-square-foot dedicated to corporate offices (sales/marketing/administration) and 110,000-square-foot for a warehouse and distribution centre.

The Belvedere Hotel-California

The upper lounge is flanked on two sides by curved plaster banquettes that define the shape of the room. Hand-carved weathered wood screens that resemble rippling water with voids and curves are located behind the banquettes. These screens also appear on the lower level in the centre of the main dining area. The main restaurant on the lower level spills into an elegant pool area. This landscaped setting is designed to transform over the course of a day. During the daytime, there are single lounge chairs covered in terrycloth slipcovers with retractable sun shades. White matchstick screens shade large teak wood single and double cabanas.

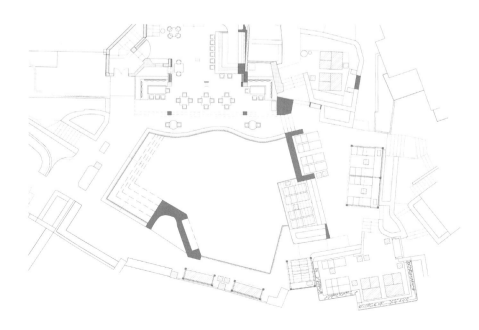

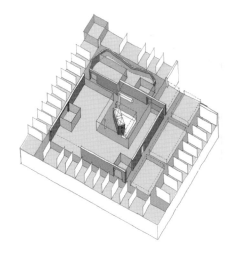

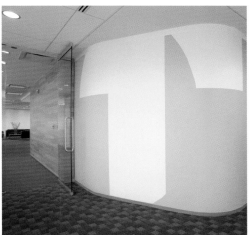

Torcon World Headquarters

The design challenge was to reinforce Torcon's corporate identity, while creating a new open office environment that houses a variety of offices. The new interior is highlighted by a dramatic entry lobby and visitors' waiting area that is composed of simple forms and stark materials, and creates an elegant and sophisticated approach that is separated from the adjacent elevator lobby by a monolithic glass entry wall. A custom reception desk of ebony wood, back-lit translucent panels, and stainless steel, is accented by the simple backdrop of a bright red wall with the Torcon logo. The executive suite with offices and conference rooms is located just beyond this bright red wall.

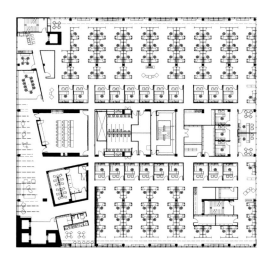

Country Music Television

Country Music Television was experiencing a growth spurt and needed to expand their Nashville, Tennessee office from two floors to three. The company also needed flexibility for future changes in a facility housing a lobby, open offices, private offices, conference rooms, break rooms, broadcast room, control room, announcer room and multi-function space. The designers' universal zoning plan, developed to increase effectiveness and enhance collaboration, represents a major change for CMT. In the lobby, large maple wood ribs frame the space from floor to ceiling. This creates a sort of homage to country music by portraying the feeling of being inside an acoustic guitar.

Paulith, Inc. Distribution Centre

As a new headquarters for a garment distribution company, this project takes the idea of constructing a building within a building and thus reconsidering the conventions of office and structure. Public spaces are conceived as exterior volumes within the overall shell. These spaces are created through the bending and folding of a continuous ribbon that unites the various stages of the distribution chain where a raw resource is converted to a finished product. Storage, fabrication, administration, and sales converge further blurring the line between programme and space. The resulting spaces create a more unified and cohesive whole, resulting in a more productive working atmosphere.

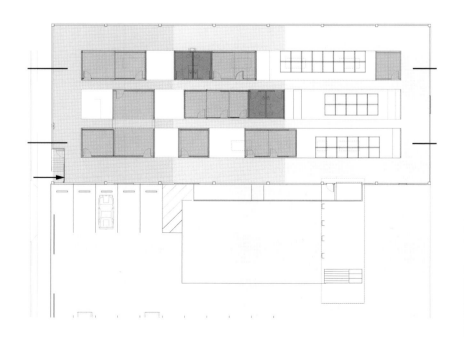

Photo: Michael Weschler

Lorcan O'herlihy Achtitects

Schindler Elevator Corporation

The interior is created with inexpensive painted drywall and indirect fluorescent lighting. The accent red used to highlight the shaft-like columns, lobby and walls is Schindler's corporate colour which is appropriated from the Swiss national flag. All other surfaces and furnishings are purposefully left neutral in colour and texture. The overall effect of the composition is like a minimalist painting where a dramatic focus is established with only a few strokes in a neutral field. Translucent acrylic resin boxes are judiciously introduced as lobby furnishings: a reception desk, a coffee table, a bench and lights. Internally illuminated, these acrylic resin boxes appear like elevator shafts piercing through the floor and ceiling planes.

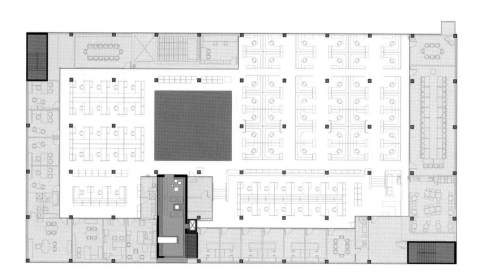

Port House

The Port House is an updated mid-20th century Steak and Seafood restaurant, serving exceptionally presented seafood and the very best USDA prime aged beef. Jordan Mozer and Associates Limited, has created a dark wood room filled with lighting inspired by sea anemones, jellyfish and cuttlefish. Jordan Mozer and Associates Limited collaborated with 23 artists to create special elements throughout the restaurant, including hand-laid glass mosaic floor murals, hand sculpted cast magnesium-aluminum ornamental metals, a wine tower of art-glass, hand blown glass light fixtures and dozens of other custom details created especially for the Port House.

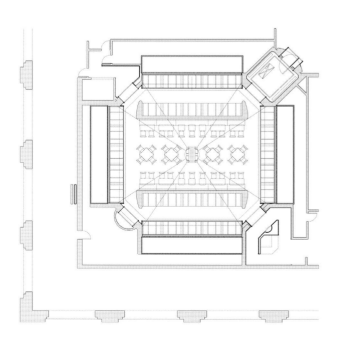

Yale Steam Laundry

The existing Yale Steam Laundry structure possesses a rich physical history that is written in its vaulted floor structure, its oddly-spaced floor framing and in its pock-marked concrete and brick. The ground floor of the annex serves simultaneously as building lobby and clubroom. Diaphanous coloured fabric sheers play off the heaviness and strength of the existing structure, screen private activities from public access and allow the space to be configured for different uses. Glass ceiling panels cut into the centre bay allow light from the second floor skylights to penetrate to the ground floor lobby, while a corten steel bar inserted into the rear of the space supports the variety of possible activities.

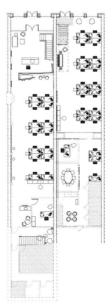

Springbox

The designer faced an unusual challenge when developing the interiors for this interactive agency. The inspiration for the design was found in the translation of the virtual to the actual, which is evident throughout the space with interior statements that mimic the playful style of the agency's own website. Since budgets were tight and there was little money left for art, the designer made the decision to use the flooring as artwork. The result was a random carpet tile pattern that has become a signature for the agency. As floors were joined together, the pixilated pattern actually unified the spaces.

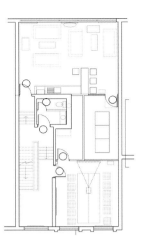

Uce/Open Advantage Offices

The building of a typical 1980s' style sits on Birmingham's entertainment strip and offers three floors of accommodation. Essentially the scheme is split into 3 clear sections which correspond to the 3 floors of the building. The ground floor houses all the public functions, predominantly a seminar space and a demonstration suite. The first floor provides staff meeting areas and staff social areas, whilst the top floor is an open plan office. Aesthetically the design responds to the client and the nature of their work, and hence the interior will be highly graphical, using graphics and text etched onto the many glass screen walls which form the different spaces.

Obsession Hair and Day Spa

This prestigious project was set in the heart of Birmingham. Designers were involved at the initial concept stage and were brought back on board for the detail design and specification stages. The high quality scheme combines a hair salon, manicure area, salon school, treatment rooms, juice bar, spa area, steam and sauna, and office area to provide a city centre retreat for relaxation and pampering. Aesthetically the design has been closely controlled and consists of a limited palette of materials which include walnut, brushed aluminum, and subtle colours, whilst the introduction of a suspended lighting canopy, plasma screens, projections, and dramatic lighting bring the subdued background to life.

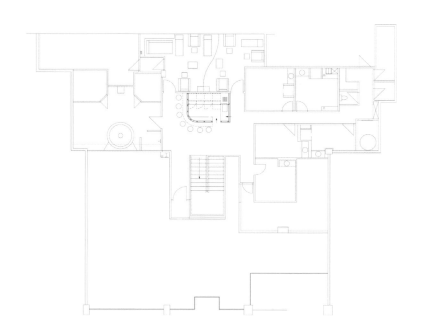

Photo: Kevin W Singh

Tony Kerby and Kevin W Singh

Chinook Trails Elementary School

This is a school focused on international studies, with an emphasis on Asia. Mandarin Chinese is taught here. Three architects were invited to submit concepts in a design competition. For this successful entry the architect linked neighbourhood parks on two sides with a green space flowing between them. The theme of the competition entry was "school in a park". Hallways are places to explore international themes. Entrance walls to classrooms have graphics displaying images from around the world. Display cases demonstrate a range of cultural and industrial objects from Asian countries being studied. The international theme is carried through the art, music performance, and computer literacy programmes.

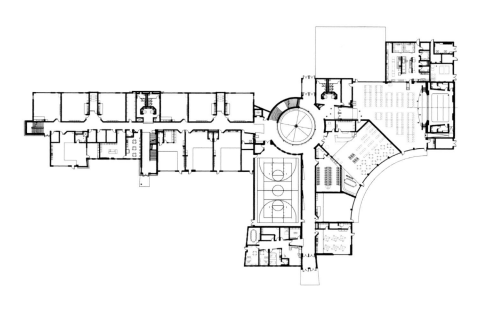

Peter and Paula Fasseas Cancer Clinic at University Medical Centre

The Cancer Centre reuses the foundation and steel frame of a 50-year-old hospital that previously occupied the site. Segments of the deep floor plate were removed, creating three courtyards to bring natural light and garden views to corridors and patient care areas. The full width of the building was extended by two structural bays to the south to form a new public entrance, lobby, and administrative suite. In the lobby, the fabric armchairs give a sense of home. Nearly floor-to-ceiling windows give an open view, making the space so close to the nature. The main palette of warm orange and cream-colour creates an intimate and comfortable atmosphere.

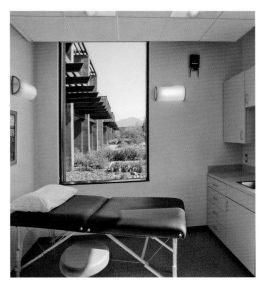

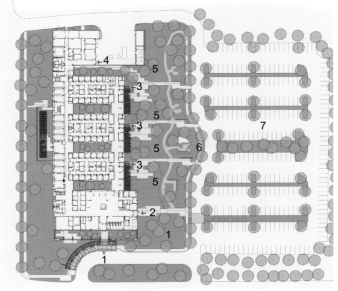

Wave-A-Wall, West 8th St. Subway-Station Façade

Like an ocean wave, like sand-dunes… As the façade waves up & down, it waves in & out: it bulges in & then twists to bulge out, until it reaches a breaking point & splits open to make a view…Here & there the wave doesn't break: it bulges in & out just far enough to make seating… The architect started a wave; designers came in later and tried to make a wave, break a wave. The façade is like a rise and fall of sand, like an ocean wave. Designers use the wave to make a view — the force of a wave — the wave forces a view. As the façade bulges in or out, it reaches a breaking point, enclosing the stairway up to the station, and it is just far enough in to make a seat. The façade does not show a picture of a wave, neither a wave in two dimensions, but a wave in all directions. It breathes in on one level while it waves onto the other level, where it breathes out.

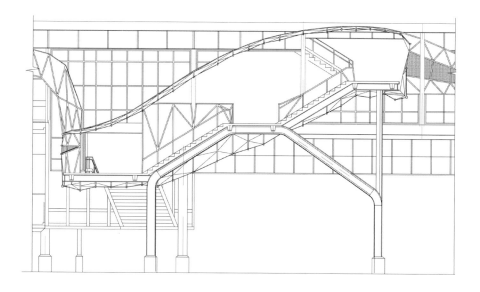

Preschool of The Arts

Child-sized zones were created utilising the lower portion of the walls lined with cork, allowing the children to display and see their work. Reading lofts look like tree houses allowing for quiet escape. A group area is more residential in feel incorporating a stone fireplace, cozy rug, and bookshelves while windows are placed at child's height so that the children can take a peak and see what's going on in other areas of the school. 80% of the materials for the project and all of the labour were donated by the contractor and various suppliers.

Writers Guild Foundation Library

The library is defined by the introduction of a box. The wall inside this "box" is made with walnut and is multi-faceted to include shelves, display areas, magazine racks, bulletin boards and the computer catalogues. The reading room is rich in woods, with a natural maple ceiling complementing the walnut wall. A long writers table made of linoleum spans from column to column, forming the primary work area. Three "script alcoves" also each contain viewing stations for remote access to archived television shows. Outside the box are the accessory functions of the library and a public lounge.

Shared Integrated Learning Centre

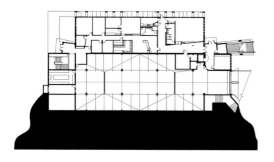

This facility is located between the High School and Middle School. On the ground floor are housed the central School District administrative offices, with an adjacent covered parking garage. The parking garage is where dancing and rock band performances happen on the weekends. Students enter the building using a dramatic staircase and arrive at the computer technology and music space level. An instrumental and choral music room shares a practice room between them that opens onto an outdoor performance amphitheater. The art studios are located on the upper level and share an outdoor deck with views of the Rocky Mountains.

NYC Information Centre

Graphic banding of floor and walls organises the interior, creating a "mapped", foreshortened space. In order not to compete with the media presentations, lighting glows from integrated "light coves" at floor and ceiling level, as well as from the digital projection mirrors hovering above each Smart Table. The Smart Tables and their digital mirrors simulate the intensity of the city experience. Layers of information, electronic interfaces, brochures, a video wall "Fly NYC" feature, and ticket and metro card vending are carefully incorporated into the design, resituating each individual experience and linking them as a unified system.

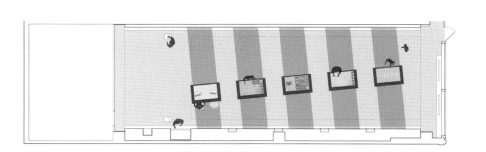

Bronx Charter School For The Arts

Through its adaptive re-use of an old factory, the school plays a role in the transformation of its industrial Hunts Point neighbourhood. To achieve a healthy environment that enhances the learning spaces despite budget and site restrictions, a simple innovative approach was needed. Colour, space, and natural light create a direct physical connection with the content and aims of the curriculum. The classrooms are conceived of as studio spaces. White and grey surfaces predominate to make the most of the north light, with colour stripes providing orientation to each of the classroom bays, towards the street and the shared arts spaces along the façade.

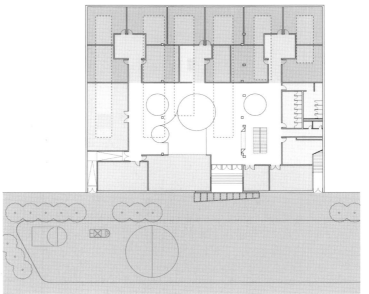

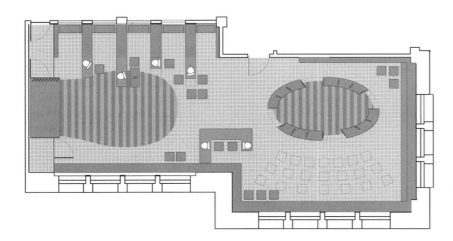

PS Libraries

PS 19 is the largest elementary school in New York City, and yet has the smallest library of any such school. Each space featured high-ceilinged painted rooms with suspended fluorescent lighting and ad-hoc furniture. Designers tested and refined the measurements and character of the chairs and tables by hosting design sessions with students in the targeted age brackets. As with the use of fiberboard for the furniture, designers employed inexpensive material for maximum effect: the existing fluorescent fixtures were humanised with a floating cloud shade made of coated fabric whose natural form inspires a link to the outdoors.

The New York Public Library, Francis Martin Branch

This children's reading room is designed to stimulate its users' imaginations, encouraging them to learn through form, colour and layout. Bold and graphic elements with a bright palette of oranges, greens, and blues are offset by glossy white. The elevated curving façade of the Library provides panoramic views that are fully realised through the new open-plan configuration. The reading tables utilise the natural lighting and outside views. A reflective fabric undulates to form a playful ceiling, at parts folding away to reveal greater height and contrasting concrete. Translucent plastic shelves display books in a clear and visibly inviting manner, while the diagonal arrangement of the shelves behind the reading tables creates a fun, dynamic series of spaces for the children.

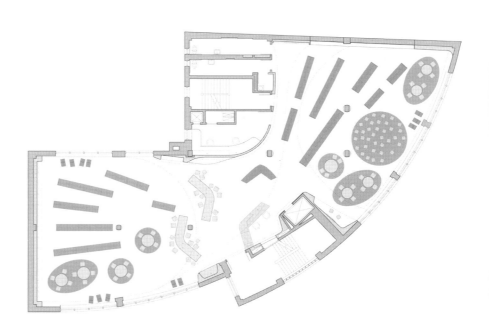

Aeropostale

Aeropostale is a well-known American brand on campus, but also the nation's hottest young contemporary apparel brand, sales force and strong pressure of Nike, Adidas and other world famous brands. The brand with the AE, AF, constitutes the leading U.S. apparel market of young people. The client desired to bring the existing brand identity, which refers to a patrician Eastern Seaboard nautical tradition, into the 21st century with a modern tone. Collaborating closely with the client, the designers facilitated the blending of the modern and the traditional by turning to the Rockefeller Centre's wonderful architecture for inspiration.

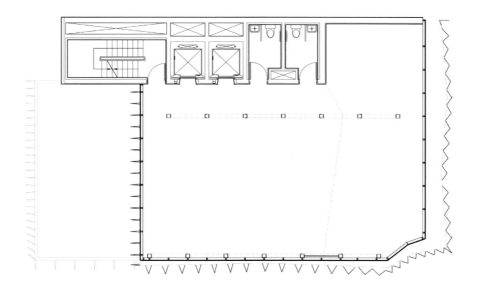

Davie • Brown

The design for DBE developed around the need to create two distinct zones without jeopardizing fluidity of space, coherence of design, and smooth, functional communication overall. The main office zone was driven by the desire to maintain a maximum amount of open space at the centre of the building. This main space acts as a kind of piazza around which all activities unfold: clients pass through, staff traverse not constrained to densely organised space devoid of a social or public gathering opportunities. A restrained use of materials: plexiglass, fiberglass, steel, gypsum board and paint contributed a lot.

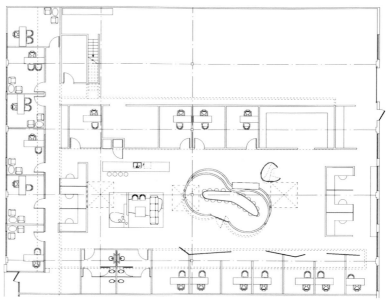

Photo: Robert Shimer, Hedrich Blessing
Scott McDonald, Hedrich Blessing

Heritage Hall Middle School

The architectural concept began as "sliding bars" and related to the excess energy of middle school kids. The goal was to make the space "exciting" and "cool" for the students and manageable for teachers. The plan concept combines a sense of energy and rigour for middle school kids and teachers. There are "connections" to nature and natural light. Just as the plan embodies both youthful energy and rigour, so does the architectural form. The building form "changes" and moves visually with the land.

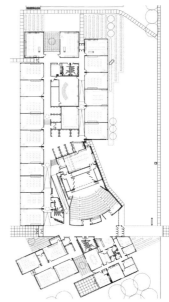

ImageNet Houston

The programme requirements included an equipment showroom, two video conference rooms, a sales area and management offices. There is also a secure inventory area, technical support area for machine repair and an inventory warehouse with dock. The project was designed to include building expandability for the future. The designer also incorporated the signature recycled "paperwall" into the project.

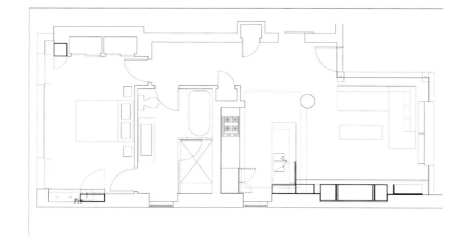

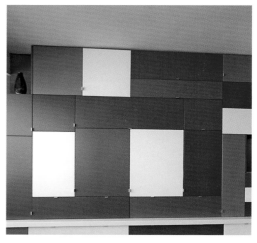

McFarland Residence

The main focus of this project was inspired by a painting the client had received as a gift which has great sentimental value to him. The designer decided to incorporate the abstract artwork composed of vibrant reds and pinks into the built-in cabinetry designed by I-Beam. The cabinets accommodate the client's large collection of CDs, DVDs and state-of-the-art entertainment system along with his collection of ceramics and miscellaneous objects. The cabinet doors were painted to incorporate the colours in the painting, and the painting served as a door within the cabinet system. All other cabinetry in the apartment was custom-built to the client's needs.

Milne Ojito Residence

The harmonic progressions radiate out from the origin point to generate a variety of spaces including a guest bedroom, a home entertainment centre, an office, an open dining area, numerous cabinets and moving exhibition panels to accommodate an evolving art collection. A prime example of this may be seen in the temporary guest bedroom which appears by opening a sofa bed that in turn releases a cantilevered wall which swings out to privatise the bed area while projecting the matrix into space. The only permanent enclosure in the loft contains closets and a new Guest Bathroom made of acid-etched mirror, which gives the impression of expanding space and suspended gravity.

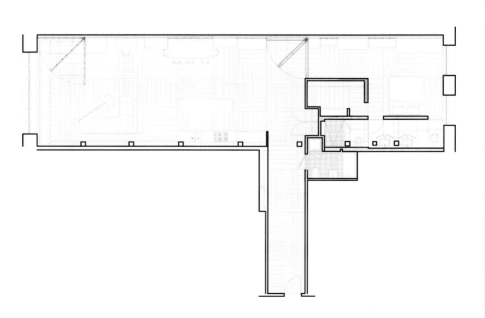

Alikhani Petroulas Penthouse

The long living space remains free of walls, using custom-built architectural elements to define the spatial character and use of each area rather than partitions. These playful elements satisfy multiple functional needs simultaneously. The stainless steel steps leading from the kitchen to children's playroom and roof garden above function as stair, kitchen cabinet, countertop and removable step ladder which may be rolled away in order to access upper cabinets, lighting or the retractable television screen and video system elsewhere in the penthouse apartment. The stationary steps are made of slip-resistant glass and appear to float above the kitchen in tempting provocation to the kids.

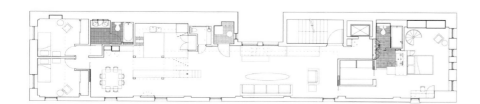

5th Avenue Condominium

Each duplex has two spacious bedrooms with their own bathrooms and ample closets. An extra studio/office off of the main living room is enclosed by a new floor-to-ceiling glass wall flooding the space with a soothing blue light. While maintaining the overall charm of the old construction by exposing the existing brick walls, the designers have created a sleek modern and pristine environment that is flooded with natural light and enhanced by solid maple wood floors and glossy white kitchen cabinets. Each unit has at least one functioning fireplace, an interior spiral stair, grey lava stone countertops, GE stainless steel appliances, Kohler bathroom fixtures, translucent Panelite partitions, and frameless solid wood doors.

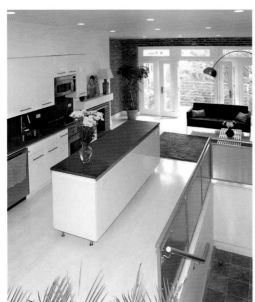

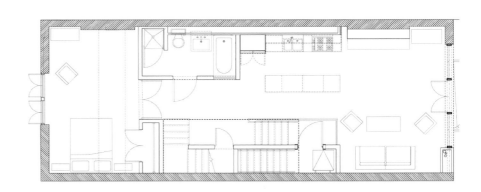

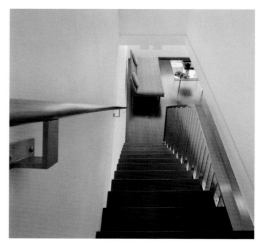

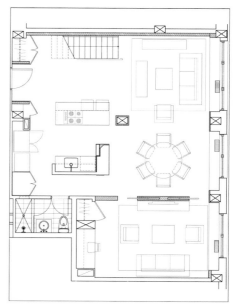

East Side Duplex

The new plan for the lower level is an open loft-like living space combining a kitchen, a living room and a dining room. A family room also serves as a guest bedroom. On the upper level there are three bedrooms including a large master bedroom and bath suite. A new, minimalist steel stair will connect the two levels. The stair is composed of a folded steel surface with simple wood treads and a delicate steel handrail. A conscious decision was made to limit the types of materials so that the unique beauty of each material will stand out and provide the client with a sumptuous, yet visually understandable interior space.

West Village Duplex

The lower floor of the duplex was completely gutted keeping only the original wood floors. The ceilings were raised to the maximum possible, adding light and a feeling of spaciousness previously missing. The new stair has a stainless steel stringer, wood treads and an impressive "hardware-less" glass railing. The stair is lit by a new skylight and a series of glass lights above. At the top of the stair, the designer created an open study with a built-in desk and bookcases overlooking the upper terrace. The master bathroom was finished with Gray stone — a dark consistent grey limestone and Limestone porcelain tile.

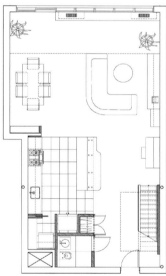

M House

The M house is an artists' work/live/gallery complex located near the arts district of Venice Beach, California. The conceptual framework for the building took the form of two interlocking L-shaped volumes, one dedicated to the art studios and one for domestic functions, configured around a central courtyard — the new focal point of the artist's compound. The painter's studio required a large, raw space with high ceilings and abundant natural light and ventilation. Facing the courtyard, the studio flows outdoors through a double-height glass roll-door and can be opened on the opposite side as well as for indoor/outdoor painting, gallery openings and video projections.

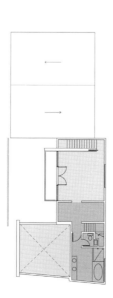

Openhouse

Front elevations of the house slide open to erase all boundaries between indoors and out, connecting the spaces to gardens on both levels. Glass is the primary wall enclosure material. These glass walls are visually counterweighted by sculptural, solid elements in the house. With the glass walls completely open, the house becomes a platform defined by an abstract roof plane, a palette of natural materials. The main stair is charcoal concrete cantilevered from a structural steel tube. The fireplace is made of dry stacked granite, which continues as a vertical structural element from the living room floor to the first storey.

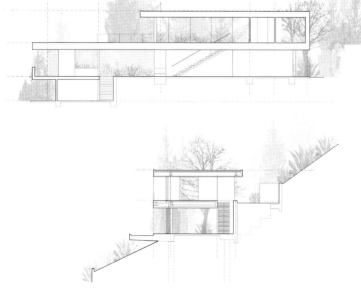

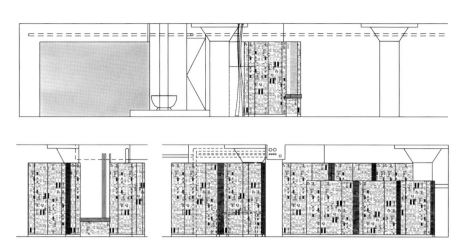

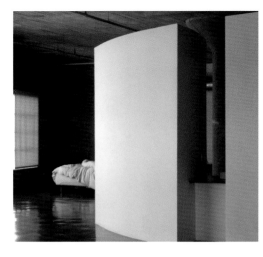

Private Loft

Emphasising the light-filled and expansive space, the designers integrated two units creating an open retreat with only a single element subdividing the expansive loft space. A sinuous double-arced wall divides spatial uses without fully enclosing any part of the unit. The wall defines a screening room on one side while providing visual privacy for the master bath and bedroom on the other. Raised two steps above the floor, the bath area features an open shower comprised of a poured-in-place concrete wall. An antique claw-foot tub sits exposed on the raised platform while the vanity and toilet are enveloped in the point of the arcs. The 3200-square-foot loft is equipped with all the goods of a luxury home.

Tehama Grasshopper

A surprising integration of old and new elements brings the remodeled warehouse alive. Three storeys of interlocked spaces have distinct personalities and functions: office, main living area, and penthouse. The rigidity of the original concrete structure is broken down in a subtle interplay of light, surfaces, levels, and indoor and outdoor spaces, making the urban living experience as richly textured as the city itself. All the new elements in the living space are treated as eight-foot-tall cabinetry, floating within the existing volume. Old and new are allowed to live together in what reads as one, large space: rough warehouse framing and concrete walls.

Photo: Richard Barnes

Fougeron Architecture

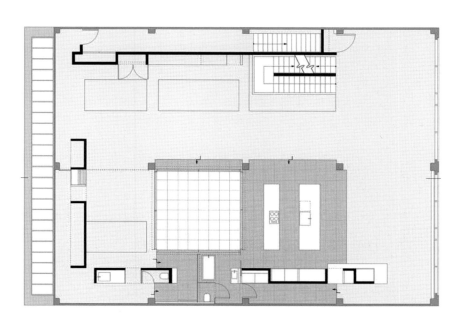

Columbia College

The exterior and interior of the Conaway Centre is dominated by floor-to-ceiling orange letters on the exterior glazing and a lime green open grid ceiling visible from outside. The computer lab is housed in a suspended blue glass rectangle. The open, lime green ceiling grid is used to allow sound to be absorbed by the newly installed black, acoustical material at the bottom of second floor structure. The acoustical material reduced the reverberation time keeping the space "lively" enough for music, but comfortably accommodating spoken communication at lectures, receptions and presentations.

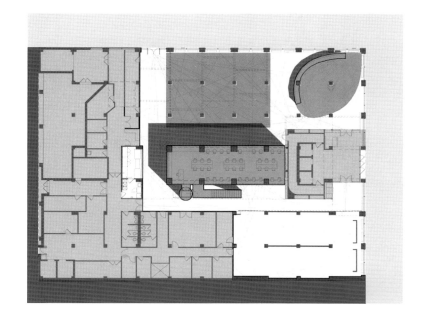

Cousins Trade Show Exhibit

The exhibit was designed with elements of the architecture used at malls and made up of different areas that can be used for different aspects of marketing. Colours were chosen that would recall to mind a retail environment. A tower is the corner focal point with glowing amber windows that can be seen across the convention centre. A servery that is covered in pillowed naugahyde and accented with dimensional letters of the Cousins name sits at the end of a common area with outdoor-like seating for informal gatherings. There are also three conference areas including a large octagonal space and two smaller rooms for one-on-one meetings.

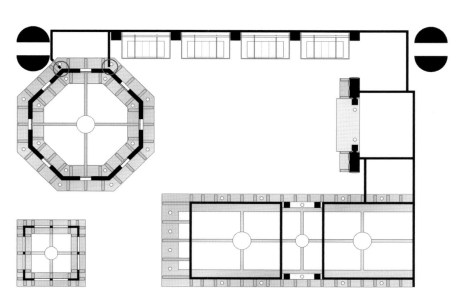

Photo: Pfau Architecture LTD

Pfau Architecture LTD

Pfau Pepple Beach House

Renowned for its world-class golf resort and incredible coastline landscape, Pebble Beach provides the backdrop for a California family's second home. The client wanted a modern home that would exist harmoniously with its environs: the nearby homes, the undulating landscape and the ocean. Pfau Architecture drew inspiration from the mission-style architecture prevalent in the area. The palette of materials is rich but understated — custom plaster and stucco, natural and bleached mahogany, white oak, limestone, and granite. The design of whole space gives the visitor a feeling of warmth, nature and comfort. You can relax yourself here far from the noisy city.

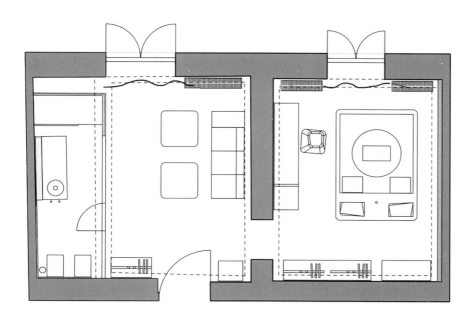

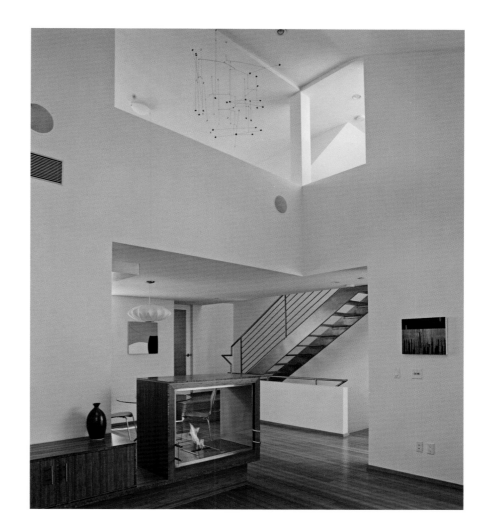

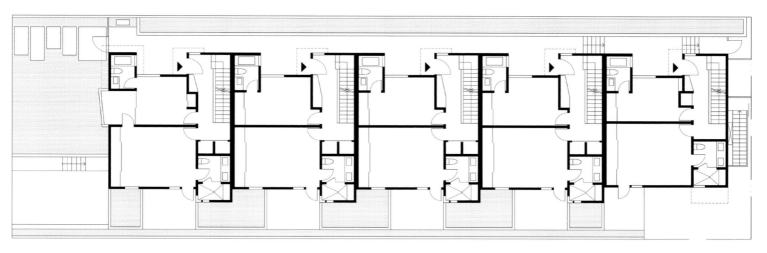

Green on 19 Townhomes

As the first green townhomes in Santa Monica, these modern, custom-crafted dwellings will provide their owners with ground-breaking green technologies that work in unison with architect Jesse Bornstein's penchant for creating harmonious spaces infused with natural light and connections to outdoor spaces and views. The project's modern, elegant detailing coupled with a sophisticated, yet simple palette of materials provides the home owner with a sense of serenity. Within this design sensibility, green features and high-end finishes normally reserved for larger, estate-style homes, represent a leap forward for value in the green building movement.

Mi-Ca Residence

With the Mi-Ca Residential Remodel/Addition, architect Jesse Bornstein has transformed a non-descript dark, jumbled and claustrophobic single-storey interior into an organized and light-filled two-storey living environment that is open to outdoor spaces and views. The architect's penchant for bringing clarity and resolution to each project was manifest here with a few deft design moves. An existing bathroom and water heater closet became the genesis for the design's service/mechanical core. A stairwell then runs alongside this core to the new second floor. The original house's hip roof is inverted; previously turned-down eaves now lift up opening up the interiors to the sky and natural daylight.

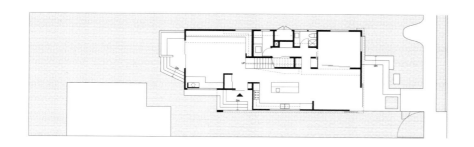

Tree House

The Tree House is constructed around the mature Chinese Elm tree. Each level of the house offers different experiences of the tree; the trunk rising from the Entry Courtyard, the ascending branch structure as one climbs through the Stairwell, the canopy of branches over the Studio Balcony, the uppermost leaves dappling sunlight into the Loft.

Walls, roof planes, beams, railing and fascia run continuously through glazed openings, visually connecting interior and exterior. Architectural elements of wood, stone and metal further tie the house to nature and imbue the interiors with a sense of calm.

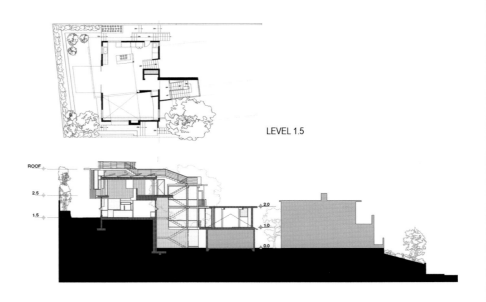

LEVEL 1.5

ROOF

2.5

1.5

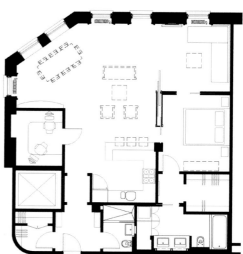

Wasch Residence

From the earliest stages of the design of the Wasch Residence, a primary goal was to bring natural light into every room of the loft. The high ceilings in the space allowed a continuous band of clerestories to ring the upper level of the main living spaces. The custom steel and glass clerestory panels became an organising element of the project; they formed a second line of windows within the loft. Many of the clerestories swivel open to allow air to circulate through the rooms. A portion of the Living Room can be closed off with two large sliding steel and resin doors to form a separate Guest Room when needed. When there are no guests, the large sliding doors disappear into a wall cavity.

MacDonald Street Interiors

The kitchen was finished off with absolute black granite countertops and birch cabinets with a nice stain. The designers located a nice porcelain tile on the floor that looked like concrete. The kitchen was furnished with modest and functional stainless steel appliances throughout. The bathrooms were decorated with glass mosaic tiles in a calm, cool colour palette, creating a modern feel. In the great room, they refinished wood floors and added some splashes of colour to brighten up the space. Custom-designed shelving was integrated into the drywall at the dining room and the living room to allow the family to display artwork photos.

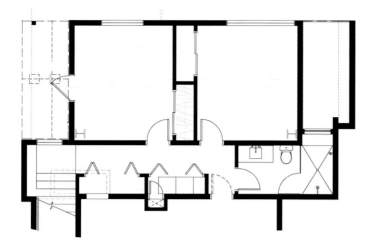

Sausalito Residence

An urbane, elegant home fused with a warm modern ambience is the main design concept. The interiors are comfortable and playful, open to the expansive view of San Francisco Bay. It has a wide open view to the sea in three sides (north, east, and south). Luxuriant light-fixture opposite to the kitchen shows modern style, green tone embraces the washing room making people more relaxing, and the bedrooms have taken good advantage of the sea. The designer's solution was to remove most of the interior walls through the use of structural steel in order to make a sense of space, create a dramatic stair event, and open the exterior walls to the views.

Hyatt O'Hare

The challenge was to breathe new life back into the space without starting from scratch. Highlights of the renovation begin with glass canopy, windows peering into the bar and new landscaping design. The property's competitiveness is also increased by providing clusters of meeting spaces and additional revenue-producing venues including the O'h American Grill and Red Bar. In the O'Hare rejuvenation, the hotel took the radical step of replacing its indoor pool area with a spectacular new conference facility, the Hub. Similar finishes and materials can be found throughout the hotel, helping to orient the guests and bring cohesiveness to the property.

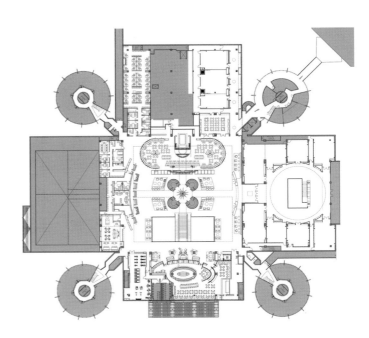

Deamer Residence

The house is for a couple who love to cook and travel, the prospect of substantially changing an existing old home, fraught with controversy and conflict. The approach to the process was to keep the neighbours aware of design progress through a schedule of meetings on one of the original crumbling wood roof terraces, which is right near the dining room and people can have a bird view from it. The interior materials used include French limestone floors with radiant heating, cork floor tiles, Anigre cabinets and built-ins, waxed and hammered copper backsplash, custom stainless sink, marble countertops and Brazilian Cherry butcher-block island top. The woodcarving in the kitchen shows a sense of Oriental.

Mirabile Gift Store

The space is divided into two radically different atmospheres, recognising opposite situations throughout the year. On one hand, the ground floor shows the programme stretching (specially the warehouse). Stretched space organisation and furniture static quality represent services that the shop offers continuously through the year. The first floor emphasises the necessary flexibility, and wheeled furniture design allows for different adaptation schemes. The warehouse is also included in overlapping, scattering through the premises as furniture of mixed use. The unattended spaces, because they are less favoured for exhibition and counter (less than 75 cm and above 190 cm) operate as storage element.

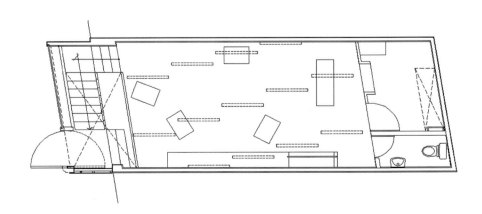

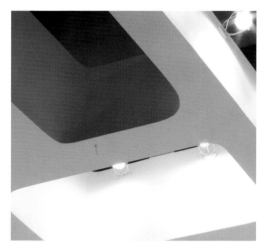

Showroom Comex Lafarge

The project was designed and built for the most important construction exposition.Flexibility, quality, vanguard and technology applications were the facts of design that promoted the development of the project, which was totally built in seven days by only using Plasterboard in order to show the constructive qualities of this product. The open plan invites the visitors to enjoy a free walk, the semi-perforated roof is visually linked to the amazing structure of the Convention Centre, and the visual communication is complemented by the use of corporative info videos.

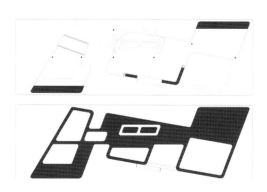

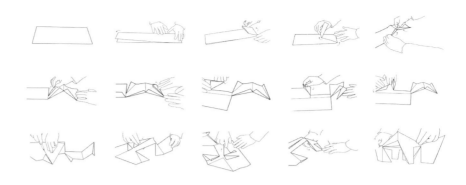

Origami Pavillion

In order to accomplish such an objective, the design was based on the art of the origami that means, in Japanese folding paper. It is composed of figures in its majority geometric-like squares, rectangles and triangles helping to create a very particular form with movements and subtle lines that go along a sense of intuition and not by a strict architectonic rationalism. The circulations of the fair were considered in the design proposal; four big openings allow people to access to the interior exhibition. The architectural elements filter the light while visitors get surprised by the different movements of shadows.

Photo: Paul Czitrom

Jorge Hernandez De La Garza

"Ave Fenix" Fire Station

The program includes, in addition to the Firemen station itself, a space of consultation and training centre open to the public; both activities must be executed separately and never the presence of the visitor should interfere in the work of the firemen. In the case of the main access, the double stair proposed, separates the flow of the employers and the visitors and goes from the level of visitor access to a heliport in the roof. This vertical circulation was complemented by the classic tubes where the firemen descend faster. Thus, making them coexist thanks to the views crossed in the main patio the proposed solution is able to resolve both uses — the station requirements and the public areas.

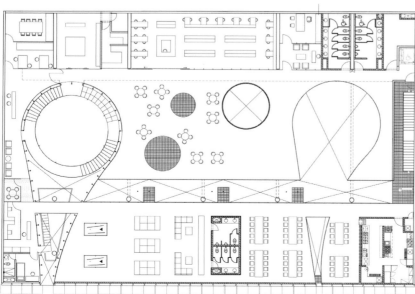

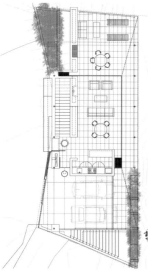

Black House

This covered roof garden becomes the most important part of the house. The most crowded area in which the family will spend most of the time is also the most ambiguous place of the house. One-half-house is then one-half-terrace, protected from the exterior conditions when needed by means of 4-metre-tall sliding glass panels towards the landscape and a wall as high as the garage doors towards the street always detached from the concrete canopy to turn it into a fence more than a wall. The exposed concrete canopy emphasises views and deals with an anachronistic local code on context which calls for typical-construction looking elements and materials such as pitched roofs.

Pc House

In search to create an architectural piece that comes from innovative forms and finds — in that quest — the paths to perpetuate this condition, Ricardo Agraz and Karina Castro combine efforts and imagination. The result is the House, a dwelling based and tailor made for a programme that takes the land as the perfect frame for doing so: it takes the river's length for self adaptation. Spanish ivory marble slabs allow the continuity into the frontal areas of the house, centred by a water fountain that shall play the main role of this first floor. Whereas the main entrance is guarded by a steel art piece done by the architect, specifically made for this house and named "Family".

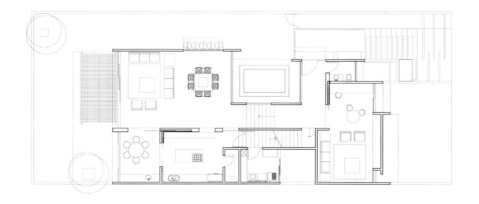

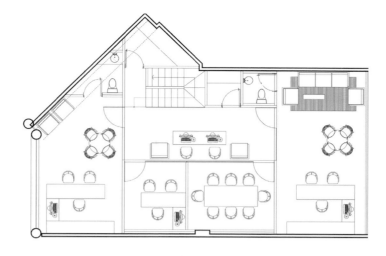

Exhimoda Office

In the present case, an insurance company decided to share its premises with a construction firm, establishing themselves on a site in a mall with an excellent location. The key of the project lies in the re-assignment of the premises for the operation of this strategic alliance, whereby the ground floor is assigned to the insurance company for the better attention of clients. The major problem to be solved in this case is how to adequately distribute the natural light for all working in both companies: the isolation of offices is solved using glass sheets and grinded fringes, allowing the passage of light without impairing privacy.

Photo: Mito Covarrubias

Ricardo Agraz

N House

The "N" House is based on three levels: the garage area is located in the basement together with service areas and a game room. The stairway, attached to the central wall, creates a spatial connection between all these different levels of the house, also acting as the meeting point for dwellers right in the moment when they exit the private rooms. The ground floor is where the hall, dinning room, and kitchen are, surrounded by a minor patio where a tree offers peace for these areas. Right on the side, the living room and family room are also framed by this patio. Last but not least is the first floor where the three bedrooms enjoy both the patio and garden views.

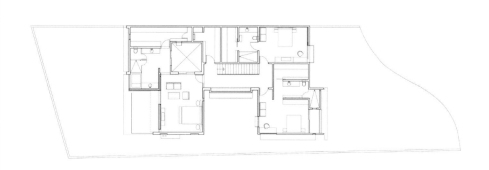

I House

Having privacy as a primary objective, the architects pursued the solution for a unique way of dwelling, bringing out a space where programme sequences come to a minimal expression. Therefore, endless interior spaces are the basis for the architectural solution, where a central patio vanishes in between the different atmospheres of the house. The inside extends to the outside, creating a place that gives a beginning for a light and shade dialogue, a continuous flow between transition and contemplation, and a balance between the user and observer. Scale plays an important role in the spatial sequence in order to link the main scheme in intimate relation with the patio.

Suntro House

This house is located in a residential area of Oaxtepec, a place of exceptional natural beauty. It is contiguous to the north with the hill of Tepozteco and to the south with a highway. The lot is oriented to the northeast with a splendid sight of the Tepozteco. The natural light is filtered through the folds of the house in shape of rays that softly flood the spaces. The shape responds to the hard hotness of the site, to place every space in the best way inside of a curved skin that opens to the immediate context to obtain the best climate and views to allow the wind circulation.

Mirror's House

A large house built during different periods of the 20th century has been adapted to current functional and esthetic needs, without neglecting its historical and architectural value. Original architectural elements of this house were restored and in some cases reevaluated with a contemporary vision, which, added contemporary design and new materials to the existing architecture. A mix of new and old was the goal of the interior design, contemporary furniture with clear and simple lines coexisting with antique pieces loaded of all the ornamental value of the époque. Old concepts like "wall stencils" are the inspiration for a 20th century version; free style and bright colours outstand the neutral white walls.

Sheraton "Centro Histórico" Hotel Spa & Fitness Centre

On the site where for decades stood the Hotel del Prado, which suffered damages during the 1985 earthquake and was later demolished, the construction of an office building was planned. Later, given market conditions at the time, it was decided to build a modern design hotel that integrated the latest technologies and would have the possibility of adapting to new developments in coming years.

In order to extend the business traveller's stay over the weekend, a Fitness Centre & Spa, and 3,000-square-foot garden were included. This gardened area match in a certain way with the original design of the old Alameda, but with a more contemporary landscape design; it overlooks the Alameda Park, sourrounds the cafeteria, the lap pool and paddle tennis court. The Spa services include massage and beauty treatment salons, a gym, an indoor swimming pool and social events open area. All areas are decked in teak wood and they are secluded from the main street but at the same time they participate in the urban context.

Finishes selection was defined by their cost, efficiency, durability, maintenance, reposition, and stock availability while staying within Starwood's specifications and standards.

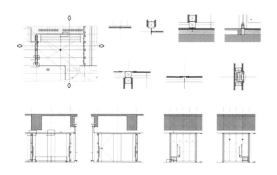

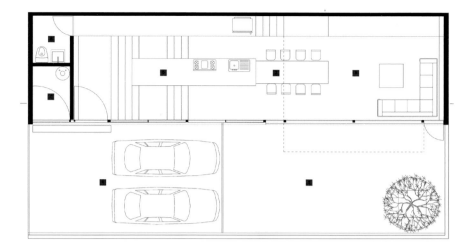

Casa Y

A corridor begins in the access and is placed above the cupboard before reaching the bedroom, which floats over the empty space crossing the crystal façade, and flies towards the garden looking for the view of the sweetgum-tree on the west. The bedroom splits itself from the edge generating a strip of light that descends all the way to the living room. All the spaces are connected to the garden but with different hues of light. The walls and the concrete roofs enhance the feeling of protection. The experience of intimacy is improved by the depth, by the concrete, and by the light.

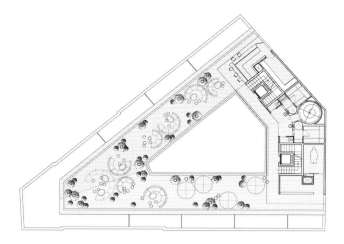

Hotel Condesa Df

This hotel project recycled an apartment building dating from 1928, catalogued by Mexico's National Beaux Arts Institute. The perimeter of the building was preserved up to the first corridor, which was restored to its original state. The inside of the building was demolished to build an opened patio, which is the central space of the project. A dialogue between architectures went on in here; the circulations leading to the hotel rooms were turned facing this open, public space, where the building was connected to the outside. Folding aluminum shades open into the patio, infinitely transforming the space. The shades virtually extend the corridors and offer a play of seeing and not being seen.

Linda Vista

The house is like a shell that takes care of the interior life. A plan in "L" shape takes the street sides of the site and becomes the perfect way to organise the programme towards the centre of the site. The first thing designers did was remove the wall between the existing kitchen and the living room to open up the floor plan and take advantage of the amazing views. They designed a new stair to connect the upper level to the lower level and then completely re-envisioned the lower level. The new roof respecting mid-century modern style was part of the new vision for the home.

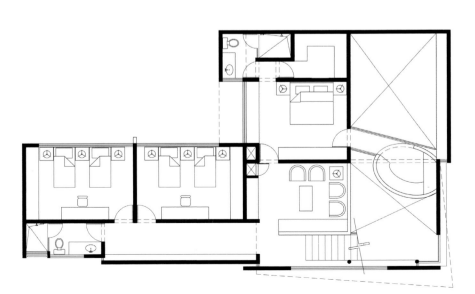

Specia Gourmet Shop

With a limited funding, it was proposed to redesign the company's run-down local premises to improve its image. A design was proposed which would make an architectural invitation to users to fully explore the premises. The solution was found in structural cardboard pipes which are primary used as centring of construction; this is a flexible and economical system that makes it possible to carry out a variety of detailed operations at an affordable price with an original image. The special layout thus achieved was especially attractive to new users inviting them to enter the shop, to explore it and buy something as it displayed the company products to better advantage.

Photo: Antonio Vilchis

Gustavo Slovik/Miguel Sanchez

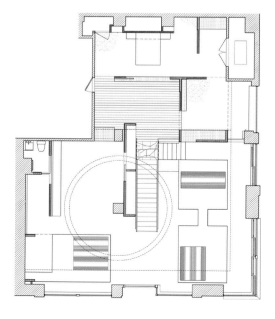

Ms-borbon House

For entry, you cross a water mirror where a glass volume floats over the lobby. From this, one can, by a ramp more than a half level, arrive at the social area that surrounds a central space fed by zenithal light. There are no windows in the traditional sense of the word; the glass is treated as independent volumes or as transparent extensions of the game of walls that are interlaced in the central space. Each space was thought for a specific aim of contemplation of the landscape where the "Cerro de la Silla" with the city on their feet is the drop curtain for the most important spaces.

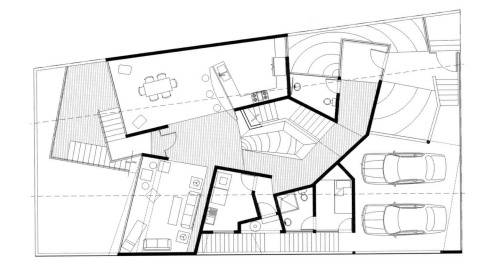

Cidade Jardim Mall

Cidade Jardim Mall is an outdoor mall, such as Ball harbour shops in Miami, but in addition to first-line international brands, the new shopping centre goes further when the subject is the design sophistication, taking care of the project, choosing the material... mainly for being opened and not using very expensive materials to compete with the shops' projects. A low profile-chic Fougeres floor, brown aluminum handrail, ceiling fans and furniture especially designed to be in an elegant and safe street atmosphere, are exactly the difference just said above from this mall and the other malls in the city.

Studio Manolo

In this little project, one can see the explicit inspiration of Sao Paulo architecture from the 1960s and 1970s. That architecture lost its strength at some point during the 1980s, perhaps due to its thermal-acoustic discomfort. That can be solved by today's modern technology. The imperative need in this photographic studio was to create parking spaces for at least fifteen vehicles. The solution was to bring the offices up to the first floor and free up the entire ground level. Another important issue in the project was the building technique: the designer chose precast concrete panels, a metallic structure and drywall to enable construction within a period of three months.

Primetime Nursery School

This project is the first Brazilian nursery developed from a programme specially directed for children aged from zero to three years, based on an exclusive educational concept. The priority was to conceive of an abstract non-stereotypical space with a ludic character that would meet the functional demands of the numerous procedures involved. The technical team involved offering ideal solutions for the best air and water quality, floor heating and balanced lighting. The landscaping was equally conceived to guarantee the safe interaction among the children. In addition to natural materials, the colours yellow, orange and red were selected to create a stimulating atmosphere.

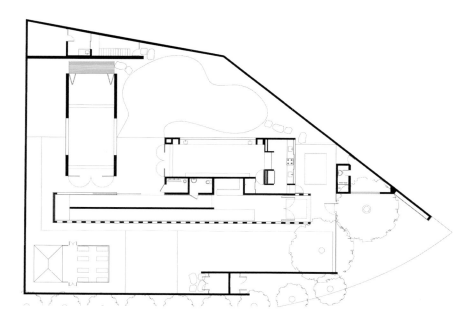

Iporanga Beach House

The project was built as a vacation house for a couple with two children, and was brought to life during the visit to the land. The house includes such features as suites, living rooms of the Guaruja Sea. Landscape and vegetation were preserved, with the structural platform becoming the base of the new area for development of the project. The client's desire for an external area where his children could play was integrated into the house, and the house itself is structuralised in steel, while the closings are all done in glass and wood.

Photo: Leonardo Finotti

Studio Arthur Casas

Dr. Helton's Medical Clinic

The space for the private practice specialised in orolaryngology must (nourish) provide well-being to all the patients who attend it. The search for this objective was carried out through the constructive/building elements already at use there. The white ceramic floor provides freshness; the walls, also white, indicate serenity; the fluctuating coating of plaster shows lightness; the furniture in seedlac and glass adds the sense of cleanliness. This space, built for the Reception and Waiting Room for the patients, is also composed of a small area for entertaining children, in a way of keeping them serene and quiet in an orderly fashion while waiting for the service.

Volume B

The shop was built using rustic material and rustic executions. Rustic and modern. Micasa Volume B recalls the artisan processes of popular civil construction, and, above all, the modern Brazilian buildings, brutalist projects in a brutalism reinvented south of the equator, attentive to the local knowledge. The façades of the shop were made in a not-very-common manner using exposed reinforced concrete: the outward appearance of the material, generally done very precisely with new lumber, is used here randomly, chaotically, and some wood was not even removed after curing. The brises-soleil in the offices are made of a net of reinforcing bars used for the concrete.

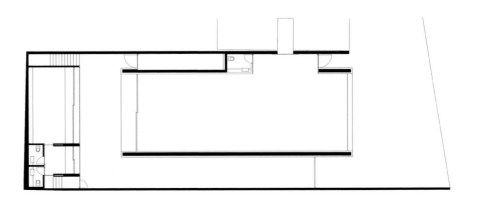

Alphaville Residence

This luxurious apartment is designed to create a harmonious atmosphere. A perfect combination of robust, warm and pure materials like wood, stone, glass and marmoleum and the use of sober colours with colourful accents make it a timeless and stylish residence. If there was a piece of furniture not exactly suitable for this place, the designers would redesign it and had it produced. For example, the grey furniture in the studio, the bed, the bamboo bathroom furniture and the high gloss white cupboards in the living are redesigned. What is special about this project is that the apartment is designed "upside down": the design studio is placed on the ground floor, and the sleeping rooms on the first floor.

Panfichi Beach House

Located at Honda Beach 130 kilometres south of Lima in the coast of Peru, this beach house is conceived as a floating structure which houses the architectural programme while the sloped natural site remains as innate as possible. The connection between architecture and territory is limited to the minimum necessary only to structurally hold the house while it creates outdoor places such as a small pool, a sand garden and a natural rock patio. This "floating box" is separated from both neighbours allowing ocean view to the rooms located in the back of the site to satisfy one important objective in the design: "to provide ocean view to all rooms".

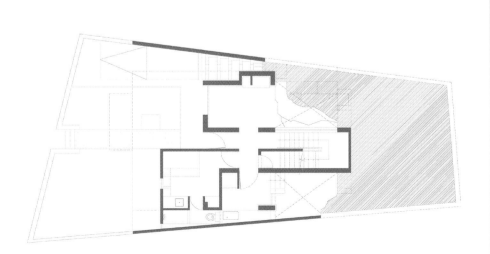

Tienda Naturas

The architects had cleared that the project should have a very clear picture, with the fewest possible elements. They divided the site into two. The new area, which reaches nearly five metres tall, has a wall lined with glass screen printing segments, in allusion to the shadow of the trees that enter the local level. The sky of this new body appears to float in the air, separated by glass walls favouring a high brightness. At the centre of the cube architects placed a large lamp, which resembles a crown of thorns. More light sources provide sausages and two colourful screens cylindrical falling on the top box.

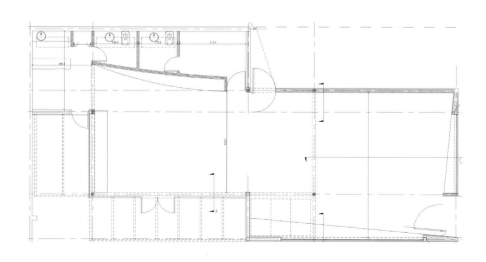

Restaurant Dominga

The project was awarded first place in a private architectural contest. The restaurant is located I a major shopping complex facing a high speed track. From the outside, the existing façade is affected by the projection of images from the inside through a large translucent screen. Thus the visitor can be transported to any scenario based on digital imaging: Tokyo, New York, Kualalumpur, the cabin of boeing or the bow of a cruise. Given the visual noise caused by the nature of commercial concentration, this project was conceived as a counterpoint of abstract expression.

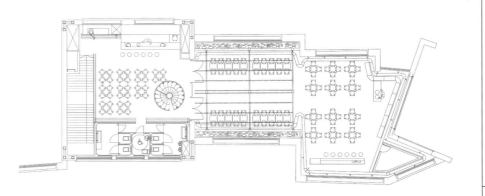

Amandita Bar Restaurant

Located in the town centre, this country-style house, which used to be the local club, is situated in an area that has little relation to the coastal spirit of the town. That is why the design of Amandita aims to build up that beach atmosphere that all vacationers are looking for when they escape from the city to go to the coast. The remodelling keeps the original structure of the house, leaving the adobe, brick and native woods on sight. Being a very low-budget project, it favoured a "soft" terrace by building a deck and a wooden roof structure, which, controlling the different light intensities, would support the exterior programme.

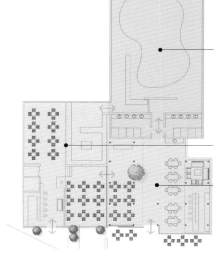

Baraona Marre Attorney's Office

The project aspires to exemplify the ideas of efficiency and classical avant-garde through the management of noble materials such as marble and crystal. The generous and open spaces have been abundantly illuminated with natural light through translucent office closings as well as artificial illumination that dramatises perspectives and focuses relevant points. The massive preexistent structural pillars were covered in mirrored glass, in order to visually lighten their presence, and in addition, vertical ducts, storage zones and cafeteria equipment were added.

Pauta Entrevista

The room is designed with transparent structure to make the user close to the nature. The evening glow makes the red wall beside the stairs dazzling and the environment passionate, which is just to express a welcome to visitors. Large glass windows are used in the living room, which makes there spacious and bright. Thus, the user can save much energy and feel the power of nature. A characteristic element is considered for bedrooms. This volume will be connected to other areas through a glass connecting bridge. Through these design elements the designer wanted to get a relationship between dwelling and land.

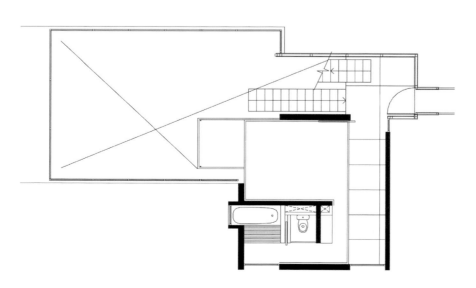

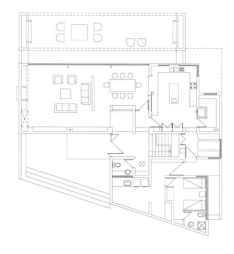

House in Marbella

The house is a white and hermetic object from the outside, but well lit and warm from the inside. This is achieved by a combination of large glass planes to the north and specific light entry-points to the south, east and west. To potentiate and guarantee more privacy, the house closes up its other façades, presenting a hermetic image towards the street and the neighbours. All the windows have concrete awnings which contribute to extend the feeling of space. Finally, there is an emphasis on potentiating the public areas of the house, including the kitchen, by giving them a greater height and interrelating them.

Muse Club

Muse is a club that occupies three different spaces overlooking an atrium in the newly redeveloped Tong Le Fang factories in Shanghai. In a neighbourhood where new nightclubs abound, Muse must differentiate itself by asserting an architectural identity through inventing a spatial experience unlike all the others. Drama here is achieved not simply by appliqué or ornamentation, but an experiential theatre that is at once monumental and sensual. The insertion of a cocoon takes centre stage both physically and metaphysically, serving an array of functions in terms of spatial organisation, yet always reminding the transformation that every club-goer secretly desires.

Photo: Neri & Hu Design And Research Office

Neri & Hu Design And Research Office

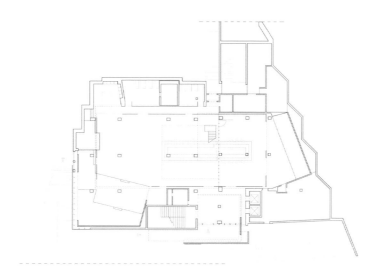

Beijing Whampoa Club

Beijing Whampoa Club is situated in a reconfigured traditional Chinese courtyard house amidst a cluster of modern high rises on Beijing's financial street. Upon entering the restaurant and travelling through the corridors, one is surrounded by a completely white space. Solemn and serene, the purity of the space draws attention to the Chinese construction details rather than obscuring it with colourful imagery, as in history. The white corridors provide rest for the eyes before their transition to the various decadent destinations. In contrast with the white corridors, the Bar is all black. Here, the traditional Chinese screen has been replaced and re-interpreted with a custom-made pattern.

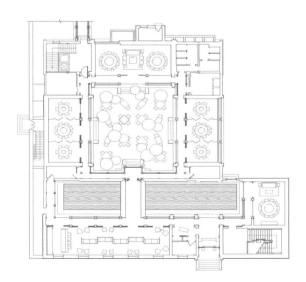

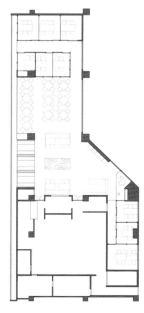

Sato Restaurant

This project was for a Japanese Family Restaurant Group to open its first Chinese branch in Shanghai and to start its branding and design its space. This Restaurant Group already operates on 217 locations in Japan. First of all, the designers wanted the restaurant to be reachable for ordinary Shanghai people in their daily lives by providing foods in reasonable price and good service. In addition, the designers valued open air atmosphere, so that people can feel ease to step into the restaurant. For this reason, the designers worked under the theme of "Consistent Art" in order for it to be able to deploy the same style and quality after their success in Shanghai.

2k Games

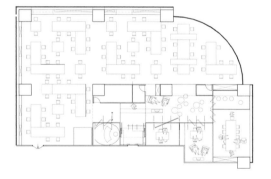

The designers mixed both the mental of game players and the childhood memory, using the souvenir of playing games under the shadow of an immense tree as a key-element. The simulated tree is composed of big vertical lacquered metal elements at the lower part, used as hangers; these are forming the body of the tree and slender elements at the upper part recovering the ceiling, forming the lamps. The red colour symbolises not only the logo of the firm but also the figurative world of computer games. The random arrangement of the ceiling lightings gives an impression of infinite expansion, forming an absolute landscape, not only transcribing computer game world but also giving a sense of natural environment.

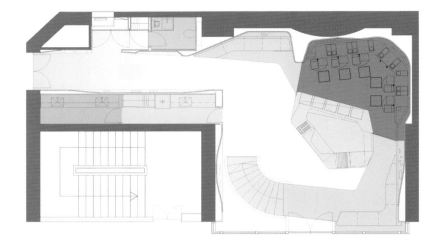

Erics Paris Salon

The remodel of Eric Paris Salon started with the need for a connection between the newly acquired second floor space, which will house the hair cutting stations in the future, and the existing saloon entrance, retail space and reception located on the ground floor. GRAFT introduced a continuous fluid staircase, linking these two spaces together and creating a vertical"cat walk". This main vertical circulation becomes the central spine which branches off and connects the different functional areas throughout the salon. The manicure and pedicure stations are set off as galleries for clients to admire the other roaming customers.

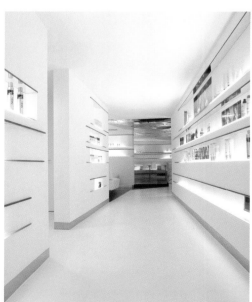

Red Box Karaoke

Various tones of grey and magenta were chosen as the key colours to provide a darkened envelope and to create the right mood for singing pop songs. Glossy and matte finishes were applied on ceilings, walls and floors in different zones to create illusion and mysteriousness. The corporate colour of hip magenta tone was superimposed and washed on various grey surfaces by glowing room directory or concealed lighting. Spatial rhythm was created by the transformation of intangible musical elements (e.g. rhythm, tempo and pitch) into tangible spatial elements of geometries (lines & circles) in various treatments of the envelopes of karaoke rooms of different sizes.

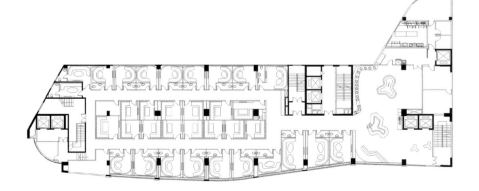

Branch In Changchun

One corner of the Changchun Library of Jilin Province is a culture exchange centre founded by International Exchange Foundation devoted to introduction of Japanese culture to Chinese people. Changchun, a city with extremely high percentage of Japanese language learning, is the city that really loves Japanese cartoon and popular music. In order to create a relaxation space with easy access to people for party or personal ease, SAKO Architects designed it by centring on trees. Any designs in the room are characteristic of a forest, attracting and charming, with people seating or leaning on the branches and hiding between branches.

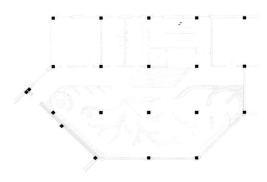

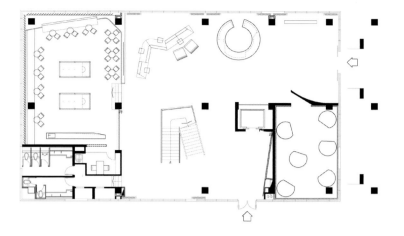

Mellon Town Now Club

The designers carved out volumes within this 12-metre-high box and created different shapes of floor plate at different levels that promote visual interaction. Visitors no longer need a floor guide for this club house because architecturally it is already a three-dimensional map. All these inviting elements lead the visitor to explore the club. The various slab height, slots opening, dynamic walls and white form create different scenarios at different points at the club. The streamline reception counter is visually light and promotes a floating feeling. Even the main staircase is not a standard one. The two landings do not fall on the same vertical grid.

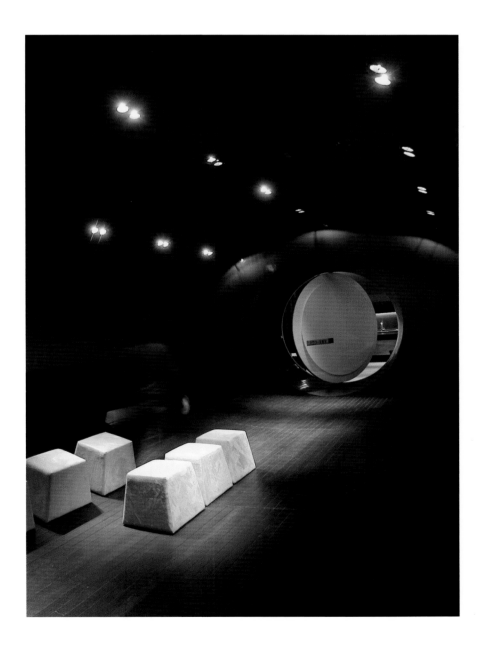

Photo: Virgile Bertrand

Zstore

The designer tactfully applies visual elements in the design; successfully make the 8,000-square-foot showroom into a fashion furniture gallery space. French windows of both two floors organically integrate the interior design with the outdoor view, attracting much attention of passers-by. Glass display shelves and lamp post highlight features of the displaying multi-colour and multi-style seats, meanwhile, creating multilayer vision enjoyment. Walking into the shop, people would be surprised by the special display of the furniture which breaks the barrier of traditional furniture displaying manner, as if entering an art gallery.

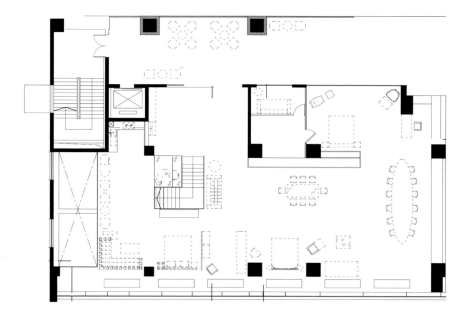

Gream

FELISSIMO in Beijing

The client wanted to create a shop that has different combinations of merchandise to suit the season or the feeling of the times freely. Generally speaking, a shop needs a variety of furniture such as showcases, checkout counters, tables, chairs with different dimensions, etc., all of which should be changed as per the season's requirements. Should we regard all these different furniture and the changes without taking into consideration each factor independently in our design?" Considering these requirements, Keiichiro Sako, SAKO Architects developed a very flexible unit furniture termed "cubic furniture" by considering boxes with two sizes (400 mm x 400 mm x 400 mm and 400 mm x 400 mm x 800 mm) as the basic sizes.

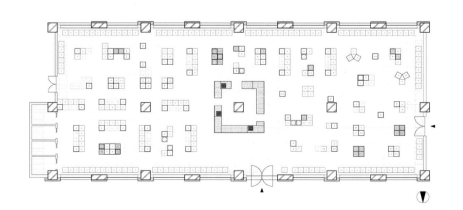

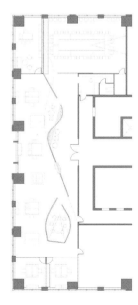

Swissnex

Originally the idea was to open the ceiling to gain more height; the room height was 2.4 metres. But the canals, cables and the huge air conditioners have taken up almost all ceiling space. The strategy became to make the space higher only where it was possible, then all in-and-out ventilation can be hidden in inner sides. The interior is divided into two spaces, public space and private working space. The two parts permeate into each other. There is the curved partition wall in between; the public side is in Swiss red, and the office side in calm white; the curve floats and shapes a waiting space or a discussion corner, and wanders to a space of meeting room in the end.

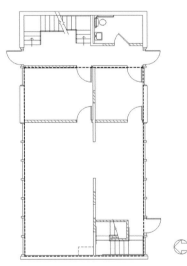

Ogilvy Beijing Offices

To creat a creative yet brutally honest space, the client did not want the all too predictable design gimmicks associated with advertising agency offices, offices,opting instead for a design which is pared down and soulful. An open, light and professional environment that encourages staff communication and reflects the corporate culture of this respected and businesslike consulting firm, whilst subtly including a Chinese touch incorporated in such elements as bamboo flooring, wood screens, and water. A refreshingly modern and elegant interior infused with references to local cultural and architectural heritage. The texture of Beijing is imaginatively re-presented.

La Rossa

Stylish red and pure white are the skeleton of the design direction. Flower graphics around the home form a very warm atmosphere for this 3-bedroom sea view unit. A red TV cabinet acts like a red carpet, to serve as a foil to a contrasting tree wall. This makes this square-like living room a romantic place. A tree-like bookshelf in the study is not only functional, but also becomes a focus of the unit. Its grey square boxes and big red translucent flower on the door create a dramatic contrast. In the master bedroom, bedding, wallpaper and the wardrobe doors are covered by flowers. This continues the theme of "flower" for the whole design.

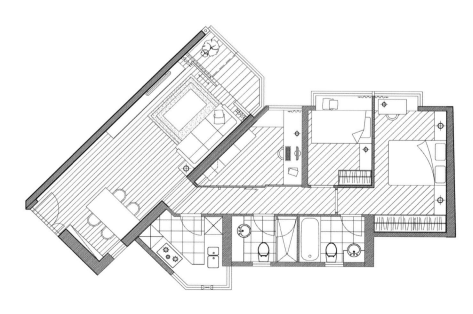

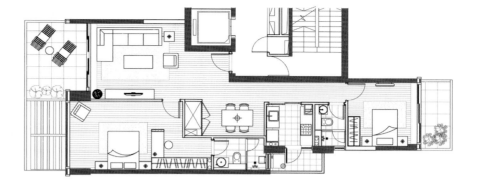

Mangrove West Coast

To give a deep impression for all visitors, the designer chose "flower" as a theme of this flat. Flower graphics and patterns can be found everywhere, on walls, glasses, accessories, etc. The fresh feeling is reinforced by the bright red and white colour combination. Red cushions, chairs, and artworks are becoming the focus of the flat. Flower graphics create shadows and add layers on the plain wall. Besides, the bird graphics on the corridor act as a guide to bedrooms. The "flower" continues in bedrooms on beddings, artworks and wall graphics. They create a refreshing and warm atmosphere.

Photo: MoHen Design International/Maoder Chou

MoHen Design International

Metropolitan Chic

For this project, the uses of design and materials are more controlled. From some point of view, it is also clear and not too much. The spaces are separated clearly. The hallway divided space into two sides. The living room faces the kitchen and the master bedroom faces the quest room or the study room (the small room is either for guest or study). Extra decorations are to be left out in this case. Only the main wall at the back of television is left. The wall was embedded with steel bars making a strong contrast of materials and details of design which is mainly for the reason to hide the CD cases inside. Spacious visual effects of lines, uneven surface and lightings are used on the ceiling to separate spaces.

The frequent use of mirrors widens this small and compact residential apartment which you can see from the entry cupboard, back wall of sofa, kitchen and the back wall of the master bed. The brown colour and the mirrors make a good combination (light yellow and light brown), making the space look simple . The materials are also affordable and easy to get. It is suitable to use these kinds of materials for ordinary households. Simple luxury is the right expression for the living character of such group of people living in Metropolitan Chic.

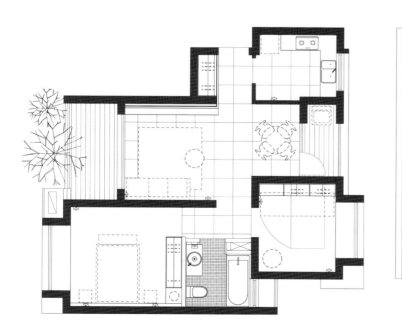

Natural Organic Space

The central body line and the horizontal active line on the ichnography separate the ground floor into few main areas; one half is the living room and the other half is bedroom. The designers don't want any obstacles to cut the public area's view and try to expand the vision of the public area to its utter size. The doorway extends to the end of the hallway in order to combine with the dining area and move its extension to connect with the kitchen. The lower side of the Television wall in the living room is left with an open hole, because it wants to connect with the study area in the master bedroom as a breathing tunnel in the visual prospect.

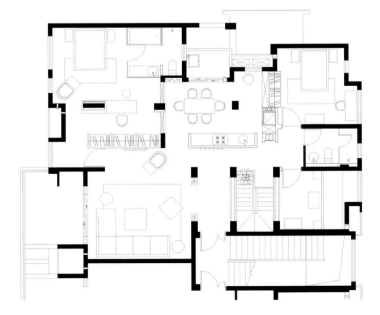

Kid's Republic in Beijing

Kid's Republic in Beijing is composed of an event room on the ground floor and a picture book shop on the first floor. The event room is a rainbow space connected by 12 coloured rings with different perimeters. Activities like story telling sessions and animation shows are periodically held here. The section gaps on floor, wall and ceiling are processed as illumination or display case, as well as stage and auditorium. Along the stairs, the children can enter a world of picture books on the first floor and seven coloured ribbon starts from the hall and goes up along the stairs till the book shop.

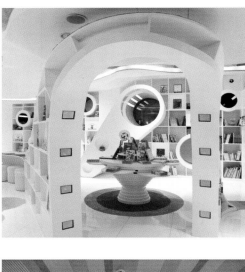

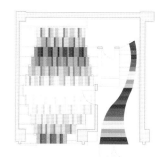

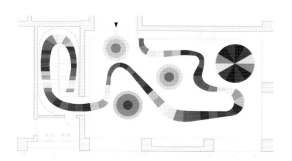

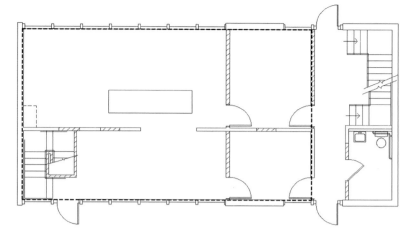

British Council

In the plan, the designer combined the reception area, casual meeting area and pantry into the same zone. He decorated this zone with British designer furniture whose function is beyond furniture. It is the key element of this office and that's why the designer minimised other material and details so as to light up the furniture. The working space is a pure open space which encourages communication and teamwork. The office is in white colour tone with decorated colour from the furniture and it leaves lots of discussion topics to all people visiting there.

Photo: MoHen Design International/Maoder Chou

Mohen Design International/Mohen Chao

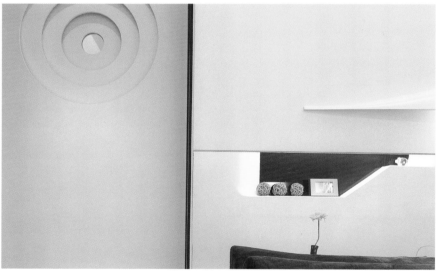

Space of Femininity

This small space is designed for a free, single woman. The designer was inspired to use curvy lines to present the space. Simple arcs and curves make the space look more lively. Even if you don't plan the colours and materials, it still looks good. However, adding a large arc or line can ruin it, if not used correctly. But using curves for small details can sometimes add a little excitement to the area. Therefore adding curves to door frames, main wall of the living room, bed heads and furniture can give the whole space a little more characters.

Having a colourful wall in the hallway and putting some eggshell-like chairs in front of it gives a clear idea of the owner's age and sex. Having no walls in between the living room and dinning room gives a feeling of a lounge bar to the guests. Besides, there is a more lively atmosphere. A few piled circles will separate private and public spaces, with a bed in air, presenting a modern home of a beauty.

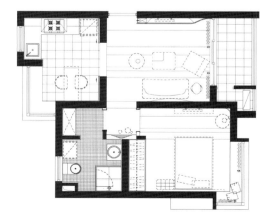

South Bay

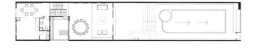

Recipient of the Andrew Martin Award, this three-storey home contains a wealth of spaces that makes it an ideal abode for entertaining. It possesses a format elegance that is enhanced by a staggered display case with recessed lighting in the living area. A central light well acts as a unifying focal point, with the staircase wrapping around this gloving niche. While the public areas are more neutral and feature furnishing such as a quartet of white marble coffee tables, the bedrooms and other private areas contain bold punches of colours. Meanwhile, a lap pool and outdoor barbecue area allow for outdoor entertainment.

Photo: CREAM Design Company

CREAM Design Company

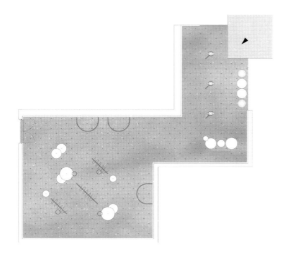

Felissimo 2 in Beijing

All that is used to display fashion dress and clothes is reduced to pits and plug-ins. Up to 1000 pits are arranged on walls and on the floor. All furniture and decorations like clothes-hanger, tables, cabinets, flower vases and posts are inlaid with steel tube plug-ins which could freely be applied to the pits. The pits are connected to power supply, which makes it possible for lighting fixtures to work. The plug-in of the circular light tube is used to rotate the face-in plug-ins by 90 or 180 degrees; the manner of node is simple and clear. As a result, the space quality is greatly improved by simply altering the way finished products are laid out and displayed.

Hugo BOSS

BOSS Orange offers casual collections for men and women. The interior of the shop is a contrast-rich interplay of authentic natural materials combined with high-gloss paint, white finished metal and brass surfaces. This combination creates an impact contrast for "radical chic". Coloured walls with finely etched graphics form a beautifully accented impression. The ground floor functions with its two entranceways and the 65-square-metre large surface area, as an opener to the ground floor. After walking up the stairs, with the wire netting handrail, you will get to the first floor, where located the two fashion boxes with the integrated changing rooms and a lounge area with vintage furniture. Hanging racks enframe the room.

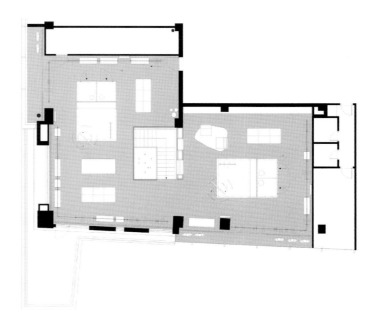

Exh Working Space

The main qualities of this Loft on the 16th floor are certainly the grand view towards Pudong, the clear height of 5.3 metres and its big free space. To create a young office space, the designers were conceiving how to change the interior as little as possible but to provide a sophisticated working atmosphere as much as possible. For a soft lighting environment, the concept was from the traditional stitch work — double wood structures tighten the fabric, shaping the huge lighting plates to filter the cold light by the energy-saving lamps and to avoid glare.

Fauchon, Beijing

Fauchon is a large retail design project that is completed little by little all over the world. It is presented as the "house of luxury culinary goods". Originally, Fauchon was established in Paris, on the place de la Madeleine, in 1886. Quickly it became the most exclusive place for food in Paris. Now, its products are sold throughout the world in more than 400 places. The new "house" is divided into three main rooms. The gold room is the bakery, the silver room is the restaurant and the black and white room, the largest of all three, is the fine grocery store. The entrance lobby and circulation spaces are pink.

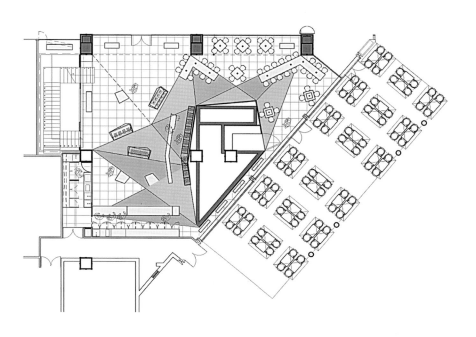

Metal House

A simple but strong visual image of a truly modern shopping window is created through the white coloured, exposed metal external wall. Track lighting is designed as an exhibition guide for visitors to feel the changes of the geometric layout formed with flowing lines and angular curves. From the reflection of the mirrors that wrap the columns, horizontally aligned shelves of metal corrugated boards display luxury accessories, and enliven the space. Together with over 300 pieces of laser-cut punched metal webs in the ceiling, the lighting, air-conditioning and hanging displays combine in clarity and simplicity to display the clean, smooth style of digital technology.

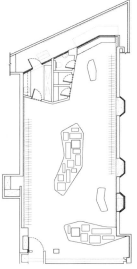

Updown Court Showflat

The designer's mission is to make the show flat attractive enough. Elegant silver and grey are chosen as the primary colours in the design. The key element to create the luxurious atmosphere is shiny and sparkling element. Glass and mirror are shiny and sparkling and a large amount of tinted glass and mirror is used here to achieve the effect and to enhance the visual impact. Geometric form and symmetric line are classic, elegant and timeless. The most successful use of it is the Art Deco period artworks. The whole design in the project is inspired from there. Wall panel with vertical asymmetrical groove lines is installed on the opposite wall surface and is extended to the TV wall. The groove lines would gradually be transformed to an abstract floral pattern to decorate the wall.

Ching Ping CHANG, Cherry TANG, Louis LAW, Chun Ern YEH, Yu Cheng Wang, Yu You Liao

Robyn Hung Wedding Boutique

This was the latest in a line of diverse shops from Robyn Hung that focused on weddings as the first try besides leisure. The shop was developed around the idea of a theatrical grand stair or the glamour of 1930s' Hollywood film. Mirror finished stainless steel faces the steps and the whole floor is carpeted in a light mauve. Shelving is treated in the same way as the step, winding along the walls and carrying both lighting and hanging systems for the merchandise. At the back top step are fitting rooms and a small lounge for customers. Its fresh design and attractive storefront gain many sales.

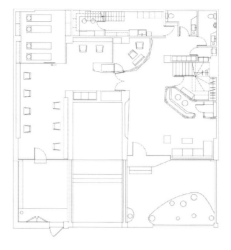

Hair Culture

Having "black diamond" as the central theme for its interior space, a contemporary and refined space is created. A multilateral geometrical cut is adopted to depict the quality of the mineral stones. The core space for both the ground and first floor is the mineral modules which are sculpted by black mirror glasses. Hiding behind the mineral modules, there are VIP rooms and other functional sections such as the washing area, the staff room, etc. Within the white painted space, the multilateral geometrical cut is once again employed on the ceilings, with the addition of brown epoxy floor, reinforcing the image of natural mineral rocks.

Bernini Fashion Headquarters

The headquarters of successful fashion retail group Bernini contains showrooms for all their main brands as well as reception, meeting areas and general office space. The brands all have show shops within the space representative of the shop designs for that brand. The in-between spaces where a pair of leather sofa stands are planned as informal meeting areas while the entire room can be set up for buyer shows at the start of each season. The reception counter forms part of a "ribbon" that connects all the areas together. Facing this is the design department screened by a full-length glass wall printed with graphics based on traditional cutting patterns.

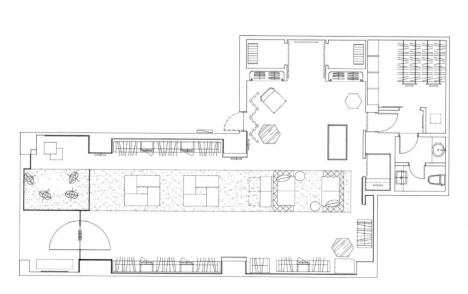

Hirose Tech Co. Ltd., 5.6f

The designer hopes that through designing the office space, it can create a positive work atmosphere. Therefore the blue belt-shaped lamp box is used from the company's entrance into the office. Displaying furniture, hanging large chandeliers and using grey aluminum wall, all present a calm work environment. In the conference room there is a large oval table and electric shutter. In the Responsible room, the use of colour-changing optical fiber for the smallpox, enables the space to have a sense of more levels.

Photo: Liu Her-rang

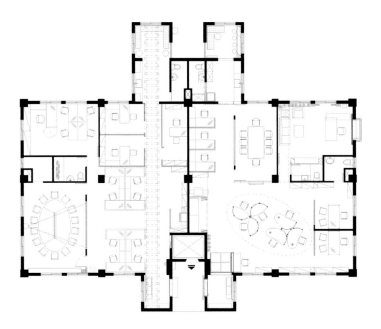

Lin Eddy E+ interior design studio

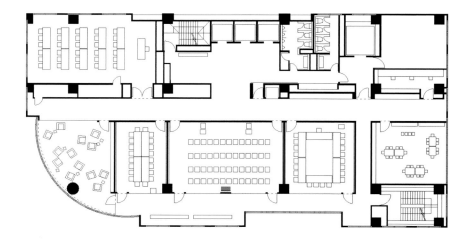

Xue Xue Institute

The aim of the interior design was to promote communication between the different groups' exchange as a basis for creative learning and working. The entire complex is structured similarly to an open loft apartment, in which people from different faculties come together and are able to design their environment according to their requirements in a flexible and functional way. E15 stands for timeless design, specially-selected materials and superior-quality production. The company was founded in 1995 in London. From its current headquarters near Frankfurt, architect and co-founder Philipp Mainzer heads up E15 as a well-known brand with an international market.

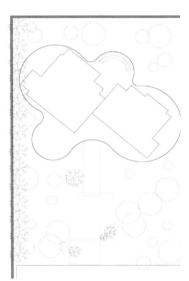

Glassware on Water

The glass bricks created totally different day-and-night views in this city. During the day time, the light inside the space is natural and during the night it turns into a light vase. To determine this project's serenity and noisiness, the designers attempted to use solid recyclable materials such as charcoal to define this boundary. The reception explains not only the void and solid of the building but also the relation of the space and view. For this project, the designers used three main recyclabe materials, for outer side, the charcoal and for the main body, the translucent glass bricks.

Residence at Goldwin Height

The designers cover a wide range of project varieties from delicate residential to commercial shop and restaurants recently. Constant style is not a major intention of their design belief but rather the flexibility and feasibility on different thinking input into the client's keen request, in which the style is a mixture with function and humanity. Very high quality materials were used to match the quality of the lobby finishes in colours that were neutral enough to house any vendor they might get in the future to operate the residence.

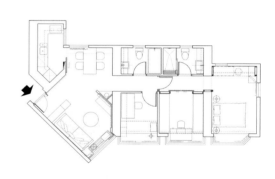

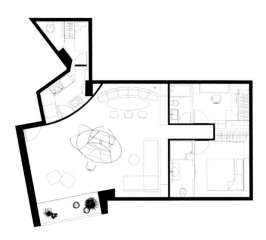

"360" Innovative Living

Johnny Wong and Miho Hirabayashi of FAK3 have created a home in Hongkong for Joanne Ooi, creative director of Shanghai Tang that took the concept of open multi-functional spaces to a whole new realm. Wong and Hirabayashi have developed an iconic elliptical entertainment cabinet that can rotate 360 degrees, which sits as the central focus to the apartment. On its two longer sides, it houses a set of keyboards and a customised study desk; the two shorter sides accommodate storage and a television. Fitted with industrial strength bearings that can support up to two tonnes, the walnut wooden cabinet rotates with the push of just one finger.

Nobu Intercontinental Hong kong

The restaurant's panoramic view of Victoria Harbour served to inspire, and now reinforces, the strength of the oceanic design elements, though the restaurant's lighting, colours, materials and layout combine to create a cosy intimacy. The low-lit stacked timber portal ushers patrons in from the hotel, leading to the luminous onyx and Ficus wood bar which showcases a dewy cherry blossom mural. Gleaming black river stones frame the inset bar and also appear in hanging cascade screens throughout the restaurant. Richly hued upholstery and iridescent plastered surfaces refer to the rainbow of colouration in marine life and enhance the warmth of the light.

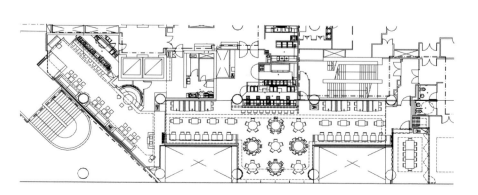

Source

The living conditions of Hongkong from public and private sectors set against the eras of 1960's, 1970's, 1980's, 1990's and 2000's are the subjects of study in this installation. Layout plans of housing from different times are etched onto transparent acrylics and installed into 5 cubic birdcage matrixes representative of the 5 decades. Superimposed chronologically, the 5 matrix walls shall take the viewers to a visual journey of time on the palimpsest of the living habitats in Hongkong over 5 decades.

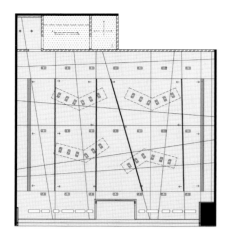

DJS

DJS is a new jewellery label launched by Chinese Arts & Crafts (HK) Ltd. selling diamond and jade. It is a total branding exercise to offer new retail experience of a jewellery shop targeted at middle class customer group in the local competitive market. The interior & C.I. design strategy adopted was to make use of the common natures/ chemical structures and cut shape "facets" of diamond and jade to generate a unique identity for the brand. To achieve this, the interior design made use of the metaphor of interpreting the retail space as a glowing gemstone to contain the two different types of prestigious merchandises for the customer to explore.

Louis Vuitton Flagship

The shop is accessed through two entry points, from the street and from the shopping centre levels. The main stair volume, designed as if carved out of a solid block of stone, organises the project by connecting three distinct levels. The sandblasted glass treads of the stair feature built-in LED panels containing video images on each walking surface, including video representing an airport arrivals/departures board to connect with the busy Hongkong traveler. Customers can experience these video images individually with each step. Customers at ground level can also view the reflected images from the mirror on the ceiling.

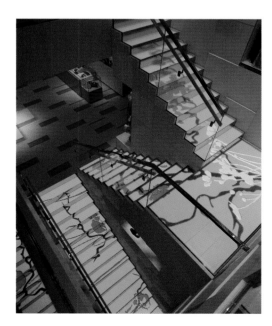

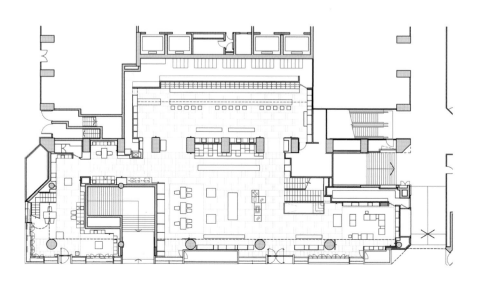

Photo: Vincent Knapp, Stéphane Muratet, Peter Marino Architect

Peter Marino Architect

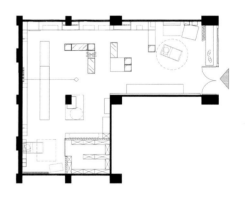

Kaloo Prince Building

For this truly international project, Axiom Oval Partnership Ltd. was asked by an international French retailer of soft toys and baby items in around 35 countries to create a design concept and implement it across shops worldwide. A distinctive retail environment embodying the company's brand values of "love, care and happiness" was created and successfully implemented in their Paris, Munich, Madrid, Istanbul, Tahiti, La Réunion, and Tokyo shops. Entering into the second stage of the worldwide project, through different form of design, the shop located in Prince Building carries a stronger message.

Bossini

This major brand revamp exercise in association with Alan Chan Design was first implemented in Bossini's 10,000-square-metre flagship shop. The redesign, which was rolled out across all shops in Hong Kong and South-East Asia, greatly enhanced the shopping experience by providing a stronger brand identity, clearer display strategy which succeeded in not only retaining existing customers but also appealing to a wider customer base.

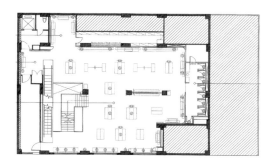

i.t in Hong Kong

This project is for the interior design of the No.1 multi-brand shop in Hong Kong in trendiness and in business. This is the renovation project of the shop where the designer designed 7 years ago based on the concept of "the future". Since the shop contains highly stylish products from all over the world, the designer tried to produce the design concept by bringing modernity and creating easy-to-enter atmosphere with the maintenance of the high quality function. The theme that the designer figured out for the concept was "the classical modern style". To that end, the designer emphasised the originality by using much materials used specially for the shop, through ordering the custom-made wallpaper, making the floor carpet in the original pattern, etc.

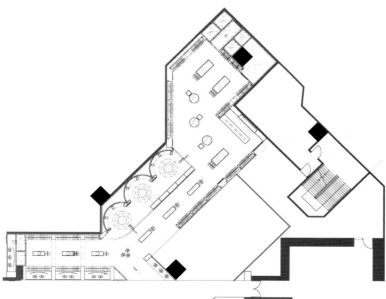

SKH Ming Hua Theological College

This project is the restoration of the 110-year-old Ming Hua Theological College. Design styles and materials are chosen to fit for the project's original style. Spaces for classrooms, chapel and conference room are redesigned and restructured for the best use of space. The veranda, windows, staircases, all the doors and the main entrance are totally revamped for the best aesthetics, comfort and practicality. Furnishings are all chosen to match with the historical architectural features of the building. Concealed lighting is employed to enhance the character and atmosphere without disturbing the original outlook and its unique style.

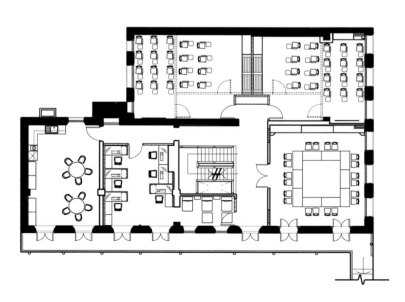

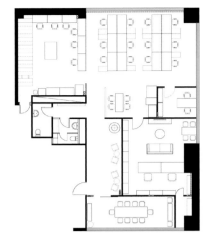

One Plus Partnership Office

Located just on the edge of Hong Kong's CBD, the new atelier of One Plus Partnership is more than just an idea factory of Ajax Law and Virginia Lung, the up-and-coming designers who established the firm; it is also one of their impressive sculpture that appears as the start-up of their new era. As a reference of their usual preference, the big black wooden door welcomes people into the designers' deep thoughts of design craft, just as what people can sense while they are being embraced by the even darker reception area. Yet black never means dullness to the owners, instead it represents the freedom space where all the creations begin.

HKJC, OMP Happy Valley

The Hong Kong Jockey Club wanted to offer their staffs a genuinely new facility that balanced healthy living, training, information access, and relaxation. The guiding philosophy was to integrate knowledge, health and fitness in a corporate environment. The result was OMP, or "Our Meeting Place", which comprises a modern canteen with a specially devised healthy menu, a fitness centre, a library and a music corner. The resulting design emphasises a casual, contemporary ambience that helps to enhance the employees' sense of belonging. All of these are contained in a three-storey rectangular space with each floor characterised by its own distinct colour scheme.

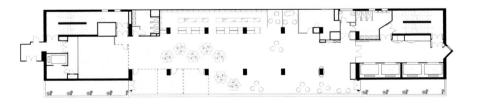

Photo: Axiom Oval Partnership Ltd

Axiom Oval Partnership Ltd

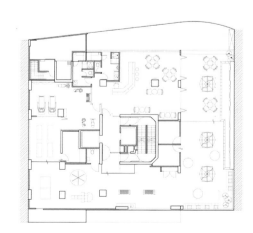

Club Morrison

The Morrison is located between Causeway Bay & Wanchai and it is a unique residential building. SEA Group give a free hand to Another, creating an original design for all interiors including club house, lobbies and finished flats. Mr. Pal Pang, design principal of Another believes that they do not provide typical design as the other buildings or accept international direction. Inferring from the legend of modernist Arne Jacobsen, the design element should be long lasting and valuable. Scandinavian style Showflat expresses a young and Cosmo living. The usage of materials let the interiors feel like a showroom.

East Asian Games

The exhibition for the East Asian Games (EAG) was created for the Sports Federation & Olympic Council of Hong Kong to promote public awareness about the 5th East Asian Games which will be held in Hongkong in 2009. Work in associate with UK Architect "MET STUDIO", we used bold primary colors to delineate display areas which are heralded by arches cantilevering into the open space above the badminton courts. On these, a series of light boxes with powerful images of renowned Hongkong athletes emphasize the content and route of the exhibition.

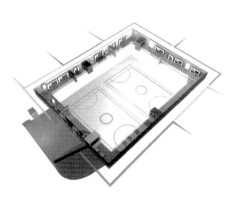

Showroom

China

Hong Kong

Photo: Aximoval

Aximoval

Photo: Barrie Ho Architecture Interiors Ltd

Youth SPOT at Tin Shui Wai

The site is a rectangular loop of angular and solid space, ironically also a literal expression of metaphor of the orthodox the target users of the space — youths of Tin Shui Wai are facing everyday. To tackle the site context and to bring new energy to the young users, dynamic elements were introduced in order to make the space look less square and more intimate. Inspired by young children running in the corridor space, decorative elements looking like a rubber band were added as a feature to the ceiling, linking the whole space. The rooms were also partitioned in fluid organic forms.

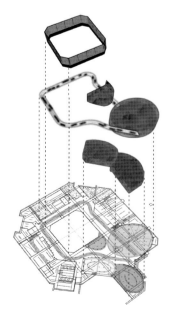

Mr. Barrie Ho

APM

The concept and design of this destination centre could very well become the norm for cities facing space issues, a 24-hour culture and the need for "third space" - everything in-between work and home. APM is more than just a mall; it is a breath of fresh air. Covering an area of 60,000 square metres, with 52 escalators, 18 restaurants and 6 cinema screens, APM is a destination specifically targeted at the youth and with a strong regenerative mission for its surrounding neighbourhood. Its architectural design creates strong links with existing transport networks, provides ample and dramatic event space, and creates a vivid and expressive stage-set that celebrates the vitality of commerce.

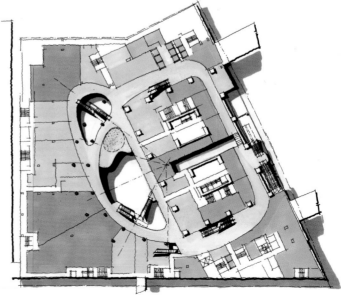

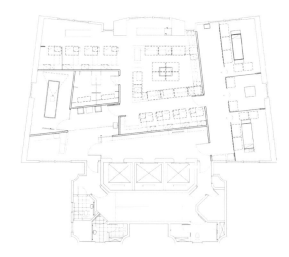

Boutique Office

The Barrie Ho Architecture show us a boutique style gallery office which is reserved for multi-functions such as exhibitions and cocktail events and it is equipped with multi-lighting levels catered for different events. The inclined Black-Textural Tile Wall intensifies the strong-sense perspective towards a reception counter, where Asian style settings are placed as a waiting area, creating a noble and graceful area. The Directors' Rooms are thus conceived as "Glass Boxes" along the Hall of Fame and are elevated for accessible storage, embodying a multi-function concept. In between the two elevated "Glass Boxes", a peaceful and luxurious VIP lounge performs as an accented space for visitors.

The Eight at Grand Lisboa Macau

Adopting a Chinese Treasure Box theme, "Eight Restaurant" effortlessly captures both the aura and mystery of Chinese culture in an elegant and modern reinterpretation that achieves heady mood of opulence always in harmony with tasteful furnishings and magnificent fittings. A unique and outstanding restaurant constructed of the highest quality materials, "Eight" is bathed in a breathtaking arrangement of gold, red and black tones, everywhere complimented or offset by intriguing and auspicious symbols taken from ancient times and mythology. In Chinese society, the number 8 is a symbol of good fortune and luck.

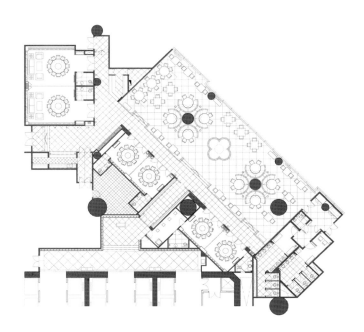

Photo: Andrea Buso

Dominic Kozerski & Enrico Bonetti

DKNY Flagship Shop

Upon entrance, the customer is presented with a ribbon of natural oak planks connecting the entry, split basement and mezzanine levels. This stands in dark contrast to the grey basaltina stone flooring. A mannequin presentation platform flanks the right side of the ground floor, which houses Women's Wear. To add organic elements for showcasing merchandise throughout the shop, hand-shaped powder-coated metal rods with wire-brushed oak bars were installed for hanging clothes, framed by white texturised plaster walls. To contrast these organic elements with a more urban feel inside the shop, white polyester lacquer was used to create the cash wrap area and used as a backdrop.

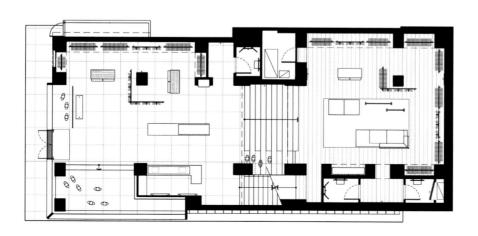

Busan Paradise Hotel

The overall concept of the Busan Paradise Hotel is modern classical. It has some of the elements of traditional classic spaces with a modern GAIA touch. The lobby has a traditional colonnade that leads into an open vertical area with sunken seating living rooms and over size modern/classic chandeliers above every seating area. With the hotel's geometry "grid", the space flows tranquilly into each other. Every niche and space has its own character. The lobby entrance acts as a contemporary art gallery. Bright materials, smooth surfaces and luxurious stone flooring are selected for this area. The lighting is mostly indirect, creating a soft, warm ambience.

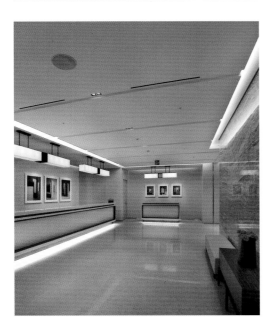

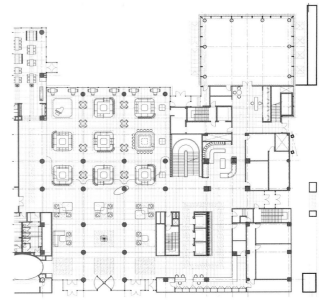

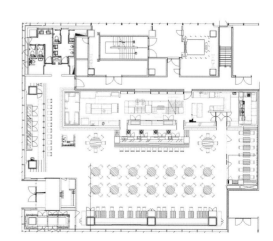

NOBU

NOBU's cuisine style is perceived as a stylishly creative approach introducing not only Japanese ingredients and food preparation method but also those with western elements. As for the design, it is necessary to have an international sensitivity to express the western techniques and architectural materials interpreted by "Japanese" design aesthetic, rather than just expressing Japanese elements in a Japanese way. NOBU's cuisine is not only food but also like an art painting and in the similar fashion the spatial design is functional and an art work at the same time. For this reason, each element and material which compose this space must have functional and artistic quality, which then will represent NOBU's concept.

AIP Restaurant

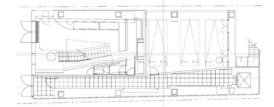

By inserting an inner wall made of thin steel plates within a French restaurant that faces Jozenji street in Sendai city, the designers were attempting to design a soft boundary surface that spatially mediates between the first and second floors of the existing building, and links the inner space of the restaurant with the space defined by the famous roadside zelkova trees that symbolise Sendai. For the inner wall of the Aoba-tei restaurant, the difficulty of welding complex shapes from thin steel plates within the existing building led to the use of shipbuilding technology for the actual manufacturing. Craftsmen who were highly experienced with the unique characteristics of steel plates were able to freely deform the steel by heating and chilling key points, and thereby producing complex curved surfaces.

Itsutsuya

"Itsutsuya" is a shop selling various Japanese craft goods such as the lacquerware. It is located at the centre of the old commercial area in the castle town. The designers wanted to design the shop which activate the excursion of the people who visited the town by combining with the street. The floor planning was decided based on the following rules. Do not put the fixture or furniture disturbing eyes in the centre area. And, install different fixture or furniture of the form in each area. The articles are displayed to various height in the floor where the prospect is good. And, the perspective changes according to the movement of eyes.

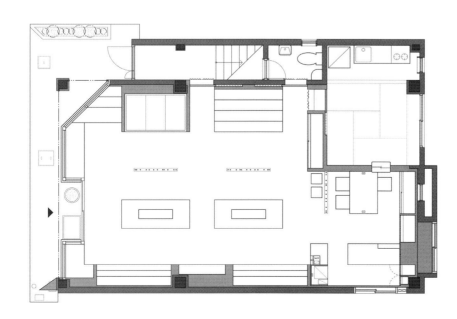

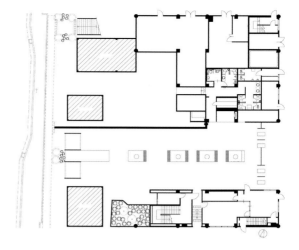

Keifuku Arashiyama Station

Approximately 30,000 natural bamboos have been applied to the concourse like a bamboo grove. In Arashiyama, there is the famous, traditional Togetsukyo Bridge, whose name means "moon crossing" because of the resemblance to that phenomenon, and the designers have added a little Togetsukyo-like bridge inside the station to enhance the elegance. In front, there is the curtain with traditional pattern which is to be replaced to suit each season. Each curtain has distinctive and fresh expression. At night, the place becomes even more dramatic and moody with lighting effects.

Lanvin Boutique Ginza

"Lanvin Boutique", located in Ginza Central Street (one of the busiest fashion district in downtown Tokyo), is a flagship shop of a French fashion brand that has a long history in couturier fashion. The designers were chosen by the brand's designer, Alber Elbaz, as the architect for interior and exterior design of the shop. The design was inspired by a contemporary French maison (residence) where the modern and the classical meet. The designer proposed a façade of continuous steel plate with 3000 clear acrylic cylinders inserted as windows, to look like a Lanvin's party dress on which diamonds are embroidered. The designers typically use window frames, sealants, and many other materials for window details.

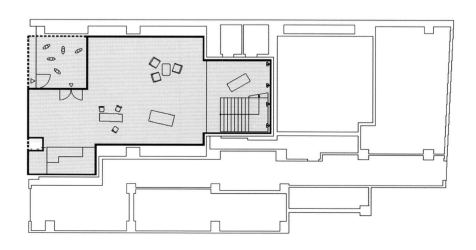

Immanoel

Immanoel is located in Kobe, a small port city in Japan on Osaka Bay in southern Honshu. The total area of this shop is only 24 square metres. Though it is cute and small, it contains lots of charming goods which grasp female's eyes tightly. Immanoel is a specialty shop of jewel or accessories. For the view of the brand, chic and cute images are needed. The designers prepare the shop as a jewellery box, with black walls and tabletops to suit the jewellery. It was simple in style but the designers considered material very well, black stainless steel, black flooring and so on.

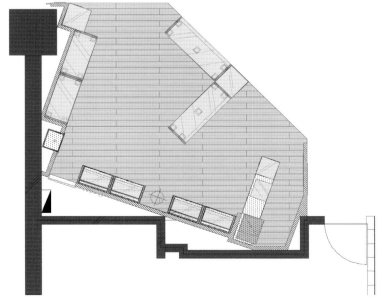

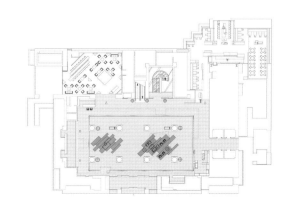

Ana Crowne Plaza Osaka

The project is full of dynamic, contemporary, and luxurious feature. The lobby is designed to create a shift: when entering the space, an impression of dynamism, elegance and refined modernity is created with the combinations of special materials and lighting design. The rhythm of thin vertical louvers creates a metallic curtain that wraps the lobby space with a soft and warm light. The large pillars in the centre are covered with mirrors, reflecting the metallic louver that seems to disappear within the space and emphasise the height of the lobby. It is multi-layered, behind the "metallic curtain", the different functions appear, such as the check-in counter, the access to the different restaurants and lifts.

Studio Graphia Marunouchi

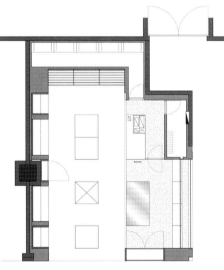

"Studio Graphia Marunouchi" is a general shop selling the goods with excellent design (stationeries, bags, clocks, books, etc.). The client is a company dealing with editorial design and stationery production. The attention was paid to the main creative work of the client being developed in paper mediums. The interior is divided into white side and dark grey side. The left side obtains a vague expanse by indirect lighting. The down lights in the right side emit the narrow light and emphasise shadow. The space of both sides have the steel pipes of the polygonal line form. Two objects which are not functional face each other, and disharmony is given to the space.

Addition

The masonry in turn, has been applied with a transparent high-gloss urethane paint finish, adding a contrasting sheen to the industrial surface. Thick layers were applied to the floor resulting in a highly reflective and intriguingly blurred finish, and diluted layers were applied to the walls and ceiling offering something more subtle. Three of the walls are offset with floor-to-ceiling façades of glass panels. The particularly thin hanging rail is a very poignant detail of these units, with its discreet and slender form and its aesthetic language in relation to other elements of the interior design such as the overhead slim-line lighting and the reflections they cast on the glass panel.

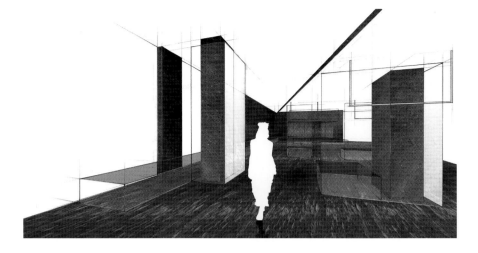

Sunaokuwahara

Essential to any high-quality interior, the different material's balance and combination have proved a key to the concept. This project has created not only an engaging contrast of roughness and smoothness, matt and gloss, depth and transparency, permanence and ethereality, but has also formed clean divisions and intersections of coherent light spatial volumes. It is the analysis between visual and physical boundaries of environment that suggests a new language of the built domain within a commercial context. This affords visitors with a subtly shifting environment as they journey throughout the shop; a series of dynamic views emerge and encourage exploration and anticipation.

Alook (Shibuya)

The designer differentiated the building from other buildings with normal façade by the designed façade. The narrow frontage can be disadvantage on the ground floor, however, the designer made the maximum opening section on the frontage so that people can see the inside of the shop as much as they can. Moreover, the designer inherited the usual interior design of each brand for the first, second and third floor. Therefore, the designer built the walkway to the upper floors in the centre so that each brand could make an appeal on right and left side of the wall respectively.

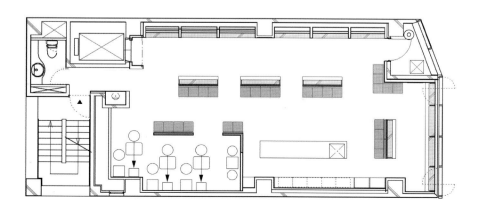

Alook (Osaka)

What the designer referred to create an actual design for the shop was the image of the recent airport. The process that the customers visit the optical shop, choose the glasses, have an inspection, and wait to receive the complete glasses requires a complex operation as a shop, in a way. The designer thought that the process is similar to the process at the airport that the passengers check in, check the baggage, and wait for boarding. The reason why the designer referred to the image of the recent airport to create the design is that the designer felt that the recent airport provides the above complex process comfortably and easily for people to be able to follow.

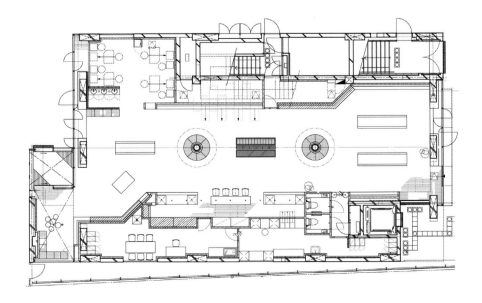

Lotus Beauty Salon

The seamless continuous space is realised by connecting the circular rooms with private space in order to resolve a feeling of closeness and oppression that is the issue of private rooms. The wall height of the rooms except haircut spaces changes according to the sloped floor, the function and the meaning of the wall tops changes seamlessly like a reception desk, waiting chairs, counters, and display boards. The designer made the joint disappeared by curving process. Though tangential lines of walls, floors and the textures usually give us the sense of distance, removing such information made the walls less oppressive.

Live Design

This project is for a personal computer school concerned with both graphic and presentation design. The designer wanted to create a space where one would feel comfortable and relaxed with no tension or pressure, so that the space encourages people to drop in. In order to create as much open and fluid space as possible, the designer created edgeless circular forms to ease both movement and flexibility. All interior elements both fixed and moveable are organised as a circular plan. Both addition and subtraction are performed with ease. In order to give the visual appearance of more space, the walls are made of milky-white acrylics only 1.5- metre- high.

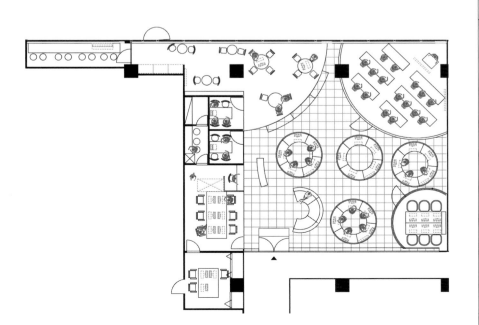

Photo: Kaori Ichikawa

Ryuichi Ashizawa

Meguro Office

The office is located near the Meguro River in Tokyo, on the fourth floor of an old office building. The clients wanted the usual spaces and functions — meeting space, management, workspace and storage to be separate, but also to maintain a sense of connection between them. Employees can move between spaces by walking over the parts of the walls that "sag" the most, thus emphasising the contrast between the uses of the different spaces. The spaces that need more sound-proofing are enclosed with the kind of plastic curtains you might find at a small factory so that people can work without worrying about noise but not feel isolated.

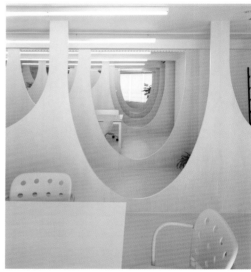

Photo: Daici Ano

Oki Sato

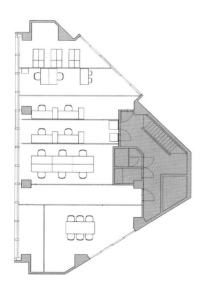

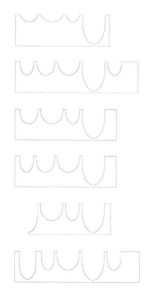

Hotel Screen Kyoto

Hotel Screen Kyoto is a study project in modernity. Smooth grey stones and large glass windows fit together in a series of overlapping planes, creating an irregular façade full of balconies and terraces. The reception area inside is clean, straight-lined and unadorned. Natural light floods through the area's floor-to-ceiling windows, providing a pleasant contrast to the all-white walls, sofas and tables, which in turn highlight the lobby's few strategically placed elements of colour, most notably, an elaborate gold and sapphire chandelier and a lacquered red reception desk. A different artist or designer individually conceived each of Screen's 13 guestrooms and, as such, each has a completely distinctive feel.

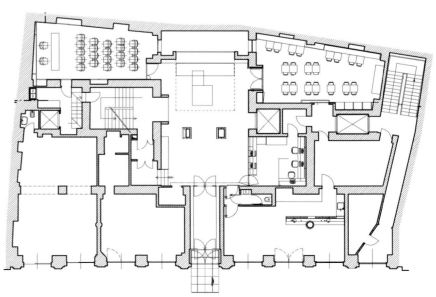

House for Mr. Romeo

This residence is built on the south slope of Mt. Moiwa in Sapporo, the capital city of Hokkaido. For this client who loves cars, it was very important to consider how he can look at his own car from his daily living space. Instead of locating the car garage and the living room next to each other directly, the designer's proposal was to provide a "reflect-garden", which brings the seasonal beauty of Hokkaido in between the living space and the client's car. In the "reflect-garden", a shallow water board is installed to amplify and take rain shower, snowfall, sun lights, and wind movement into the interior space.

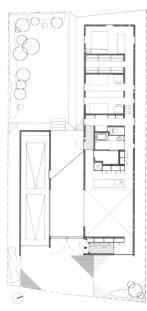

Nike

It is because that the direct management design office for Nike headquarters is set up in Tokyo. It draws up a plan as the strategic foothold for launching out from Tokyo into the global market. In its interior, the designers respect for Japanese traditional design and integrate modern colour of Tokyo and identity of Nike. The whole space was divided into different regions with different functions by Tailor-made shutter. The sun through the curtain against the background of mottled shadow, becomes a bright spot of the design.

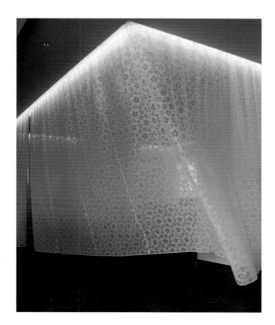

ROYAL ORDER

This is the first shop project of ROYAL ORDER, which is a mainstream jewelry brand from American East Coast, breaking into apparel business. The designers have thought that ROYAL DESIGN images are luxurious and rocking, and they focus on high-end consumers. Using materials which have a presence such as mortar and a black glass, they have couched the design with simplistic European motives. And for the functional capability, they could simplify and couch "Zen"-like ROYAL ORDER.

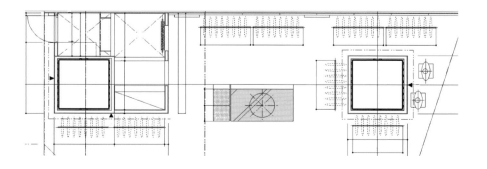

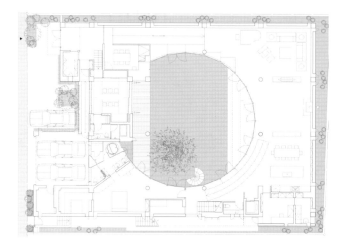

"House like a Museum"

The rectangular silhouette of the house was pushed to the boundary limits of the 776-square-metre property, in the centre of which was placed a 15-metre-diametre circular patio for each room to face and have a view of this central garden. Finish material for the exterior is basically diatomite over exterior insulation, while for the interior is predominantly Japanese stucco-paint for walls and ceilings and either bamboo laminates or limestone for the floors. The designer applied traditional Japanese house design vocabularies, and selected evergreens and non-evergreens roof gardens for extra geothermal insulation for natural energy efficiency.

Photo: Edward Suzuki Associates

Edward Suzuki Associates (Edward Suzuki, Toshiharu Nanba)

Photo: : Chikao Todoroki Sasaki Studio Inc

Keiichiro Sako, Yuichiro Imafuku---SAKO Architects

FlatFlat in Harajuku

FlatFlat in Harajuku is the store with the concept of "the future park" and aims to combine virtual elements with real space accessible to anyone. The designers attempted to create a space that people feel like snuggling up to the organic form that curves based on human body dimensions. On the other hand, "Inorganic principle" consisting of white wall surface fixtures, neon tubes of ceiling illumination and mortar floor creates a virtual character. They used lines which let neon tubes and the prevention of crack seam of mortar offset the forms of the wall surface fixtures. They stimulate curiosity of the visitors by synergy with the forms of the fixtures and lead them to the inner part of the narrow space.

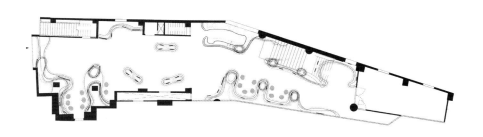

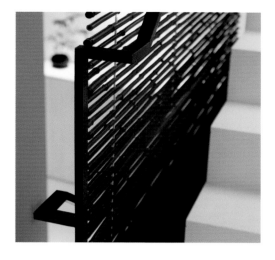

House at Shimogamo Yakocho

In order to meet the requirement of "To be able to see green from every room", the concept of "Interface" was again used here. The project brings typical Japanese apartment style — simple, spacious, and bright. They also use lots of bamboo and tatami; beds are used in bedrooms. The house is multi-functional with almost all kinds of spaces such as family room, Japanese room, study, guestroom, related sanitary rooms, kitchen and a pergola-clad moon-gazing terrace. The façade of the house is masked by a circular screen of frosted glass. At night, the whole house is illuminated by one large "Andon" or Japanese candle lamp which also sheds warm light to the neighbourhood.

House

Japan

Kyoto

Photo: Edward Architects

Edward Architects

213

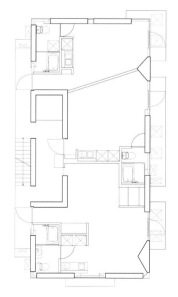

Grucks Garten

This building consists of the wife's art studio and car parking space on the first floor, rental rooms on second and third floors, and residential spaces for the owner's family on the forth and fifth floors. Plan for the second and third floor rental spaces are totally the same, completed with new structural system where the square measure stays the same even if the shape of the cross section changes, but the incoming light varies with change on the outer wall presenting an entirely different facet.

Magritte's

The site was just 45.61 square metres in area, located in the middle of Tokyo. The width of front road also restricts the size of construction machine, so the condition was not good to build the residence. The client was a young married couple aged around 30, and their simple request was the use of concrete for every part in the house including floor, wall, and table, etc. They didn't even care for storage space. To satisfy this request, the architects chose to use a Precast Prestressed Concrete which stress the preinstalled steel bar, to separate the volume between the ground floor and the basement.

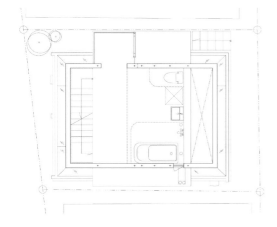

T in Tokyo

Sunlight, lighting of the surrounding buildings, signal lamps, vehicles, etc. are reflected and refracted, and various expressions are created on the façade. A change in the "surroundings" is more evident because "duplication" coexists with "transformation" on the façade. In addition, an "illusion" is created through the refraction by the mirrors. Designer scratched lines of another type on the stainless steel mirror of a worktable in the shop. When a spotlight projects light on the worktable, many circular patterns will appear at the surface, creating an illusion that the worktable surface consists of two layers.

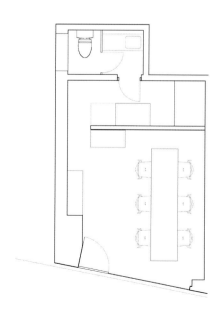

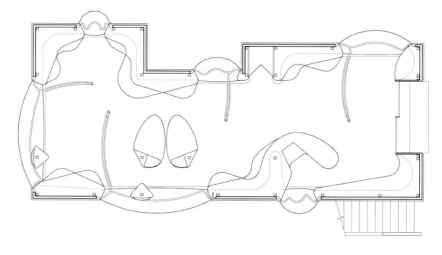

United Bamboo Shop

An Old Building Re-Clothed: the outside of the building gets a second skin... A Clothing Shop As Soft As Skin: PVC is pushed & pulled to make walls, counter, shelves... Fashion Without Models: if you like how you look, push a button at the mirror — it's you who's projected on the store façade, out on the street... The exterior of the building is given a second skin: a screen of stainless-steel mesh that encloses the balcony and re-shapes the building; the framework crosses the mesh in diagonals, radiating from some unknown point and traveling around the building, re-orienting the building. The interior resembles fabric, like the clothes in the shop. The PVC is pulled down and arched down, from the ceiling onto the walls; it is pulled out from the walls, and pushed back in, to make shelves — it is pulled out and around to make a counter. At the front of the shop, the PVC is pulled up from the ceiling, over the second floor façade; it makes the projection screen.

Photo: Acconci Studio

Acconci Studio (Vito Acconci, Peter Dorsey, Stephen Roe, Julia Loktev, Sehzat Oner, Larry Sassi, Dario Nunez, Gia Wolff)

Citrus Notes

Usually, the interior design of "Citrus Notes" is expressing nobleness under relatively square plan with the theme of high quality and glamorousness. However, considering the creative characteristics of Omotesando, this time the designer tried to produce the creative space that stimulates imagination through using the custom-made rose motif print carpet for the floor, producing the different viewpoints with the height difference on the floor, and reassembling the chandelier designed by Angelo Mangiarotti in a glamorous way.

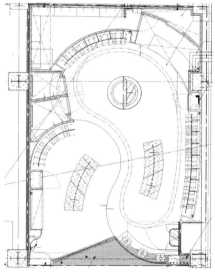

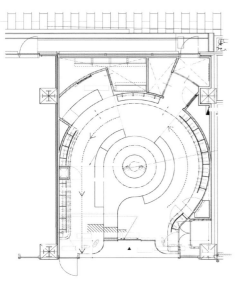

Une Vie Avec Elle

The most attracting point for the designer was to be able to design the shop without domestic sense. The whole design ignores the unique current Japanese trend, and creates the space with the international trend, namely, it could leave the Japanese trend as an antique and a retro-modern boom to challenge the futuristic design. The designer could create the fluid organic space that people couldn't see for a long time in recent Japan through the spiral-shaped plan and making the whole walkway slope. As a result, the space has become unique in a good way in the fashion mall with so many tenants, which is differentiated from other shops.

China House Restaurant

Inspired by the vibrant 1930s' Shanghai Art Deco, The Oriental, Bangkok's China House restaurant has been re-designed and revived into an avant-garde eatery that serves classic yet contemporary cuisine in a refined atmosphere. The concept of the design rests on a re-thinking of "period" decoration and how one is able to convey the spirit of a time without being overly literal. The end result is a fresh evocation of this cultural period, mixing very few actual Deco furnishing with modern pieces against an interior-architectural setting that aims to balance a new experience of fine dining with a reluctant dosage of nostalgia.

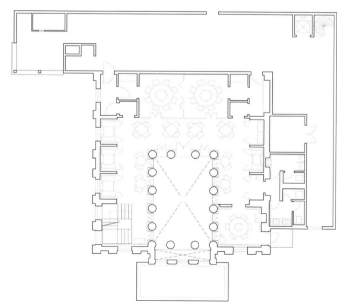

East Coast Trucks

The new layout is an evolution of their corporate identity and a departure from a traditional truck sales yard. External colours and materials were carefully selected to reflect the updated corporate image of the company and served as a backdrop for the building's signage. The new office included a reception and customer waiting area, open plan office area, partitioned offices, kitchenette and lunch room and refurbishment of existing amenities. A simple three-colour palette was used to create a modern interior. White was used as a base colour to accentuate the red bulkheads and green wall. The patterned charcoal carpet and ceramic tiles reflected a sophisticated corporate image.

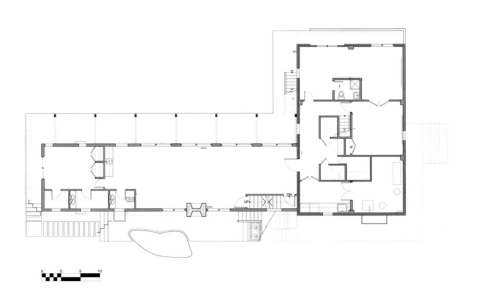

X2 Kui Buri

X2 Kui Buri is located on the Gulf of Thailand, approximately 3 hours' drive from Bangkok. It relaxes the eyes with uninterrupted sea views and engages the senses with a combination of indigenous materials and modern lines. This is feng shui meeting utopian community in a design by Duangrit Bunnag, for whom simplicity means spatial economy and a lack of complication. Guests can absolutely unwind in 23 villas. These are largely identical with understated furnishings and floor-to-ceiling glass doors that open onto the beach, yet certain individuality lies in their proximity to the bordering terrace, adjacent pool and neighbouring garden areas.

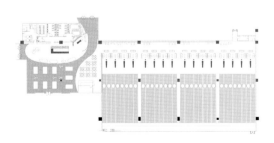

SM M.O.A Bowling Club

Turn a 34-lane bowling centre into an entertainment hub which included a billiard hall, pro shop, café, KTV. The space had to be flexible in order to transform itself into an arena to host major competitions. The bowling centre is located in Mall of Asia, Manila's largest shopping mall. The entrie of the bowling centre are exposed to a semi outdoor space of the mall. At certain times of the year, the space is exposed to strong typhoons. Therefore all external elements had to be properly secured for these conditions. The requirements for a 34-lane bowling centre meant that designers had a large floor space of approximately 2000 square metres to design.

Perfume Gallery

Located on a department store in south Jakarta, one can see Perfume Gallery in perfume and cosmetic area, side by side with another brand. Based on this reason, the design must be eye-catching and recognisable. With a large range of products, the design must be general, and should not focus only on one brand. Bright colours are chosen to differentiate this outlet with others; shelving mirror is used as product display to maximise its use. To give a cosy and relax feel, one unique-shape chair welcomes customers to sit down and get tester and service in a comfortable way.

Daniel Amarta's Luxury Beauty Salon

The concept is minimalist luxury, by using vintage craving sticker on the mirror. Minimalist style synchronised with the saloon functions, combined with glossy black glass and natural wooden material, creating a luxurious and elegant impression. Feminine round stair works like a magnet to attract people's attention and neutralises the minimalist design. Lighting concept is also considered to create romantic ambience by using warm light. For the ground floor, the main purpose is to make the regular customers feel cosy and relaxed, where the saloon function locates. The first floor is designed for VIP customers who want to get more privacy and also gives more space to design to pamper the customers.

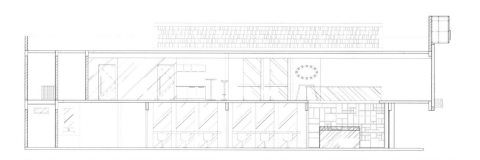

Photo: ESPERTA architecture-interior

Erwanto, Ir. MT

Photo: Esperta Architecture-interior

Mr Affandy's Apartment

To catch the nice view clearly, the designer uses glass as a mirror combined with black walnut wood to give modern accent and to catch sunshine as much as it can. The dining room and living room are connected by niche decorated with modern fancy ornament to make those two rooms look larger. Every room also has sea views to pamper eyes. Large window is made to catch the sea breeze for good air circulation and reduce light expense. Each room gets minimalist design, not to compete each other. The whole design completes each other giving modern homey environment. To reduce budget, the designer tried to keep the floor construction and existing ceiling by giving modern accent to wall and furniture.

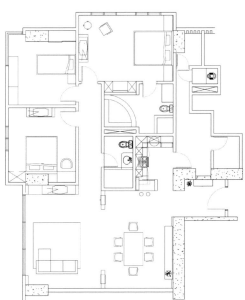

Toys City Flagships

As a usual children shop, the designer comes up with colourful design and child-friendly materials. The shape is also designed with lots of round or half round, preventing a sharp shape to reduce injury for children. The designer try to create funny, funky, colourful, and energetic environment and atmosphere by creating a basic shape that children like, such as colourful stars back lighted, colourful flowers to cover the column display, circle drop ceiling and other unique shapes like leaves, sky and square that are finished with colourful picture as promotional advertisement. To get the most attraction on façade and interior, the designers presented a colourful and attractive visual with a strong image and unique ornament shape.

The Nam Hai Spa

Among a range of natural therapeutic treatments are the Nam Hai Massage and Warm Stone Massage plus a menu of rejuvenating holistic beauty rituals including the exclusive "Neem and Go Tu Kola Healing Envelopment". Invigorating and romantic bathing rituals are also on the pampering menu, such as the "Herbal Steam", "Herbal Clay Bath and Love" and ultra-romantic "Nam Hai in Villa" — a romantic candlelit bath for two with flowers and love potion in the privacy of villas, celebrated with champagne and canapés. A retail section stocks a wide selection of spa and beauty products specially created for The Nam Hai.

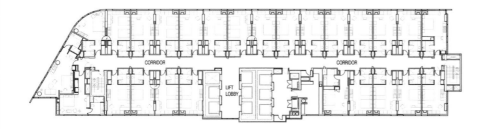

Bahrain World Trade Centre

The Bahrain World Trade Center (BWTC) stands as an icon of sustainable design and includes the first installation of large-scale wind turbines into a commercial building. As well as offering 38 floors of premium office space, the BWTC also houses the boutique shopping facility MODA Mall, providing nearly 16,500 square metres of high end retail space. The shopping mall has been designed in keeping with the iconic nature of the BWTC, incorporating sweeping staircases, impressive glass domed courtyards and relaxing water features. Themed from a distinctly nautical flavour, each tower of the BWTC is visually anchored to the ground by a concertina of curved, sail-like forms.

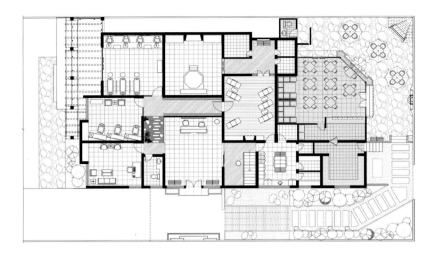

Nirvana Day Spa & Salon

The interior of the Spa drives a flow of moods, collectively shaped by natural elements, manifested through an amalgamation of rich textures and earthy hues. The interior's perspective binds together in perfect harmony all constituents of design, while each element maintains its mutually exclusive relevance. The Interior flaunts textured walls, part wooden, part tiled floors, smoothly lacquered in some places, rustic and weathered in others, detailed with rugs, thus wholly emanating a rustic allure. Natural material such as white gravel, stone, pebbles and plantations are made to blend with man-made features.

Office of International Business Machines Corporation (IBM)

A distinguishing feature of this office is its open plan concept, largely dictated by its curvilinear form — a curved corridor leading from the reception to the board room, with blue LED lights on either side of the corridor guiding visitors along. The built environment is designed to meet the distinctive needs of a fully-functional, technology company and presents a mix of workstations, management offices, waiting areas, tea and coffee stations & a series of meeting & project rooms. The Board Room is a communication-friendly, sophisticated room, equipped with the latest multimedia features, hi-tech Audio Visual systems and LCD monitor, not to mention exceptional presentation facilities such as lighting dimmers and pre-set lighting arrangements.

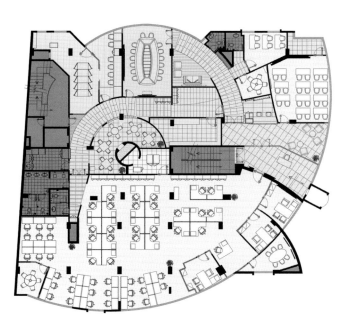

Photo: IDS Design Team

Team IDI

The New Majestic Hotel

The "New Asia" style of hospitality finds one of its most rarefied expressions in the New Majestic, located in the heart of Singapore's Chinatown. An open-concept period-inspired lobby shows the imaginative possibilities of this marriage of old and new, or "heritage chic", as the hotel calls its particular design savvy. Individually designed rooms, 30 in all, continue the mix of vintage and designer furniture, customised baths, and include private gardens and six-metre ceilings in attic-style suites. Five rooms have also been personalised by some of Singapore's most influential talents from cinema, theatre and fashion.

Photo: DP Architects Pte Ltd

DP Architects Pte Ltd

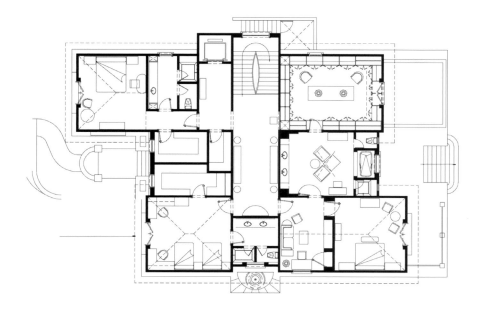

59 Blair Road

The house sits on an irregular trapezium-shaped site, making it much wider than its neighbours. There is a swimming pool and deck surrounded by a lush greenery of bamboo trees. When one overlooks, an integration of modern contemporary design fuses with subtle oriental vibes. All areas looking into the pool are fronted by glass doors. When light reflects off the water, the atmosphere metamorphoses into a calm, private sanctuary, invoking the feeling of a beach resort. The balcony on the second level continues the theme of light and shade. The deck is a unique feature, made up of three individual wooden slabs, using a motorised pulley and winch system and each is controlled independently.

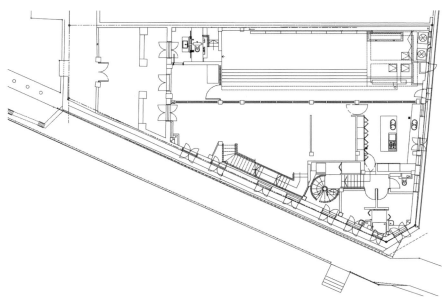

The World's First Underwater Spa

The underwater spa, which forms part of the luxury Huvafen Fushi resort in the Maldives, comprises two double treatment rooms and a separate relaxation area with mind-blowing views under the Indian Ocean. Guests enter the underwater spa along a passageway lit with colour-changing lights in the ceiling to enhance the overall sensory experience. Once inside, reconfigurable sliding walls allow the space to be opened up to make the most of the spectacular views or closed to create a more intimate space for treatments. The resort itself is comprised of 43 naturally modern rooms located both on the beach and on stilts over the Indian Ocean.

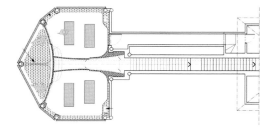

Photo: Richard Hywel Evans Architecture & Design Ltd

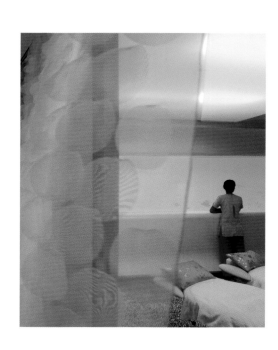

Lover's Night Lounge Bar

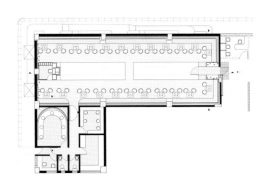

The linear footprint of the central space dictated the layout having a central aisle adaptable to versatile use with tables and seating on either side. A D.J's cabin and an entry vestibule at the two ends of the central spine were the only encroachments allowed into the main hall. The designers lit from below the entire length of the aisle and the tables on either side with colour-changing LED lights. These, along with some ceiling mounts were linked to programming devices, controlled directly by the D.J. The aisle and the tables were engineered and constructed entirely out of toughened glass with frosted shatterproof film conforming to safety requirements.

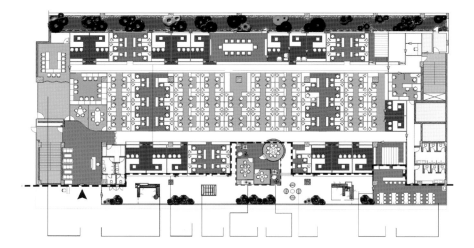

Gunnebo

The designers were surprised to know that some people in the sales team spent on an average about 15 minutes in the office everyday and preferred the flexibility of working at any place where they could hook up their laptops to the server. This opened up 'Hotdesking' possibilities and potential reduction in the number of dedicated workstations. The designers did not question their need for formal workspaces. They managed to fit in the requirements as described by them in the most efficient manner and consequently freed a large bit of space that could be used for something else. The design provides an entire zone that becomes a breakout, hybrid use space.

Shoppers Stop Rajouri

India's retail industry has been enhanced further by a new shop format, developed by JHP. The consultancy's Indian client, Arvind Brands, has just opened a discount fashion shop, "Mega Mart" in Chennai. The 30,000-square-foot shop is a new strategy for Arvind and will provide customers with an entry point for brands in a contemporary department shop style environment. The shop is spread over two floors, and as well as men's, women's and children's casual and smart clothing, it has a marketplace and a café. The project also involved JHP creating a new brand identity, mark and graphic communication suite within the shop.

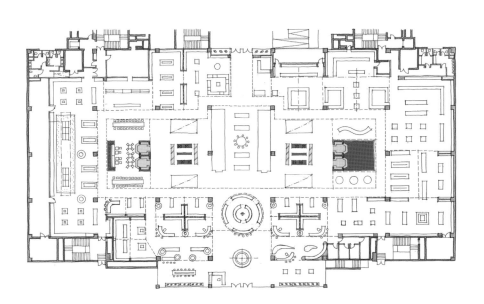

Photo: Planet 3 Studios Architecture Pvt. Ltd

Planet 3 Studios Architecture Pvt. Ltd

Eyelex Multiplex

It is the first and yet the only two-cinema-screen multiplex in Jharkhand state. The cinema lobby is accentuated by an abstract composition of trapezoidal planes that appear to fold in and out like crumpled paper across the varying heights below the cinema halls. The ceiling folds down to encapsulate the columns merging them as unified elements across vertical and horizontal planes to create a sculptural feel to the entire space. Mirror towards one side and glass on another reflect and heighten the depth of the small lobby. Although much smaller in size, it has a distinct identity by virtue of the sculptural quality of its spaces in both the interior spaces and its built form.

Silver Tube

The programme briefly defined the requirement of four different dining experiences and offerings in a single hospitality destination. These were to be accommodated on two levels. The challenge for designers was to first manage the requirements within the given space, second offer dismountable construction solution to cover the terrace in conformity with local bylaws, and third, create experientially rich and varied interior experience to address different patron need-states for different spaces within the singular entity. The designers understood the need of creating a lounge that allowed patrons to truly relax, soak in the environment and immerse in music.

Photo: Planet 3 Studio Architecture Pvt.ltd.

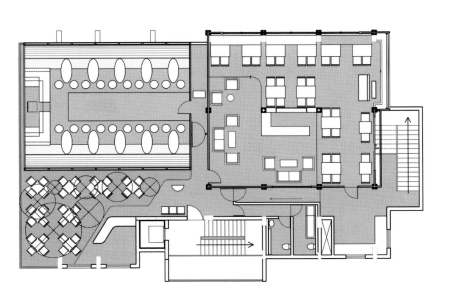

Planet 3 Studios Architecture Pvt Ltd

Dawnay Day India Land

The ceiling in all areas of the office has been designed in a way to avoid direct lighting. The lights in cabins and open office provide an even wash all around. With all the white, it was important to have a darker floor to set off the furniture. A dark grey patterned carpet with straight-line, clean contemporary design does the trick. Choice of chairs was limited to mesh backs in work areas for the lightness of the pieces.

Photo: Mrigank Sharma, India Sutra

Kalhan Mattoo, Santha Gour Mattoo, Dimple Toraskar, Gauri Argade.

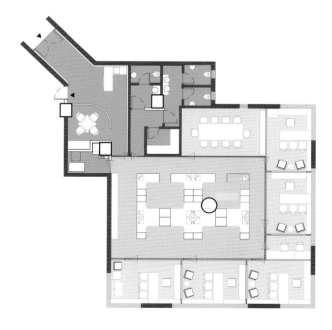

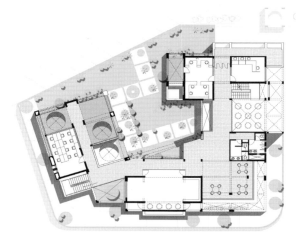

ITM Management Institute

The concept is based on the principles of an Indian Courtyard where the liveable spaces look into the semi shaded landscaped court and receive soft diffused sunlight. There is a beautiful symphony of light and shadow and the interplay of textures and surfaces throughout the building which accommodate a lot of transitional spaces much like the transitional state. The context is ever present and the occupants of the Institute are encouraged to be a part of it and accept this context on both micro & macro level through the Architecture of the building.

Photo: M:OFA Studios Pvt Ltd

M:OFA Studios Pvt Ltd

The Park Hotel

The brief for the public areas was to create a four star hotel with flexibility allowing weekday trade to convert to weekend tourist stays. Therefore two free-form pods on the ground floor were designed containing the bar, the snug and back office. The orange plastered bar breaks out to address the terrace, while the reception/snug is clad in hand-made plaster jail work addressing the lobby and coffee shop. The bedrooms are characterised by their bamboo floors, teak furniture and brightly coloured fabrics.

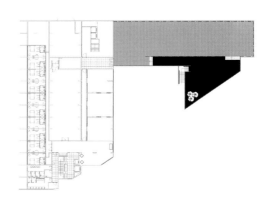

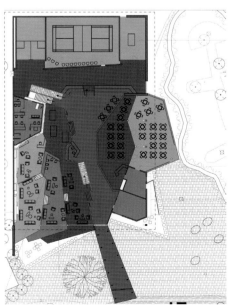

Amby Valley Leisure Centre

The whole design passes a peace and spacious feeling to the guests. Floating panels in the ceiling that are linear and trapezoidal in shape and suspended at varying levels enhance the meandering movement of the low wood partitions. The stepping ensures unobstructed views creating separate areas as well as providing privacy. The orderly seats enjoy beautiful landscaped surroundings in all directions. The ceiling roof with AC ducts, structural system and electric cable trays painted in black, floating trapezoidal panels in wood and shades of white create a sculptural effect. The layout with its abstraction allows uninterrupted views of the exterior landscape with gardens and hills.

Leisure

India

Maharashtra

Photo: Vinesh Gandhi

Sanjay Puri

243

Cinemax-Mumbai

The designers created an undulating curvilinear ceiling that unified the entire space while connecting the low height areas to the higher height areas at the opposite end in a fluid seamless manner. This ceiling constructed of gypsum is punctuated by varying lengths of indirect light troughs that accentuate the undulating curvatures. The entire flooring of the cinema lobby is of yellow vitrified ceramic tile punctuated by varied lengths of black granite strips.

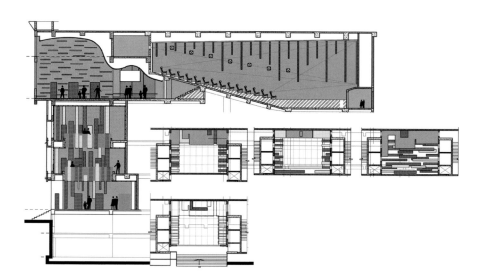

Jewel World, Mumbai

Located in the heart of Zaveri Bazaar, the diamond and gold trading market of Mumbai, Jewel World occupies three levels of the legendary Cotton Exchange building which is an exemplary example of Art Deco style architecture. When approached for the design of this landmark structure given its iconic destination, Arris Architects were assigned an exigent task — not merely to maximise the retail footprint in a taut layout but also to offer the patrons a visual gratification never experienced before. Visual communication was the key design focus while conceiving the retail area and the final design succeeds in exploiting individuality for each and every shop front; this becomes a commercial and experiential asset.

Patrons are gradually cocooned into the shopping experience — a 115 feet long and gradually curving corridor, interspersed by sinuous curvilinear elements, which "de-scale" the long corridor for the patrons, while bringing a sense of identity for each shop. The shop fronts on either side of the corridor are treated with distinctly different materials – white acrylic solid surface, and veneer — each individually elegant, yet together strive to connote the wonderful union of different eras and the unique cultural flux of the city.

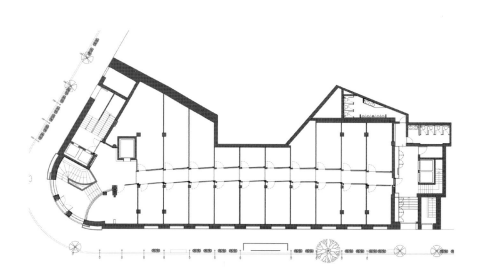

Mapfre Assistance

A very lateral thought was put across to actually lower down the reception backdrop wall to a half height partition which resulted in achieving the prime maximum openness that the client desired for and also showcase the complex yet clean designed ceiling. The other design element incorporated was the 'logo wall', the idea anybody could have thought of, yet it came out to be the most integral and corporate identification. The recreation zone and the cafeteria were treated differently from the rest of the office space through the use of bright coloured gradation in the cafeteria wall, bright colour chairs and tables and importantly the Spanish caricature laminates.

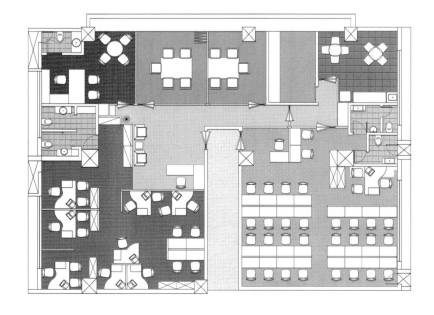

Forest Club

An upscale contemporary housing in Noida literally sitting on a water rivulet was the context for Forest Premiere Club in Noida. The River, the central greens, the swimming pool, the landscaping all became the entry. Functionally this Club houses the Club Premiere Lounge, Restaurant, Cards room, Billiard's Room, Spa, Squash Court, Fitness Centre and multiple indoor & outdoor courts in its folds. The Restaurant & Bar sit on the River as a glass bridge with glass flooring letting the water body make its presence felt. The Squash court flanks the Premiere Lounge as a Concrete Structure with a smoked polycarbonate roof taking in optimum light during the day.

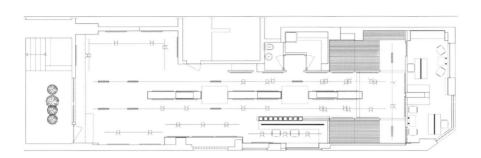

X-ist Art Gallery

The gallery is situated in the basement of an apartment in Nisantasi, with five bedrooms and a living room. The designers wanted to create an open art gallery having white walls that would make the paintings prominent. For that reason they have created one big main exhibition area and a closed back office area out of five bedrooms and a living room. Epoxy was chosen to create a cold atmosphere that will go in contrast with the paintings. Although the art gallery is in the basement, there is a small courtyard in front of the main exhibition space that lets the sunlight as well as the pedestrians' attention inside.

"NYLO" Hotel

NYLO Hotel is currently the most popular category of lifestyle hotels. One feature of their hotels is conceived as "full of art and design of the driving force behind quality, rich social atmosphere, filled with surprises and fun personality of the civilian-style luxury hotel". Young people use the popular LOFY space design, the wall of the Park by the rough brick or cement block wall from the base, landing windows to dilute the indoor structure function of the regional sense of space, bright, open, open, pristine. The designers delete the commonly used stone, brick, wood flooring decorative layer, and the ground directly to the polished concrete finishes.

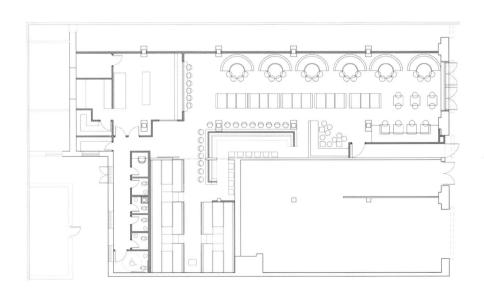

Kemerburgaz House

This project was designed for a family of two with a different kind of living habit. The starting point was to make the spaces open, spacious and flexible. The three-floor house was designed with a great relation to each other, connecting each space to another or referring it to the following one. The spaces in use with each other are kitchen-living rooms and bedroom-bathroom. Natural materials were mostly chosen and came into prominence. Natural timber and stone were the main elements used in designing the house space with their original colours and natural styles as well. All the natural appearance of walnut timber was preferred to be left untreated.

Bodrum House

The idea of creating shadowed open spaces came from a high influence of the climate on defining the physical environment. Different effects the sun gives during different times of the day helped experience the same spaces differently. Simplicity, the dominant concept in the whole house, was the starting point for creating a calm and quiet atmosphere. Different types and colours of wood were used combining simplicity with different details and materials turning the house project into a "home". Cutting the joints of the ceiling, walls and the floor, gave the opportunity to perceive each important element separately which meanwhile strengthened the effective fullness-emptiness in the whole space.

Habif Mimarlık Office

By looking for the answers to the question of what kind of a working environment people would like to be in, Habif Architecture Team has concretised their effort to create a very calm, serene, tranquilising, luminous and warm environment by designing big wooden study and meeting elements without any separations.

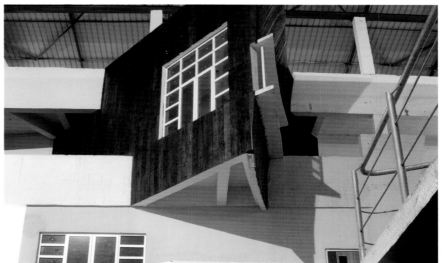

Zone

Zone is a private airport lounge in Istanbul Ataturk Airport, designed and built by GAD in 2007 for the American Express & Life card holders of Garanti Bank. Zone is 580 square metres and consists of an entrance area, lounge area, a business centre area, and two bars, one for drinks and the other for open buffet bathrooms. The main idea behind Zone is to give a comfortable area and colourful environment to the visitors before their long, boring flights. They can have their delicious food and drinks before the flight, use the business centre, watch TV, play billiard, and their children can enjoy the play station in a special room designed for them.

Ritz Carlton Sharq Village & Spa, Doha, Qatar

The planning has been based on a traditional Qatari village-ornate courtyard and beautiful furnishings and treasures that may have found their way here from the seaports to make this experience steeped in detail and tradition. Lobby and public spaces flow gently into one another while allowing for intimate seating groupings and moments of interest along circulation corridors. All aspects of detailing were to refer back to authentic Qatari motifs — handrails, stone carvings, and inlaid mosaics created a sense of continuity and refinement that help to reinforce the storyline of the project.

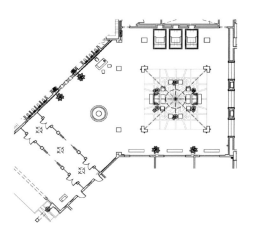

Almyra Hotel

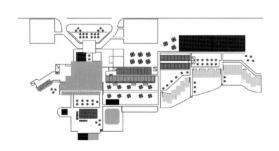

Splashes of the 1970s' boldness — such as white leather sofas and ottomans — are enhanced by a combination of natural and artificial lighting. Seeing as the hotel places as much emphasis on a successful family experience as on a good design, the concept focuses on the practicality as well. All of the hotel's guestrooms and suites are generous in size, so as to provide ample space for families — who will most certainly also appreciate the Almyra's two freshwater pools, both built with Italian slate. Auer and Pleot have gone for lots of natural materials as well as glass and Carrara marble to create a calming effect in the rooms.

Saudi Arabian Airlines Ticketing Offices

Crea International has designed the new ticketing offices for Saudi Arabian Airlines, giving new strength to this brand with a new concept "Discovering the other side of the moon: the Saudi Arabian Airlines' moon experience". The scheme was thought to take advantage of the maximum line of vision from the public spaces within a land of 87 square metres and with limited budget. The colours of the logo, particularly related to the King's culture and customs were transferred into the space so that the whole concept guarantees a unique and high quality "travelling experience" which starts from the first approach with the agencies, through the aircrafts until land services.

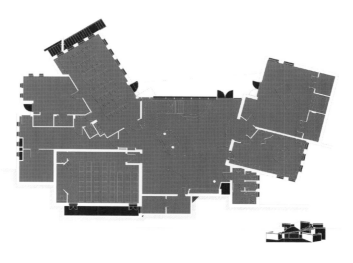

Zichron Menachem Day Care Centre for Children with Cancer

At the centre of the "mound of blocks" is a central space, three floors high. The space acts as entrance lobby, circulation space, and central orienting feature. The cladding of natural Jerusalem stone, required by law on the exterior, continues on the interior surfaces of the blocks. The space is transversed by horizontal circulation in the form of bridges, and vertical circulation elements, stairs and glass elevator shaft. The circulation elements are designed with soft, rounded lines, in contrast to the angularity of the stone cubes.

Photo: Chaim Ehrental

Oster, Lang, Architects, Jerusalem, Israel

The Uterus

The Uterus project was designed for children with special needs, who took part in the design process of The Biological model called Uterus in which the embryo grows and develops. It inspired the design of the children's room and living area, while the children are the embryo and the surrounding area is the uterus that prompts the evolvement of the children. This fruitful process led to the creation of a childish and enjoyable environment where every child defines his own private space over and over again. The kitchen and living room area have turned into a meeting point between the children's bedroom and their family and volunteers'.

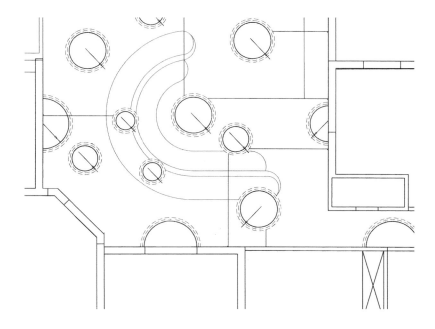

Peres Peace House

Peace is a spiritual condition, an aspiration: tension and utopia. The projection of will into the future is also an expression of hope that children and future generation will live in a better world. The designer has thought of a series of layers, a building that represents TIME and PATIENCE in strata of alternating materials representing places that have suffered heavily. A stone basement to raise the building, a meeting place from which two long staircases lead to a place of rest whose size and height, full of light from above, helps us to forget the troubles of the world, and fills us with the positive attitude that is needed for our meeting with other men and other women.

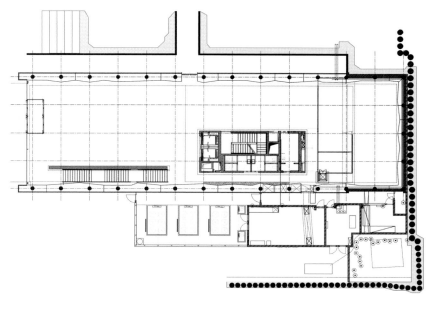

Barber Shop

Hair adheres to the gravity of earth with a dynamics of its own. This concept was adopted for the interior design to create setting and atmosphere. The work posts and hair styling preparation areas were adjoined in one function, starting in the barber work posts continuously leading in its other side to the hair styling preparation area. The process was divided to three stages; each one as a partition between spaces begins as a barber work post. A first partition ends as a hair wash post, the second as a sitting area for clients and the third as a secretary's post. Separated areas were thereby created between the barbers' posts.

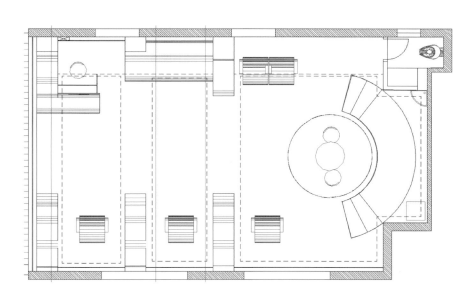

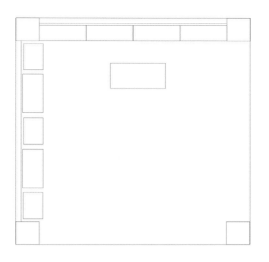

Exhibition

This furniture design exhibition took place in a large exhibition hall, showcasing all of Israel's major furniture companies in September 2007. The space is 30 square metres. Many different elements were taken in consideration for designing this project. The hard task is: fitting so many different kinds of products in a small space, and also the designer should make them feel harmonious. Tusks of 4 metres high are employed to make a consumed space, and to allow light fixtures to hang down. Covering the tusks with gold fabric sets the stage for a glamorous, eye-catching space. The space is an explosion of texture, patterns and colour, which gives you a unique experience.

Makuleke Region Kruger National Park

The brief for the project was simply 12 free-standing units with a main building, housing reception, a restaurant, lounge areas and a swimming pool. The main aim of the project was an architecture that would sit subtly in the remarkable landscape and would provide luxurious accommodation and a compelling relationship with nature. The 12 chalets are connected by a long teak walkway, raised above the site that also conceals the water, electricity and phone lines. In order to keep the environment undisturbed, the buildings are all raised on stilts. The limited material selection consisted of local timber (teak and meranti), concrete, steel members and pre-painted corrugated-steel sheeting.

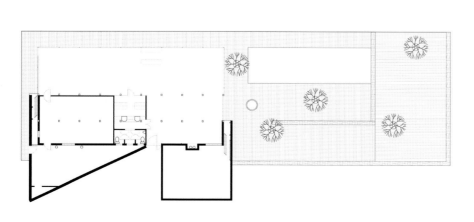

Ksar Char-Bagh

The courtyard is homage to the Alhambra: carved plasters, marbles, and murmuring water and perfumed scents, the spectacular swimming pool as a huge basin surrounded by giant palm trees. Everything here is in the architecture, the materials and the light, a labyrinth of salons, corridors, staircases, high vaulted and painted ceilings, terraces, large windows opening on the gardens. Walls are made of marble powder with pigments and clay, painted plasters with quite white and earthy colours, the floors of stones, and desks with a touch of marble.

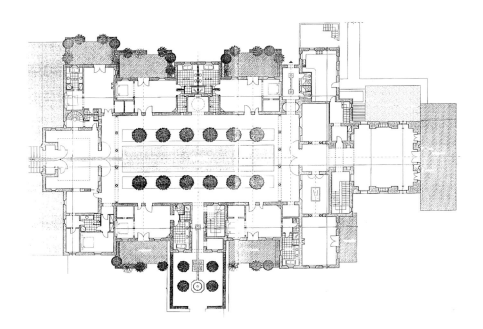

Photo: P de Grandry, M Zublena, J Silveira Ramos

Patrick & Nicole Grandsire-Levillair

Apartment With A Nile View

A private apartment is located in a large apartment block in Cairo, with a panoramic view of The Nile and the city below. The concept was to transform this conventional space into a place with a unique identity. This apartment was designed for a client with quite specific lifestyle needs; it is a home of a well-travelled and busy professional man. It incorporates the interest for a cultural architectural references and the necessity to accommodate a modern European lifestyle. Here a fusion of both cultures penetrates each other and creates a new design language, a language which makes a balance between functional demands and the aesthetical experience of the apartment.

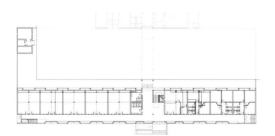

Lusofona Baltasar Lopes da Silva University

The July 5 hotel, which is the municipal patrimony of Mindelo, will house the Lusofona Baltasar Lopes da Silva University. The project foresees the phased restoration of the built set and the transformation of the spaces according to their new use. In the first phase, the visible reflex of the intervention is centred on the interior circulations and on the elevations, in an attempt to attribute the appropriate sense of scale and formal dignity to the building. Seeking the maximum results with minimum intervention, the rooms were adapted, the corridors were widened, and the façades were reformulated, with new light entrances and air circulation.

Photo: Jacob Nielsen

Jackie-B: Interior architect and furniture designer.

Cubion Office

Located in the heart of Copenhagen, the consultant company Cubion a/s now occupies the lower floor in a protected house dating back from 1793. The main office supports and stimulates the exchange of knowledge. The office space for eight employers is suitable divided into two groups of juicy green tables. The office is lit up by two (100mm high x1500mm long x1000mm wide) suspended lamps also designed for the room by Jackie-B. The office walls are habited with synthetic grass islands that allow the possibility to lean into and help to secure a dreamy and calm atmosphere. The kitchen is designed as a social meeting room with a bright yellow table that centres the room.

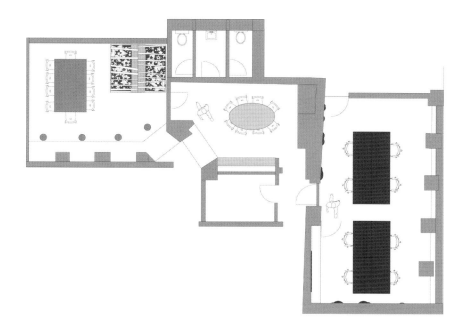

Fuglsang Cuts

The five housing units are established around a central core which consists of the staircase, parking and a combined garbage, storage and bicycle room. On the conceptual level, the thought is to place the flats from the wishes of size and internal coherence. The conceptual cuts are added after the placement of the flats. The cuts add character to the buildings and are placed according to daylight and external views. The diagonal cuts act as terraces and bring a contrast to the regular interior of the building. In the combination of the number of flats and the cuts, the five Fuglsang Cuts gain a great variation but still in an architectural coherent relationship.

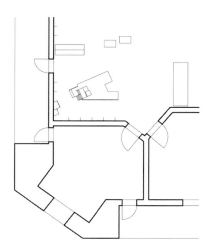

Won Hundred Showroom

Won Hundred is the first Danish brand to take up the challenge to step up to a significant position in Denmark not only by the way they design their clothes, but also by the way they want to represent them in the shop. A multidimensional space with twisted box-like figures emerges from the floor and shelving disappears through the walls. Everything is covered in white paint to give the illusion that all objects are extruded from the same material. This small installation in Copenhagen is designers' investigation of how to produce retail spaces by combining custom pieces with low-cost standard furniture that is cut up and reconfigured.

Orestad College

The college is interconnected vertically and horizontally. Four boomerang-shaped floor plans are rotated to create the powerful super structure which forms the overall frame of the building "C", simple and highly flexible. Four study zones occupy one floor plan each. Avoiding level changes makes the organisational flexibility as high as possible, and enables the different teaching and learning spaces to overlap and interact with no distinct borders. The rotation opens a part of each floor to the vertical tall central atrium and forms a zone that provides community and expresses the college ambition for interdisciplinary education.

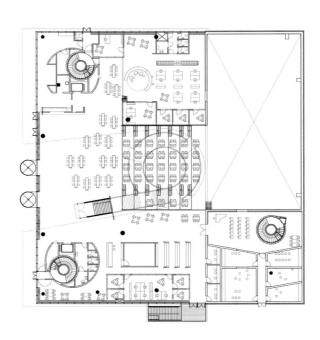

Photo: Adam Mork

3XN Kim Herforth Nielsen, Bo Bøje Larsen, Kim Christiansen

Risor Hotel

It is the first design hotel in Norway. A salt-water aquarium divides two hotel rooms, with an electric adjustable glass screen in the middle, which can be opaque or transparent. An alternate version features an electronic aquarium, featuring a VersaTile low resolution screen for interactive electronic art and inter-room communication for the new generation. The floor is inspired by forms of the Risor peninsula, where jetties have formed huge pot-holes for swimming in, and waves have polished the rock silk smooth for sunbathing. The floor, bed and bath form one continuous bathing-sleeping landscape — a private spa.

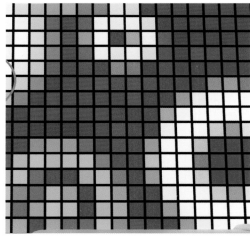

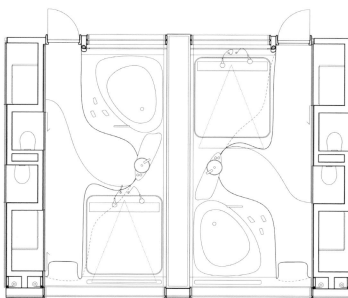

Bergen Fire Station

Four elements form the main architectural composition: the base, the shield, the tower and the bridge. The "base"(ground and first floor) houses the garage and the heavy-duty working areas. The main material is in-situ concrete. The "shield" is the dominating feature of the building covered with copper housing the offices, sleeping rooms, alarm centrals, all within a singular shape opening up towards the courtyard away from the motorway. The "tower" is given an asymmetrical position to mediate between the courtyard and the main building. The tower is part of the fire station's training premises. The "bridge" spans from the 'shield' and connects the tower to the main building.

Photo:Silje Katrine Robinson, Bergens Tideride

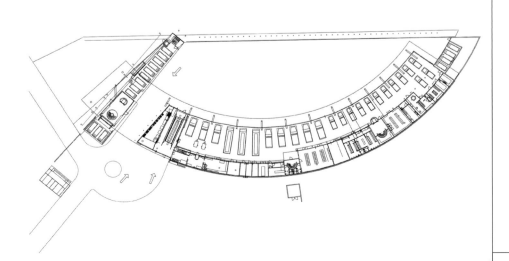

Stein Halvorsen Architects

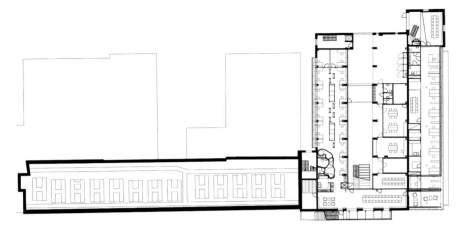

Doga - New Headquarters and Exhibition Space

The Norwegian Design and Architecture Centre decided to move to this old transformation station. The building consisted of a conglomerate of different additions and alterations from around 1860 until 1980. The designers thought it would be appropriate and interesting to reveal this intense and dramatic history of continuous physical change by uncovering as many as possible of the "voices" from the past. This was done with different techniques that the designers developed during the building process, like removing only the plaster that was in bad shape and never covering anything that was uncovered.

Oslo International School

The primary goal of the building project is to upgrade the existing areas, replace the temporary structures and establish new educational areas for specific needs. The project is divided into 3 phases to make possible continuous use of the school during the construction period. The architecture is developed as a new vocabulary of soft and organic forms, softening dense spatial relationships between new and old areas. At the same time these new areas contain special programmes framed by the rectilinear structure of the old. Daylight fills the rooms from narrow slits from floor to ceiling combined with circular roof lights.

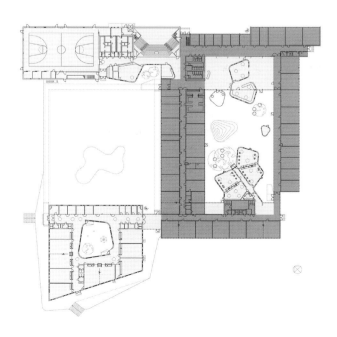

Photo: Ivan Brodey

Jarmund/Vigsnaes AS Architects MNAL

Photo: Wingårdh Arkitektkontor AB

K:fem Department Shop

If the exterior is dressed in a red gown and white lace, the interior shows the fancy underwear. The semitransparent theme continues. A pendant ceiling transmits a diffuse light, and the white pattern on the balustrades evaporates like mist in the morning. The large opening in the core of the building opens up toward the light. To ascend the space shall be a travel to the light — as an airplane rising through the clouds. The scheme was simple and straightforward. Orthogonal blocks with shops on a large horizontal base, were decorated with circular pattern in paving stones and fountains. These elements are all present in the plan.

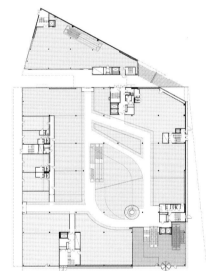

Wingårdh Arkitektkontor AB

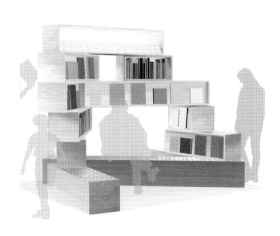

Dylan Kwok-Jenga'em

In order to achieve the competition requirements to provide 10 metres of bookshelves in a 17-cubic-metre reading space, Dylan Kwok and Yuko Takagi filled the space by attaching bookshelves on top of wooden benches. Thanks to the unique construction, the system can be assembled without any hardware. It gives the designers maximum freedom to reconfigure the units into various independent and interconnected reading spaces based on different spatial requirements. The material not only excels the design with optimum strength, but also highlights the vivid publications on shelves.

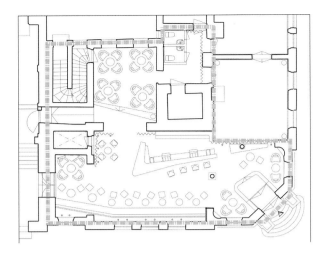

Bar Grotesk

The interior of Bar Grotesk is done in white, black and gold. A custom-designed white leather sofa stretches luxuriously for 14 metres under the windows, sharing the space with black designer plastic chairs, black leather chairs, and black glass tables. The bar is the heart of the nightclub. The designers wanted it to be a freeform, bone-like element, as if a spaceship had landed in the middle of the room. The designers like the look and the satiny feel of the material. Solid surfacing is ideal for creating complex, yet stable shapes.

Talo Kekkapää – Puuta Kivessä

The house was built in a historically significant agricultural landscape in North Espoo. The simple form topped with a pitched roof integrates the building into the wider context. The western slope of the woodland site is divided into two areas of differing character; the back part with pines and the rocky ground, is covered with moss. The main building comprises three zones: living and working, and a glass-roofed conservatory linking the two. During the day the living area is used for in-home child-care; the conservatory acts as a shared dining space and as the meeting room of the office. The office can later be transformed into a separate apartment.

Photo: Katariina Rautiala, Architect

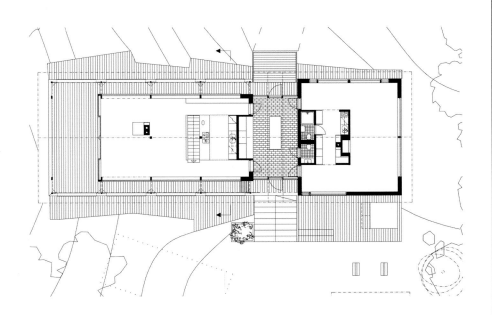

Pentti Raiski, Architect

Vogaskoli Secondary School

The building is centred on a double-height hall-surrounded on the lower floor by a library, music, kitchen, teaching zones for the youngest and middle age groups on the upper. Divisions between areas are minimised and if necessary are of glass or movable partitions. A grand stair connects the hall to the upper level and this can be used either as an audience platform or a stage. The entrance is located at the junction of the existing building and the new extension; it also connects to the school grounds on the south side where the land has been lowered to create an external space for teaching and play, sheltered from the inclement weather.

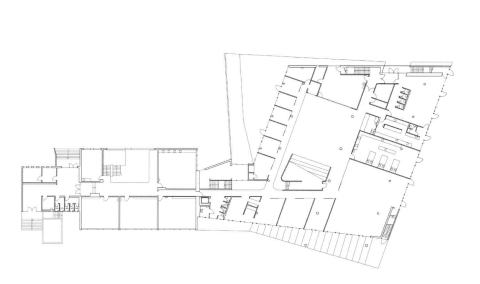

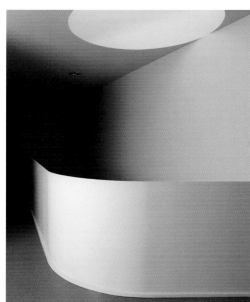

Skrudas

This family house is located on the northern edge of a new neighbourhood with panoramic views over the capital region and the Atlantic Ocean. On the private garden side, the volume of the house is cut away into a series of interconnected terraces with large sliding doors. The entry is from the south at a mid level that also serves the garage, au-pair and family rooms. The bedrooms are located on the lower level whereas the kitchen, dining and sitting rooms are all placed on the upper level to benefit from the magnificent sea views. The internal finishes are a simple palette of black walnut, limestone and stainless steel in a series of white volumes.

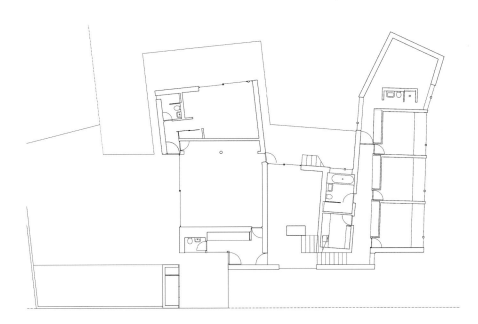

Modular Lighting Showroom

RHE took advantage of his client's proclivity for the extraordinary to design this showroom. The open space of the original showroom was broken into smaller spaces by the introduction of six sculptural walls, all of different heights and forms, custom-made using fibreglass with a shiny gel coat. These walls wrap, slice and enclose the areas, creating a narrative journey, built on by the hi-tech theatrics of Modular's lighting and dimming systems. RHE then took these walls and punctured them with a veritable menagerie of animal cut-outs, an idea sparked by the exquisite photographs in Modular's cult catalogue. These apertures allow the viewers a small glimpse into other zones of the showroom.

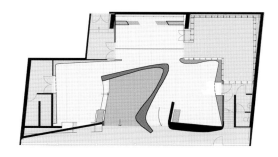

Photo: Richard Hywel Evans Architecture & Design Ltd.

Richard Hywel Evans Architecture & Design Ltd.

Landmark Spa

The greatest challenge was planning: trying to unlock the under-used space, ensure spaces connected better, and offer increased facilities without increasing the area. The designers "squeezed" the entire plan for possible space, and made every attempt to improve the sense of both space and drama in the venue. The critical addition was a new glass corridor running between the pool and gym. This allowed views of the pool when walking down the main corridor (through the heart of the venue), created a contemporary feel, increased the sense of space, and "opened up" the gym by providing views across the pool.

The Birmingham School of Architecture

The main feature of the design is a "hub" area that acts as an informal breakout space for tutorials, seminars, and independent student working. A 15-metre-long bending, folding bench feature houses student lockers beneath a continuous oak worktop which encourages informal sitting. The hub space features a workbench along the perimeter which is articulated by a series of orange perspex fins defining computer workstations. The design is supported by a range of contemporary furniture which supplements the design, particularly by bringing an injection of colour with items such as high and low folded orange stools to mirror the geometry of the bench feature.

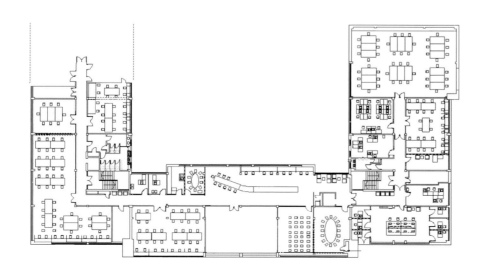

Lexmark

This project was shortlisted for the Design Week Awards 2010 – London. The design concept is a visually engaging tech-landscape to reflect the evolving brand position of Lexmark: from a mid-range technology brand into a more appealing lifestyle product. This high impact fit-out has helped Lexmark stand out next to well-established companies such as Microsoft & Canon. Materials were kept to minimum in order to emphasise the seamless and sculptural nature of this display.White curved Corian plinths with LED edge-lit satin acrylic tops meld into anti-slip Amtico flooring. Energy-saving lighting was utilised throughout this concession.

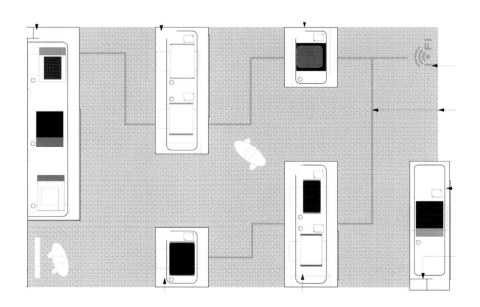

Queen Mary University

Queen Mary University of London's Blizard Building, a new world-class Medical School breaks new ground in the design of research facilities. Aiming to create an outstanding new building for the College, plus a significant landmark and educational resource for the local community, the design team developed the building's form around two primary concepts; Firstly to foster better integration of the science disciplines through the provision of an open-plan environment; secondly to create a building which broadcasts its purpose, achieved by the development of a seductively transparent building envelope.

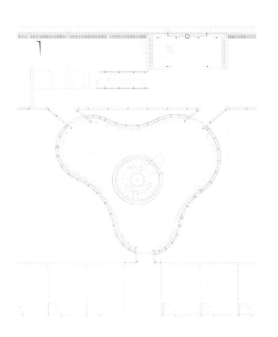

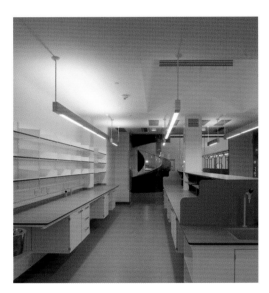

Photo: Morely von Sternberg

Alsop Design Ltd/AMEC

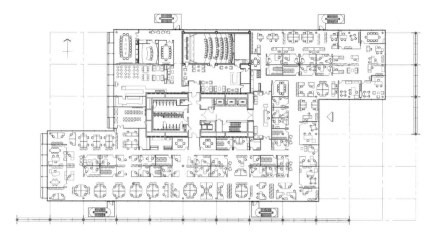

Paramount Pictures

The creation of new headquarters for Paramount Pictures International and associated companies is the reinforcement of new status and identity for the organisation in new premises with a distinctive character. The designer tries to make the building and internal layout allow for future growth and changes. The project provides a 45-55 seat Preview Theatre with state-of-the-art facilities and a reception lounge, as well as an in-house Café and informal meeting/break-out spaces. Conference and meeting rooms are for marketing presentations and film launches, including full video conferencing facilities. It also provides a new ITC systems, latest audio visual installations and M&E services.

Photo: McFarlane Latter Architects

McFarlane Latter Architects

Malmaison Birmingham

This hotel occupies a contemporary building, a new retail and residential quarter in the heart of the City. The intimate reception and spa areas at ground floor are linked to wonderful double height space of the bar and brasserie on the first floor by a beautiful elliptical, stone staircase that is a contemporary interpretation of the traditional main stairs found in French Chateaux. The hotel is conceived as an urban oasis, providing a restful haven within the busy city centre. Rich details of velvet cushions and wall hangings, vivid rugs, leather furniture and wood paneling all contribute to the calmness, enhanced by the crisp elegance of coloured glass, polished chrome and limestone.

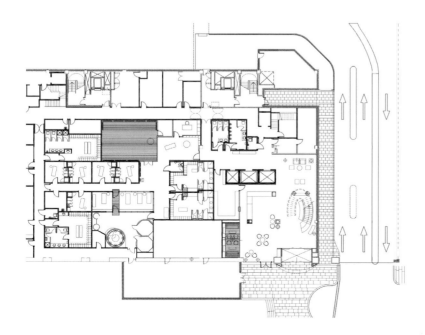

Delicatessen Shop Olivino

OLIVINO is a delicatessen shop complementary to the newly-opened restaurant Olivomare, with which it shares the appealing aubergine-coloured shop front as well as a graphic taste for its interiors. Of rather small proportions — if one only considers the part of it accessible to customers on its left side, as to the entrance, a staircase protected by a full-height frameless glazed partition leads to the storage in the basement and is adjacent to a perimetrical wall entirely covered by a cladding finished with a double layer (white and black) of thick opaque laminated plastic on which has been engraved a decorative pattern of variously oriented bottles and glasses.

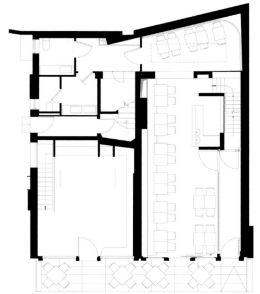

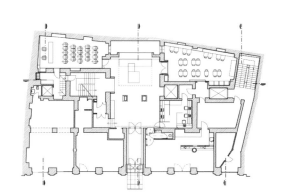

InterCon

On the ground floor, total re-planning and internal re-building, together with the introduction of oversize windows, transformed the public spaces and harnessed the quintessential London panorama beyond. A full height infill on the Piccadilly elevation substantially increased the lounge area alongside a new bar which, in turn, had been made possible by removing the business centre to a more logical habitat on the meeting room level. On the top seventh and eighth floors, a stunning duplex suite was created out of a void captured by rationalising the top floor Club Lounge, both now commanding magnificent views.

DFGW

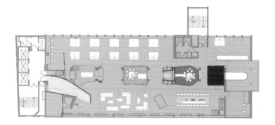

The project consists of: The Birdcage-Formed Aluminum tubing around acid catalyst sprayed MDF cabinets and Spray booth; The Burger Van-Scrubbed Ash timber kitchen table; Plasterboard kitchen enclosure with sliding hatch; The Forest-Sawn Untreated Pine timber construction suspended from ceiling; Exposed Stainless Steel dome head fixings; The Foundation-Plasterboard meeting room enclosure with coloured Perspex vision panel set in recessed aluminum channel; The office, the kitchen table and the reception.

Photo: Rory Carnegie & Tom Foster

Richard Hywel Evans Architecture & Design Limited

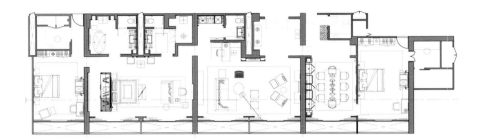

Chaya Bar

Chaya is a Bar and Restaurant. Here it offers both a large bar venue and a more intimate dining experience. The large open site is divided into more intimate areas with the use of sustainable bamboo screening, which allow vision through whilst providing privacy to its diners. The long, feature mirror clad bar is highlighted by both the dramatically lit bamboo screen behind and the ceiling raft above. The raised floor area opposite the bar provides views over the rest of the bar and restaurant. Here, a second, smaller version of the main bar sits to provide cocktails in the evenings.

Flagship Shop for Fullcircle

When viewing from the shop entrance, the clients can see a 12-metre-wide full circle at the rear of the shop. To reiterate the brand name, glowing circular halo lights on the floor surround the mannequins. The menswear wall to the right is constructed from large wardrobe-like frames, angled away from the entrance to maintain the architectural aesthetic until inside the store. The womenswear wall to the left of the store has a softer, warmer feel combining felt, grey stone and sand stone laid in a brick-like linear layout to lead the clients' eyes towards the back of the shop.

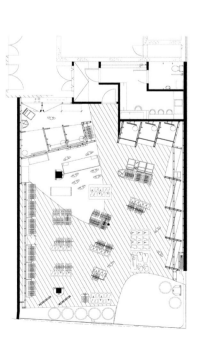

London House

The first floor plate was removed leaving a double height box (10m x 10m x 10m). A new steel armature was inserted, stabilising the box and hanging a mezzanine (4m x 10m). The minimalist impression is developed through concealed lighting throughout the house; the ceiling to the mezzanine visible to the ground floor is covered in black lacquered panels with slits of light running through to the extension, giving the unusual impression of illumination escaping from a single, solid block of light. Douglas Fur lime-washed broad planks throughout the ground floor, whilst the black oak used on the mezzanine, in harmony with the extension ceiling parallel to it, emphasises the overall warmth in design.

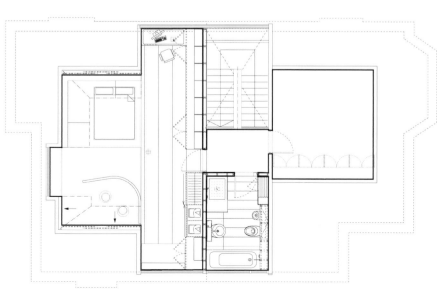

LEVI'S BB Barcelona Winter

The idea was to bring to life the new Levi's creative platform: "THE NIGHT". This is a creative territory that will inform all brand activities; from advertising to store environment. Designer's idea was to bring to life the anticipation and mystery revealed in the night. The journey takes you through a series of "nocturnal" spaces, linked by glimpses of light and shadow pulling you to a series of product stories. The journey culminates in a bar and social/meeting spaces. It was important for Levi's to make an impact and the success of the stand was reflected in a tripling of the number of people visiting the stand over previous shows.

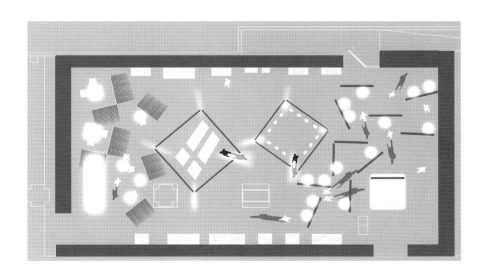

Sergi Arola Gastro Restaurant

A cool and elegant new restaurant stands at the heart of Madrid. This gourmet restaurant is organised around a space set on two levels: the high street level where the main dining room is placed, as well as a private lounge for 8 diners; the lower street level, housing the cocktail bar, as well as the wine cellar with capacity for 1000 bottles. The kitchen, fitted with the latest technologies, stands on both levels. The private lounge has the privilege to view the fun and frenzied activity in the kitchen through a glass wall (transparent/frosted). From the fringe of the main dining room passing through a suspended passage, one reaches an elevator which leads down into the very exclusive wine cellar.

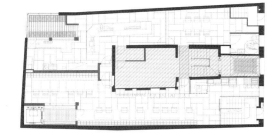

Hugo Boss Orange Shop

BOSS Orange offers casual collections for men and women. The interior of the shop is a contrast-rich interplay of authentic natural materials combined with high-gloss paint, white finished metal and brass surfaces. This combination creates an impact contrast for "radical chic". Coloured walls with finely-etched graphics form a beautifully accented impression. Loving attention to detail and the extraordinary, these attributes apply the fashion of the Hugo Boss Orange collection as well as the shops presenting them. The new shop in Madrid though comes up with more than fashionable surprises. The rooms are structured by "fashion boxes", in which the clothing is displayed.

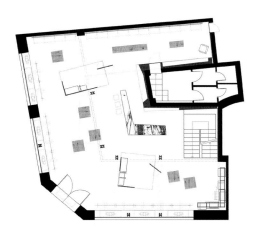

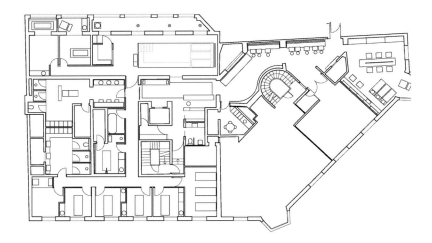

Spacio 0mm

The floor plan was divided into three different areas according to the different activities that would take place. The wet zone includes a small in-door pool, a steam room and two exclusive rooms where special water treatments and massages are carried out. The personalised treatment zone is formed by several cabins, each uniquely designed for a specific treatment. All cabins are connected to both male and female dressing rooms. A post-massage room where clients can relax after their treatments is also located on this area. Finally the third zone is a common-use area that includes a beauty salon, a small gym and a snack bar.

Las Lomas

In Las Lomas neighbourhood, a few kilometres from the city of Madrid, this detached house is located. The main characters of the home are its pieces of art; the owners have one of the most important Chinese art collections in Spain. The furniture has been designed to allow each piece as unique as it is, so the decoration hands over the main protagonist to the collection but being at the same level of its pieces. The materials used are wengué, silver paper, creamy colours and fine textures.

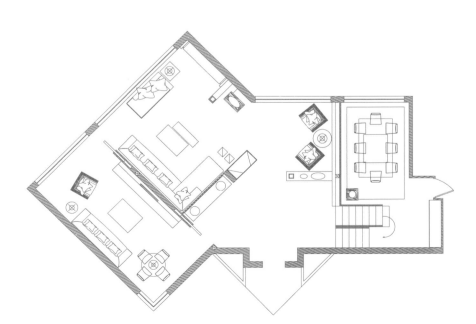

Photo: Estudio Interiors

Estudio Interiors

Duet Sports Centres

The Duet Sport Centres chain is a clear example of living club, focusing its interior design on a deeply human level. With a special code of graphic representation, these centres avoid all conventionalism: contrary to the written information, these clubs bet for a singular chromatic and image code that reflects the type of activity that is done there, with a visual and intuitive information giving life to a colourist and calmed environment of great visual richness. Close to the visual impact, the designers obtain a unitary reading in all the centre: two corporative colours identify the use areas by gender; masculine (blue) and feminine (orange), with two complementary colours that point to zones of collective use.

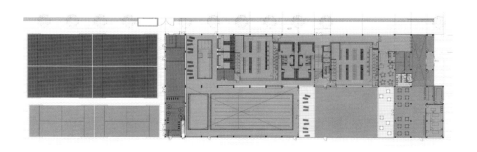

Municipal Youth Centre

The project proposes to provide different settings intermeshed by the natural lights of its patios in this long narrow strip of land. To do this it has to use colour through the whole width of the building, both horizontally (the paving) and vertically (interior carpentry and glass work). The light of the patios turns them into lanterns, the base of which are roof lights illuminating the exhibition hall and different offices. A hall for large events, a library, a teaching room, offices, meeting rooms, an exhibition hall, the youth services department and other lesser uses make up the minimal but exact jigsaw.

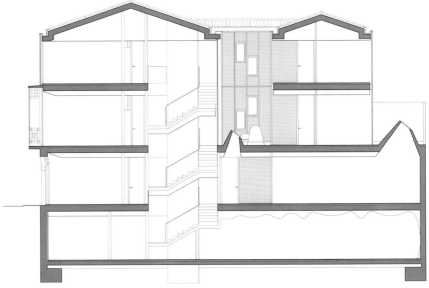

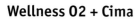

Wellness 02 + Cima

The "sports club" concept enters the world of health and comfort, with a denomination ("Wellness Centre") that associates sports with health in a way never seen before. The weighting machines stop being the protagonist, water being the prior element, with a great number of applications and treatments. All these concepts and functional differentiated programmes have been contemplated in the project, individualising each centre but keeping common points on the sharing of the diverse facilities. Therefore, people can find two buildings, two differentiated bodies that give content to both principal raised activities: sports and medicine.

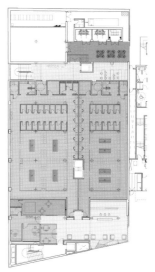

Photo: Adrian Goula, Rafael Vargas

Chic&basic Born

The new structure will keep the regimented classroom layout while aiming to create little idyllic oases which give the sensation of belonging to a wide-open space. In each room the shower, wash basin and toilet will be housed in a well-defined nucleus around which a distinctive design for each individual room is based. The walls to each of the rooms will be built in accordance with the new design while respecting features from the original structure, its plasterwork and painted decoration, but without actually adhering to the same layout. Cornice strips and wall festoons will cross the new divisions, sweeping in and out of rooms, evoking their origins in more generously spaced quarters.

Equip (Xavier Claramunt, Marc Zaballa, Martín Ezquerro)

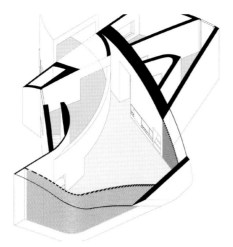

House of Convexities

Inside a house among coarse Mediterranean glades and corrugated stone walls, a slanting light, pierced by innumerable narrow repeated blades, inscribes and describes the walls with its impermanent, mutable hand. This light will tell so many stories over the course of a year. A curved wall jokes with the light. But the light reaches the moment and the place in which, going beyond the curve, it takes a tangent, deciding what will be lit and what will be dark. And this movement suggests the indefinite, mutability, shading, and ineffability. Thus, smooth, tall and still, a wall opposes silence. And such stillness paradoxically supports the preceding movement, giving sense to its being.

Puro Hotel

The concept that the owner of the hotel proposed as motive of inspiration of the design, was based on "the art of travelling" or "knowing how to travel". The team of architects and interior decorators interpreted this good suggestion trying to join in harmony. To the Mediterranean sensuality represented by the proper building, was added the Oriental serenity present in the decoration of walls, roofs and floors. The light, the water, the fire and the landscape are present constantly. The combination of these environmental elements with the system employment of facilities of high technology turns "Purohotel Palma" into a special place for rest and leisure.

Photo: Estudio de Arquitectura Álvaro Planchuelo and others

Alvaro Planchuelo

Gonzalo Comella Shop

The Gonzalo Comella Shop is situated on the corner of Avenida Diagonal with Via Agusta. The shop originated from the idea of strengthening the interior and exterior relationship, as well as creating a greater floor height. The existing large shop display windows assist in the interior-exterior relationship and provide extensive natural lighting inside. The volume of the stairs has been reduced to emphasise the different floors and also to provide a visual link between them. The use of the tensioned reflective black PVC to form the ceilings helps to double the height of the space and create a play of reflections.

Photo: Sandra Tarruella & Isabel López

Sandra Tarruella & Isabel López

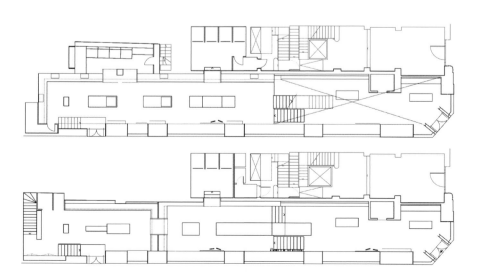

Imaginarium in Barcelona

Many of their goods and packages are in primary colour, therefore the designers filled the whole space with rainbow colour to set off the commodities and create a cheerful atmosphere. Each of the six layers of display shelves draws their own smooth curved line throughout the shop. In some places, display shelf is flying out just like "tongue" and becomes a special shelf for promotional commodity, area sign, table, chair, counter, book shelf and partition and so on. Those "tongues" create distinctive areas in the shop and then generate variety of activities around them. Since each layer has different shape, activities are distributed irregularly in three-dimensional way.

Showroom Ume Iluminación

The new space is intended to be an environment in need of "luminous objects" to take effect. The leitmotif of this company, as can be read in the uniform, "there are no shadows that can not beat the light," is evident in the exhibition space, marked by generous heights (after demolition of the old false ceiling), areas of darkness and contrasting elements: the white and red vinyl blinds, glowing fluids converted into graphs that run the walls, or the lights themselves reincarnated in autoiluminados satellites, become the undisputed protagonists of the staging. The proposed overall design extends across the graphic identity of the company, renewed by the hand of Medusateam.

Movie Space Centre

This project shows an imaginative and wonderful world. Walking on the floor of the cinema space, it's possible to estimate all the rooms represented by big numbers behind polycarbonates with background illumination, that change colour like semaphores, indicating the state of the movie. To unify visually all the rooms and to create a conductive thread, all the roofs are covered with semi-opaque skin which make the place as a whole zone. In front, the label consists from the decomposition of the own front in pixels that represent the new age of the digital cinema. All the decorations were chosen to represent the fantastic world of the cinema.

Photo: Innova::designers

Diego & Pedro Serrano (innova::designers studio)

Dental Clinic

The dental clinic was followed by the definition of an identity for the space, which was developed from two basic elements: colour and light. The project aimed to reflect the importance of colour use, as an action that configures space, and as an essential agglutinant element in the architectural and commercial image of this establishment. Despite the small scale of the establishment, colour was used in vibrant different ways and meanings in each compartment. The significant presence of natural light was integrated in the conception of the main compartments. This presence of light was continued by an indirect lighting system that linearly goes through the different spaces.

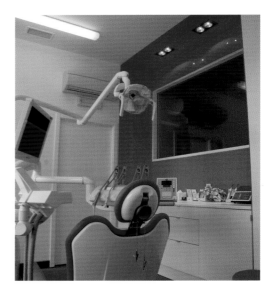

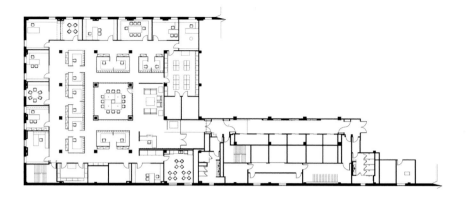

Tsunami Concept Shop

In the 19th century, when the doer opened to reveal the new "Tsunami Concept Shop" what initially seemed like an impossible mission was made possible. The expertise of the construction company BEC, was able to put a space of this complexity together in record time. This shop, just as its contents used technology to make this space possible, from high tech fiberglass paneling to CNC cut furniture. The opening was accompanied by celebrities and the presence of the press. With this proposal, the designers were able to relate several aspects of quality and above all innovation. They sought to destroy preconceptions and developed this unconventional solution.

Refuge Pavilion

The project anticipates the rearrangement of an already existent construction annexed to a small house, in a refuge pavilion of 50 square metres. The project is special for its utilisation of the small stone and its unique interior design. The designers' goal is: to design a real urban house which will make people feel that they have put themselves into a real nature. The interiors of the house are: the simple slate floor, wall, and furniture, the glass door and also the ventilating kitchen; the homely but functional bath rooms are all the method of making people feel free of city's hustle and bustle. To live in such a special house, one must feel comfortable enough.

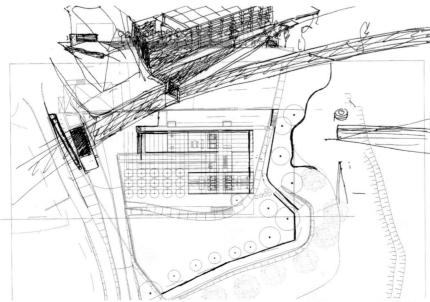

Pharmacy Monteiro

The intervention area is part of a small palace built in 1882 in Esposende (In North of Portugal). The intervention space are two contiguous spaces which have different characteristics, geometries and coverings — a smaller room with no natural light and low quality coverings and a larger main room which has a sculpt ceiling, surfaced granite walls, and the floor covering is in solid wood and several doors make the connexion to the exterior. The background supporting area (lab, ordering conference, storage and bathroom) occupies the small room. The several activities are organised in a liberalised way in an open space and the colour white has been chosen to increase the luminosity of the space.

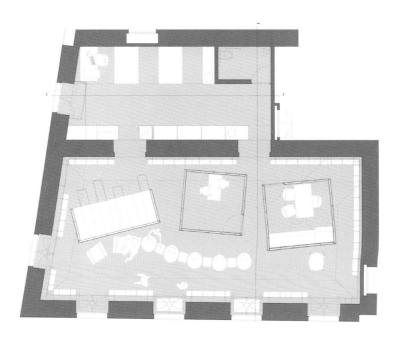

Photo: Jacques Simon, Laurette Valleix

Plaren

Superior Institute of Administration Sciences Lusofona University

The project gave continuity to the formal and aesthetical characteristics of the building Antonio Gaudi Arch. As for the choice of materials, the designers intended to establish a connection between the interior and the exterior and to accentuate the difference between restored volumes and the new intervention. The intervention is sober and discrete, allowing the architecture to stand out, revealing all of its elegance. The light and simple interiors of the classrooms and offices, contrast with the density of the woods in the atrium and library, punctuated with brass elements which call to mind the old function of the building — National Mint.

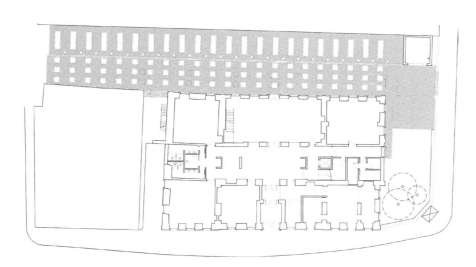

Restaurant in The Village of Brufe

The building stands in a site descending in slopes towards the Homem River, near the small village of Brufe. The roof continues the natural platform of the access road, on which the volume with service entrance is the only mark, related to the natural rocky heights. The main entrance is located in the platform below — with service areas against the terrain and public spaces wide open to the landscape. The orientation and location search for an intimate relation with the context, as well as the choice of materials: granite (in walls) and wood — in the non-glazed part of the main elevation, which continues the horizontal plane of the exterior deck.

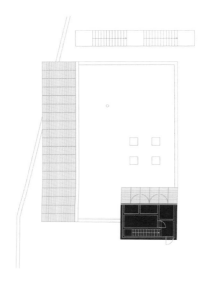

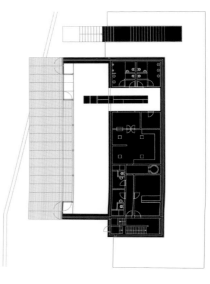

Photo: Luís Ferreira Alves

António Portugal, Manuel Maria Reis

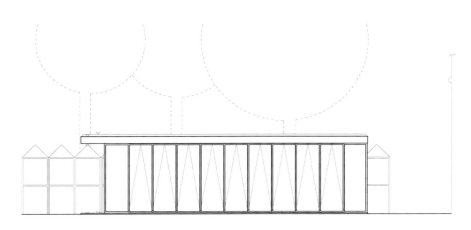

Activities' Pavilion In Lisbon College

The college is one of the famous Portugal comprehensive colleges. The pavilion is composed of a main room and a support space, and it occupies the centre of an area with trees, in the proximity of the building from the 1800's where the main school activities take place. The solution to the programme was given by a simple, potentially ephemeral composition, possessing an interior environment valued by the quality of the surroundings.

House In Ovar

On the ground-floor are the study, the living and dining spaces and the kitchen. Outside, as if spreading from the living room, there is a covered area along the concrete wall which strengthens the intimacy of the house as well as provides different lounging places. The service area, the garage and the laundry room (open to a courtyard), is connected to the house through a corridor along the northern concrete wall. This axis marks the entire distribution of the house, ending in an open staircase that connects the various floors from the basement to the first floor. The distribution in the upper deck is done along a corridor overlooking the ground floor.

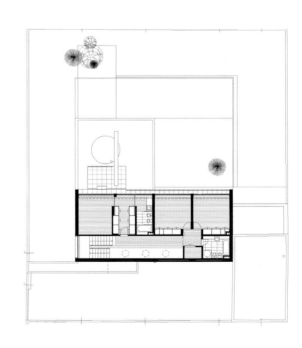

Photo: Manuel Aguiar

Atelier D!Arquitectura J. A. Lopes da Costa, Lda.

Vitae Orthos

The shop is bound to the trade of orthopedic products. The shop's ceiling is a continuous surface of light made of alveolar polycarbonate plates that hides the fluorescent lamps and uniformly spreads the artificial light towards the ceiling's surface. The shop's opposing walls have different finishes. One of the surfaces is covered with a pellicle of vinyl in which was printed a digital image of a dynamic allegory. The opposing wall and the back of the shop are covered with modular mirror panels that extend the small space of the store. Those mirror panels hide the fixation and support systems of the shelves used to display small complementary orthopedic products.

Public Library in Oliveira De Azeméis

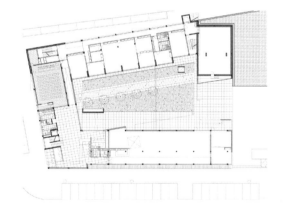

The Library is developed basically into two floors, most of the services located on the ground floor. In the north lie the main entrance, the lobby and the multipurpose room, with a privileged relationship between the atrium and the inner courtyard. In the west, and open to the view, is located the children's section, maintaining a relationship with the inner courtyard, sometimes slightly overlooking it, and sometimes completely open. The adults' section occupies the entire upper body in the north and east, opening up to the inner courtyard. The access to the adults' section establishes a relationship with the atrium through an open space that overlooks the entrance area.

Me Boutique, Issey Miyake

AEDS has worked with Issey Miyake for more than five years to create the Pleats Please spaces and me line boutique. The me line boutique is a practice in minimalism. Existing in an all white colour palette, the featured element of the boutique is a lacquered, reflective floor and ceiling with recessed light fixtures. This unique lighting method prevents direct spot light, creating an even, ambient light environment. The forthcoming fitting rooms, digitally designed and using 3-D print technology, will be an ornamental installation within the aesthetically pure me boutique space. AEDS has matched this sentiment by using cutting-edge digital technology and new materials.

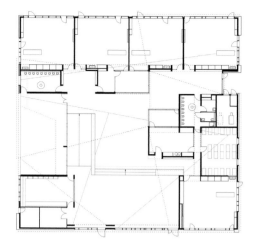

School Marmoutier

Classrooms on the north façade are intimate in scale while an activity room on the south is a larger volume, with a ceiling the slopes upwards towards the centre of the building. From the exterior, the 40-metre-long façade forms a horizontal band while sloping sections of the roof create a landscape of folded planes. The use of copper for both the façade and the roof surface unifies the elevation. Oak frames the windows and sliding doors. Concrete floors are treated with pigment; four zones of colours continue along the walls and ceiling defining angled lines, which contrast with the sloping planes of the ceiling.

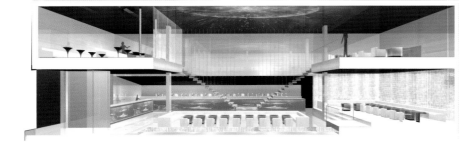

Vip Room Night Club

According to LightArchitecture's philosophy, the project of the refurbishment of the "Vip Room" is a synthesis between the virtual and the real in their game of ambiguity. By their superposing, multiplication and reflection, glass walled spaces are exploring this ambiguity; Images and information come alive on a pixilated glass, which gives them a floating and artificial transparency in a night black environment. The ambiguity created by projections is the main concept of the club which has been thought like a series of different special spaces, each one with its own design feature, to create a sort of "clubs in the club".

Tropez

Tropez is certainly the most festive spot in Paris but its transformation comes from an architectonic prodigy and technological feats, and it takes part in a reflection on our times. The basic concept was to make a new generation club never seen before with the basic principle to discard everything reminding us of a club or place already found anywhere else. An illusion is reinforced by the perpetual movement of projections on the huge image walls, which make it a place of metamorphosis, and a chameleon place which can change from one minute to the next from the Versailles chateau to the Niagara Falls. By entering this new night spot, the strict geometry of the square in the square organises a very pure graphics, broken by the big black bar as round as a flying saucer and the remarkable water walls.

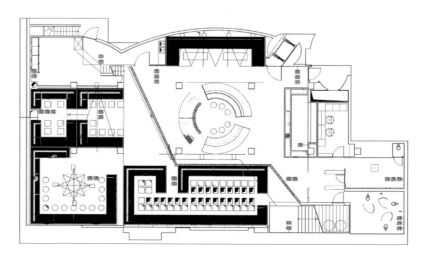

Photo: Light Architecture Ltd.

Gianni Ranaulo, Light Architecture Ltd.

Sony-Alifax

It opened in October 2006. Alifax chose Christophe Pillet to work on the permanent demonstration of the best technology of Audio, Video, and Computer automation. Christophe Pillet articulately analyses the ethics of his generous domain, aiming at "making life a little prettier". His style, elegant and sober, goes straight to the essential while never being stern. Meanwhile, the architect created a kind of welcoming atmosphere to make the customers feel at home and to arouse their desire of purchase. Showing the progress of modern high-tech, Sony-Alifax is no longer a store or showroom. The lighting, audition and structure meet together and come into a perfect combination.

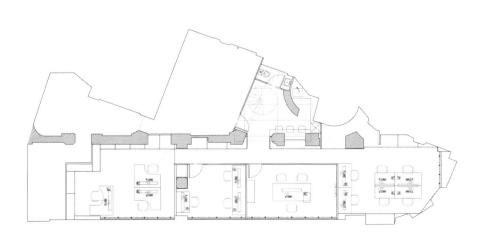

Domus Furniture Mall

The challenge was to develop the design of the interior space of the 62, 000-square-metre mall using a contemporary architectural language, which would frame and complement the furniture retail offers within. The mall stretches 200 metres and consists of three floors of dedicated retail space. The commission also included the lighting scheme for both the external and internal spaces. Daylight was an important element with an 8,400-square-metre glass roof to the main atrium adding natural light throughout the day. At Domus the landscape is not just about commerce. Some of the atrium spaces are devoted to non-commercial uses — spaces to rest, refresh, and refuel or simply to contemplate.

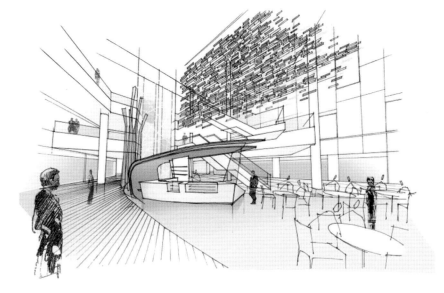

Photo: Virgile and Stone Associates Ltd

Virgile and Stone Associates Ltd

Photo: B&B Italia SpA

Maxalto Shop

The Maxalto Shop expands a 145-square-metre addition to its existing space. A leading name in the world of high-quality furniture, Maxalto uses traditional furniture making techniques, modern technologies and prestigious materials, predominantly wood, to create furnishing collections with timeless and precious lines. The dark wood floors and the soft atmosphere are in perfect harmony with the space. The latest Maxalto collections will be displayed in the boudoir atmosphere of this extraordinary space.

B&B Italia SpA

Animation Festival Place

The Centre Animation Festival Place is a new building in Paris. The architects designed it to accommodate cultural, sporting and social events. The façade is pulled into a skin made of black rectangles, white and silver. The skin folds on the roof to provide residents in the towers with views of the building. The basement hosts a theatre of 150 seats. There are an exhibition hall, multipurpose room and a kitchen on the ground floor. The first floor studios are for dance and sports activities and the second level workshops are for visual arts. The whole space is full of energy and youthful spirit with the colourful decoration.

Photo: Christian Biecher, Architect

Christian Biecher, Architect ·With Bruno Etienne, Architect

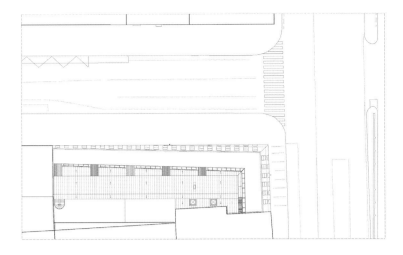

Seeko'o Hotel

The Seeko'o Hotel is positioned on Bordeaux's waterfront. On the ground floor, guests will be welcomed in a vast open hall. Certain windows, dressed in silk-screen printed panels, are reminiscent of the past activity of the waterfront. These French windows, their height exceeding their width, ensure a remarkable visual continuity in the extension of the façade of the waterfront. On the first floor, there is a bar, a dining-room, a hammam, a sauna offered to guests. The spacious bedrooms, ranging from 28 to 55 square metres, offer a sober, graphic unity. All the rooms face outwards over the streets and are served by a corridor with natural lighting from the centre of the plot.

Lamarthe Opera

Designing LAMARTHE OPERA shop, the designers applied the vocabulary of materials and the design concept of the modern idea of "classic contemporary". Here the designers find it is in a wide boulevard full of traffic and fast walking passer-bys. This is why they decided to use the same forms and materials but they enforced the expression through colour. The amber colour of the previous shop was reinforced with a strong red/orange colour. For the ceiling a mirrored film was applied, that creates a feeling of an infinite height of the shop and also becomes an instrument that controls the light and distributes the colour throughout shop.

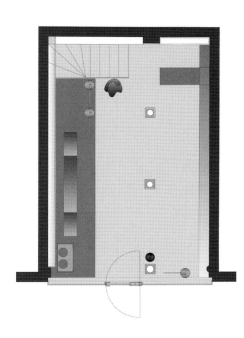

Photo: Andrea Tognon

Andrea Tognon

Closed Antwerpen

The interior is characterised by a natural, deliberately undesigned, casual yet polished and inspiring design concept. Dark floorboards create a great contrast with the signal white walls and a specifically designed long white bench element which works as a display table. Furniture elements were specifically designed Closed, which appear in all different locations. You will find one black wall with specially designed CLOSED wallpaper, the neon logo. Furniture units are plain white cubes, vintage glass cabinets and a farm house table. Mainly mobile elements were created that can be arranged according to the floor plan.

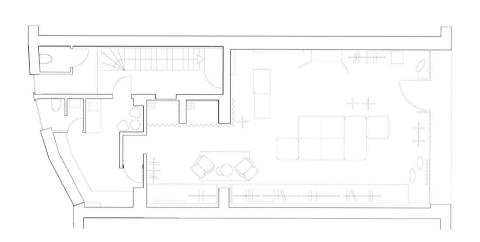

The Dominican Hotel

The Art-Deco building La Mondiale (designed around 1930): La Mondiale was the name of the former insurance company that had the corner building on the Schildknaapstraat and the Leopodstraat in 1937. The project is known as the renovation and restoration project of one of the most centrally located city eyesores in the heart of Brussels. The seriously neglected building in the heart of Brussels is located just next to shopping areas, just behind the Theâtre Royale de la Monnaie, and within walking distance of the Grand Place and lots of other tourist attractions. Residential properties are planned for the top floors of the old buildings while the ground floor is reserved for business properties.

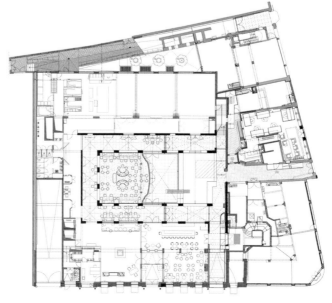

Photo: LENS°ASS Architecture

LENS°ASS Architecture

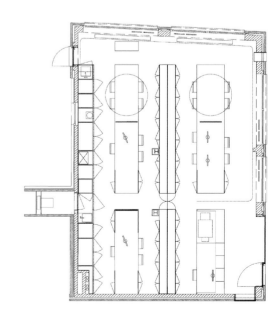

Woonburo Custers

The designers laid grey parquet interiorly and chose to go for a linear concept: with four long lines, as three long black boxes and one wall cabinet. When entering the office, you are led to the reception desk, made from the same material as the floor: grey oak. This desk was given the shape of the roof of a house for obvious representative reasons; being two V forms, in which, currently, the presentation books are stored for renting and for selling. At the back, a complete work space was installed in black MDF, also being the area where the fax machine and the coffee machine are located.

Tackoen

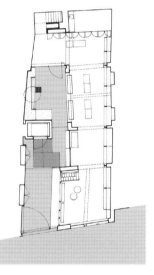

The existing ceilings, floors, timber-framed walls and roof trusses were renovated. While new details were given a contemporary interpretation, new elements are visually virtually not present. This could be achieved through the grouping of the technical and sanitary facilities around the lift shaft. Very few original structures remain at these locations so that these spaces could be adapted to current lifestyle needs without having to spoil the whole. The most important and striking element is a glass presentation cabinet which crosses the full depth of the shop without touching the floor or the wall at the rear. Spectacles and frames are presented in this cabinet that is illuminated along the back.

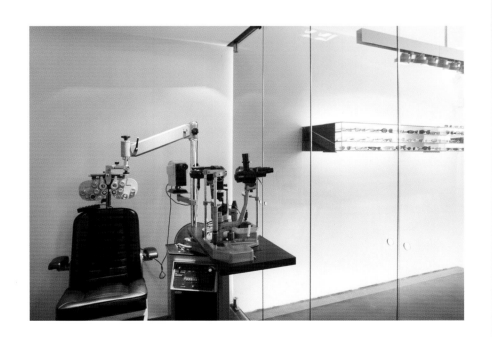

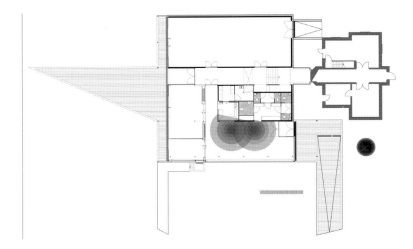

Funeral Museum De Nieuwe Ooster

The Museum is connected to the existing gravedigger house which functions as exhibit space and offices. The main entrance to the building is a ceremonial slope, a long route into the entrance hall and reception space. The visitor is made aware of the ceremony of "descending" into the earth. There are no steps leading to the main entrance. Inside the spaces are flexible, sliding walls close and open to different configurations in use. The large exhibition hall is an open space with movable interior exhibits; the interior is open, not fixed. The glass wall of the main exhibition space opens to the cemetery garden.

Novotel Rotterdam

The designers have managed to create sight-lines through the space, allowing customers in the reception to see the bar and a hint of the restaurant, and vice versa. Areas are subtly defined by use of colour coding for different areas, primarily through fabric materials: green/orange for reception areas, orange/light red at the bar, light red/burgundy in the restaurant. The reception was re-modeled to provide a more approachable desk, and allow staff improved views towards the bar, and the new business "touchdown". The wall separating staff offices were finished in curved oak slats, a material that links the "touchdown" design, and the wall divides the bar and restaurant at the opposite end of the space.

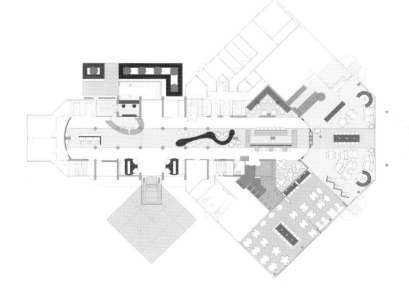

Office 03

The office is targeted to embrace the mantra of "reduce, reuse, recycle" to create a stylish space that would impact as little as possible on the environment or their wallets. The design reflects the client's personality and philosophy — simple, uncomplicated, no-nonsense, and humour. Everything in the office is white and grey. All the furniture was locally sourced via the Dutch eBay. Everything was spray painted with polyurea Hotspray. The collection of old and repaired products in its new coating has given a new potential and soul to the old furniture. The new office is a perfect case study of a smart way to fill a temporary space stylishly and at minimal cost.

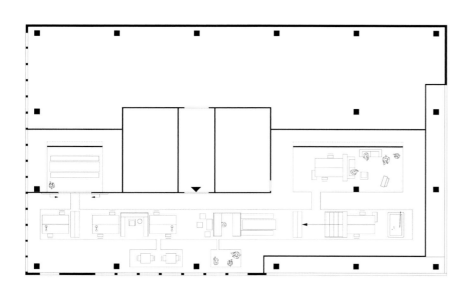

Fathom

Zeff has outfitted this vessel with some of the most luxurious interior fabrics and materials. Fathom accommodates 8 guests in four cabins including one oversized master bedroom suite stretching from port to starboard. Engulfed in white silk from floor to ceiling, the master bedroom offers separate dressing areas and a bathroom with marble walls, soothing river-rock floors and custom bronze fixtures by J.D. Beardmore. The other three guest rooms feature en-suite baths and internationally inspired decorations (e.g. Indian, Thai) tailored with exotic materials such as bamboo, leather panels and red handmade rice wallpaper.

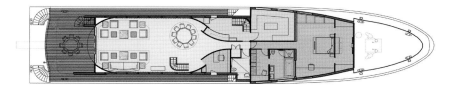

Nederlandse Publieke Omroep

In spite of the limited budget available, it was possible to create a powerful concept. The interior design is timeless with colourful accents. In 2006 COEN! redesigned the TV test picture to symbolise the National Broadcasting Channel. The well-known test picture was translated into colourful art forms on wall panels and window accessories throughout the media building. Based on the same design, a series of 16 colourful giclees were produced, which when taken, together form the complete test picture. Each giclee is available in a limited edition of 50 prints. Each print is signed, numbered and framed in aluminum behind glass. They are available via COEN!

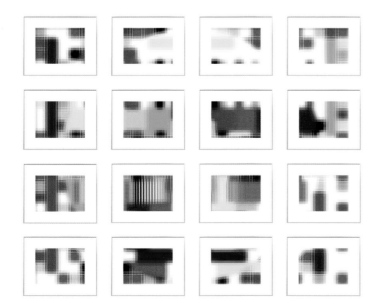

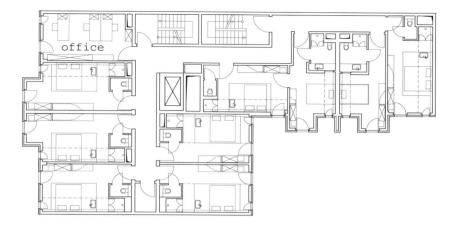

Media Academie

The Media Academie is the leading training institute for the media and is located in a stately villa at the Media Park in Hilversum. This beautiful building has been renovated to restore its original glory. The interior was designed by COEN! to create a harmonious whole. All the walls and window casings are white, which is reminiscent of the purpose originally served by the building as an asthma treatment centre. A major addition is the colourful, digital pixel floor with plant patterns, which reminds the visitor of the building's present function as a media training institute. Warm wooden accents and notice board prints round out the interior and make it ready for the future.

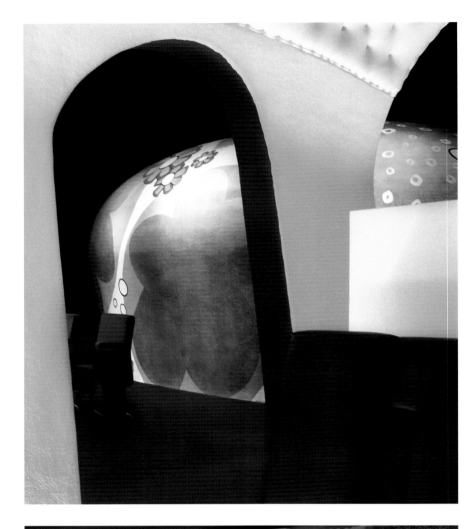

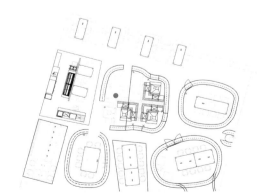

Interpolis Metropolis

Marcel Wanders studio designed the "club house" which is called Stone House. It is an office space with a special intimate ambience and out of all spaces it is the most used of the whole company. Interpolis Stonehouse is part of the main office for the insurance company Interpolis in Tilburg, the Netherlands. They are all working with flexible workstations and see their office as a city. For their 3000 employees a city is created with a centre: a square surrounded by different areas with different functions; cultural, communicative and catering are areas with functional workspaces.

Fabbrica

Every detail combines industrial sturdiness with soft colours or decorative elements. The designers chose not to intervene with the authentic industrial character of this 19th-century warehouse so they left all the structures in original state. The walls, for example, were left intact; in several places large glass panels were placed in front of them covered with Italian wallpaper, the patterns on which seem to "float" in front of the wall. Lovers can get to sit in a train structure that floats in the centre of the space. The logo of Fabbrica is based on a font in which the point on the "i" resembles the beautiful shape of a hand made pizza, but one can also see a full moon, as it enlightens Fabbrica at night.

Photo: Daniel Nicolas

Tjep.

Heineken The City

Launching on July 5th in the brewer's home city of Amsterdam, the shop comprises six buildings where special products and services will be sold in the sphere of music, fashion, travel and events and, obviously, beer. The project aims to highlight Heineken's international network, and the brand's foreign and domestic sponsorship activities. The design of Heineken The City claims to be "revolutionary", full of the latest technical devices, including speaking mirrors, 3D TV screens, an ice wall and interactive pillars. This store is the first in Europe to be 100% LED-lit. Heineken The City targets Dutch consumer and will be open seven days a week.

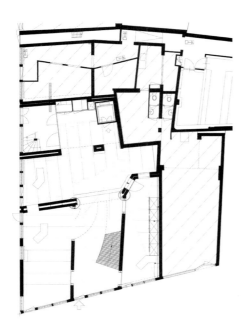

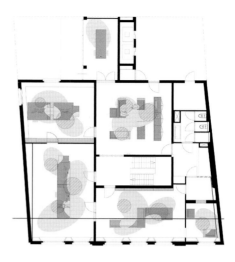

Office Herengracht

All three boardrooms and a lounge are executed in an overall design concept. Large round lampshades, spray painted gold on the inside, seem to cast light and shadow oval marks throughout the whole space. By this, a playful pattern of golden ovals contrasts with the angular cabinets and desks, which are executed in black stained ash wood. The lounge area has, in combination with the white marble flooring, these same light/shadow patterns that cover the bar and benches in silver fabrics. This area can be used for presentations or social working, with an integrated flat screen in the bar and data connections in all pieces of furniture.

Asia

First a "World Map of Cultures" was designed. In the first interior courtyard of the Museum, the widely spread-out island world of Oceania becomes an explorative experience as a walkable map. The three-dimensional green island bodies show 19 different themes of ethnology, commerce and natural history. Following from the permanent exhibition "Oceania", the idea of the island world is applied to the presentation of the Asian continent in the second interior courtyard of the Bremen Ueberseemuseum. A geographical structure shapes the design concept. Asia's contrasts and diversities are represented by six various thematic categories.

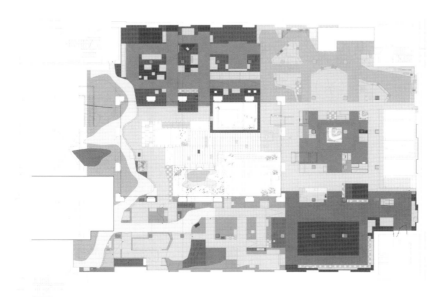

Climate and Man — life in eXtremes

The concept of the exhibition seeks to board public with an admiration for the adaptability and survivability of our ancestors who were facing extreme climate changes. By walking along a climate curve, the exhibition is arranged like an expedition, as a travel through time and space. Themes and objects such as the development of flora and fauna, climate changes and the evolution of man become a walk-through experience. The concept is structured in clear information levels, designed as a multilayered illusion of a landscape. This landscape is created by overlapping real imagery, graphics, texts and background painting and visualises the development of landscape and life over the millennia.

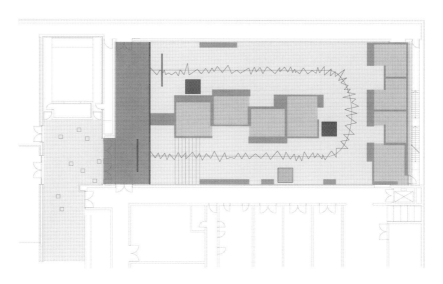

Photo: ATELIER TELLER BRÜCKNER GmbH

ATELIER TELLER BRÜCKNER GmbH

Cyberhelvetia

Inside the "Cyberhelvetia" pavilion, tradition and future, reality and virtuality, and nature and technology are amalgamated into a novel and fascinating experience of space. The glass pool in the middle of the exhibition replaces the real swimming pool. It is filled with virtual water which is enriched by the exhibition visitors both on the spot and on the Internet with imaginative life-forms. The reciprocal interaction between real and virtual people and artificial life-forms constantly creates new atmospheric images on the pool's surface almost giving the impression of a living organism.

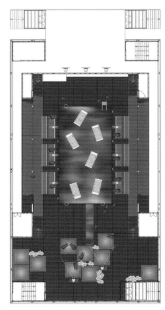

Sitscape

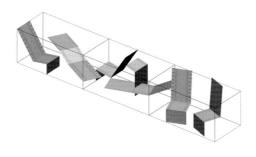

The sitscape is configured based on preferred positions of use and the dimensions of the users. As a "customised mass product", it allows different demands and forms within the same structural principle. The first version of this furniture piece was realised in a length of six metres for a client in Berlin. The form extends the usual use of a couch. The design is based on specific seating positions and smooth transformations between them. The preferred relaxing positions of the client are used to generate a "perfect fit" in the sitscape and provide familiar possibilities for relaxing. The transitional areas between these positions are undetermined in their use.

BMW Motor Munich

The first zone maintains the peaked roof typology by adding perversities for natural light. The ascending slope extended up and the other in a symmetrical manner appears high. Half a flat roof for light to flood in through the other half appears lower height. The second zone is a display space for vehicles. An intermediate level lies inside the original bays with a horizontal forging and concrete pillars. On the entrance are workshops, storerooms, after-sales services, sales and display space. On the second level is a car park. A façade with metallic structure was erected to hold the two shells.

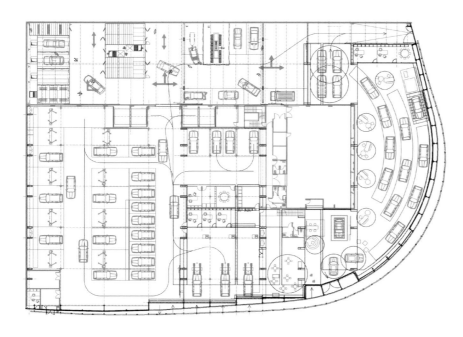

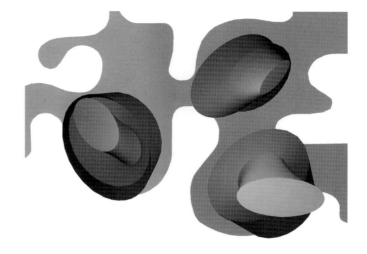

Garment Garden

Each city fabric needs space for nature and retreat. Garment Garden by Nya Nordiska offers a place for relaxation within the busy Inside: Urban context of the first Design Annual in Frankfurt. The vertical elliptical columns whose form is found somewhere between miniature skyscrapers and arboreal structures are covered with folded fabric whose reading oscillates between the curtain wall façades of a high rise building façades and the bark of a tree. The mirrored walls reflect the pocket park into an infinite display forest for the numerous products of Nya Nordiska — strolling in a park close to getting lost in the urban jungle.

Photo: Constantin Meyer Photographie and J. MAYER H. Architects

J. MAYER H. Architects

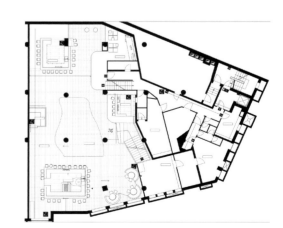

Baliha-Lounge Dance Club

The new zeitgeist of the world metropolises is combined with elements of furniture, accessories and figures from Asia by the architect Olaf Kitzig to a new, unique composition. The Baliha Lounge is from the point of view of the designer. The Baliha Lounge is based on Far Eastern elements of design, accessories and colour palettes that are in an exciting relationship with the harmony and tune of the areas of lounge, dance-floor and bar with a modern interpretation. This is developed by accentuated lighting, individual furnishing and surfaces and candlesticks that are designed exclusive for this object.

Bella Italia Weine

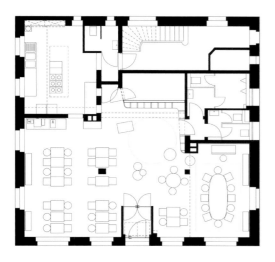

Bella Italia is a wine shop as well as a restaurant. The owner is a typical warmhearted Sicilian woman. While selling the products of her home country and offering a creative home-style cuisine on an upscale level, she transfers the Italian spirit to Germany. "Bella Italia Weine" was run for many years in a small living-room-like place with a very personal atmosphere. To extend the sales area as well as the capacity of seats, she decided to move to a new location. The new restaurant is located in an urban district which is very popular as a housing area as well as a location for offices working in a creative field. The restaurant is situated in a freestanding multiple dwelling in a charming Wilhelminian style.

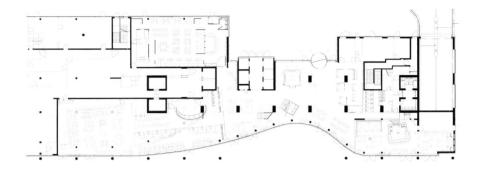

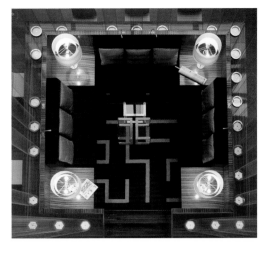

Blue Heaven

Tihany Design was commissioned with the design of 2,500 square metres of public spaces for Blue Heaven, the round-shaped skyscraper located in the heart of Frankfurt, Germany. Tihany's design concepts for the space included the lobby, library, lounge bars, all day dining and brasserie. Inside the loft-like concrete, glass, and steel emporium, the areas are defined with architectural features and furnishings rather than with division walls. The free layout allows for fluidity and better showcases the glass curtain wall of the building. An industrial luxe feeling predominates the air and complements the intellectual and financial characteristics of the city.

Bachhaus Eisenach

The highlight of the exhibition is, in the centre of the space, the so-called "Accessible Piece of Music" (APM). At the exterior walls of the oval, the fugue is explained as a musical form. Inside the body the visitor can see a large format media interpretation of three contemporary performances of Bachs opus. They refer to three exhibits as there are the first edition "Kunst der Fuge", a text notebook "Tönet ihr Pauken" and an organ manual from the year of 1702, on which Bach personally played. The illusionistic medial space performance fascinates its viewers and allows them to immerse in the respective music of Johann Sebastian Bach.

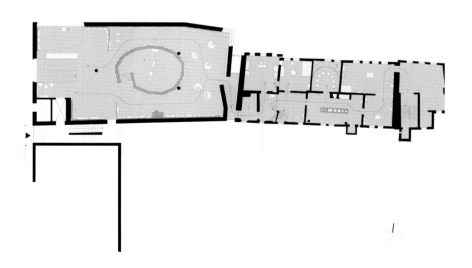

Photo: Atelier Brückner

Atelier Brückner

Uli Schneider Flagship Shop

The Uli Schneider Flagship Shop is located in a historic building in Hamburg dating from the end of the 19th century. The building's façade is preserved and forms unison with the contemporary design of the shop's interior. A peaceful coexistence is formed between old and new. The length of the shop space is emphasised by a 27-metre-long backlit wall which can be illuminated in all colours. During shop hours the lighting is set to white, at night the retail space is plunged into blue light. This curved design element invites customers to explore even the backmost area of the shop and greets visitors with a sense of openness.

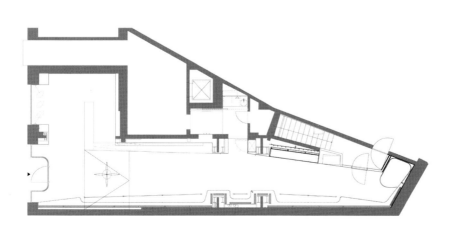

Matrix Technology AG Headquarters

The design combines the architectural concept with identity and the exclusive corporate company's values. Walls consistently separated from the façade, generous glass doors from floor to ceiling and textured back-lit glass panels used for the matrix cube support the transparent appearance of the office. The powerful simplicity of the elements of the design concept, as well as refined details, high quality materials and carefully-chosen colours create a positive team environment. Clean shapes, an intelligent lighting concept and the reduction to black and white surfaces in interaction with dark wooden surfaces give the spaces generosity, modernity and elegance.

Laurel Flagshipstore

The former room structure was completely removed. By this measure, a view from the street side to the backside water fleet of the river Alster was established. In combination with a large skylight, a brightly illuminated space with a generous loft character was created. To accentuate the label's feminine positioning, all ceiling openings to the Mezzanine were designed in elegant curves with bended glass balustrades. The shop is structured by freestanding walls with jacaranda surfaces and organic fitting rooms with curtains from floor to ceiling. Back-lit wall niches with powder coloured back walls create the wonderful Laurèl shop.

German Stock Exchange Frankfurt am Main

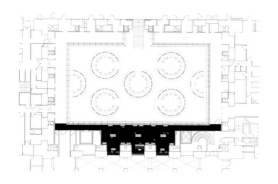

The Main Trading Hall, situated in the ancient Stock Exchange building in Frankfurt, determines the image of the Deutsche Börse AG worldwide. A redesign had to convey this message and serve the needs of brokers and visitors. The designers were entrusted with conception, interior design, lighting design, technical equipment improvements and ergonomics of the workplace.

The coherent spatial impression of the Trading Hall emanates the corporate identity of the company. The sleek design translates the brand into architecture. High-quality materials and the CI-colours, blue and white, contribute to the consistency of the design. The space-defining elements are the new backlit ergonomic brokers barriers, the DAX-Board and the stylised world map – a room-encircling light installation showing Frankfurt's importance in the international context. It is juxtaposed to the running stock price index, creating an impressive spatial narrative.

The light concept allows a flexible and dynamic use of the hall. An installed changing light mode calls attention to potential stock market flotations or IPO's (Initial Public Offerings). The brokers' barriers appear white translucent and convert to a blue backlight during these events.

Photo: Uwe Dettmar

ATELIER TELLER BRÜCKNER GmbH

Photo: Diephotodesigner.de

Plajer & Franz Studio

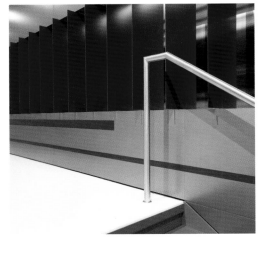

BMW iaa 2005

The BMW's motto at the iaa motor show is "the driving force". plajer&franz studio managed to design and construct an impressive temporary building and the main objectives of plajer & franz studio were to give birth to a new architectural design concept, providing an appropriate setting for the exclusive brand BMW. Both design and material expectations reflect the high-quality aesthetic features of BMW GROUP. With wall and ceiling element, the design of plajer & franz studio guides you through the exhibition in a very vivid and emotional way. All product groups present themselves according to their emotional and brand identity.

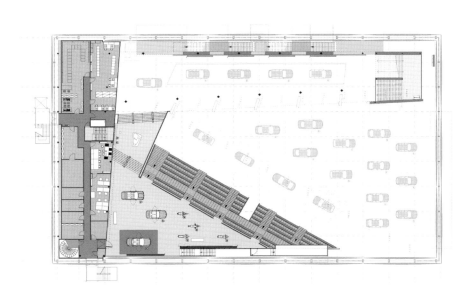

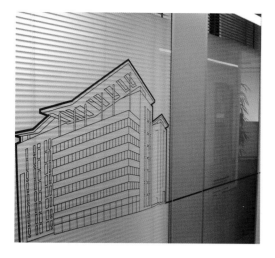

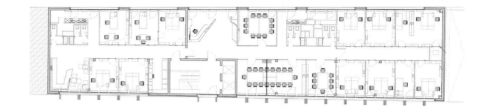

Hochtief Office

The project comprises the overall design, furniture design, the reception area and special zones such as conference rooms and lounges. The entire office storey is enhanced by a diversity of fluid furniture forms. The entrance lobby's reception desk combines shelves, a fin with integrated LCD-display and a desk for two receptionists. Facing the desk, a seating area with hidden coat rack and catalogue stand is offered for the visitors. A complex graphic design concept which joins all areas and extends across all surfaces compliments the furniture.

Serve Pure Wine — Wineworld in Change

A vineyard in the museum: For the house of the history Baden-Wurttemberg the ATELIER BRÜCKNER, Stuttgart, has realised a special exhibitition which shows the wine scenery of Baden-Wurttemberg clearly and informativelly. The expressive room narrative was derived from the structure of a vineyard. 495 ground tests presented in glass cylinders and the accompanying end product — a full bottle of wine — are rhythmicaly arranged like vines to a spatial great structure: a uniform scenery with all individuality of the regions, winegrowers and cultivation methods.

The exhibition cubes which are sprinkled like small vineyard houses into the great structure are devoted to the mediation of cultural-historical subjects all around fermented grape juice. Here it is about species of vines, cooperatives, wine drinkers and wine experts, wine measuring and about the consequences of environmental factors on the wine cultivation. It becomes clear that in Baden-Wurttemberg not mass, but variety and individuality counts. This individuality stands in an optically produced contrast to an anonymous wine shelve which forms the Entrée to the exhibit. It represents the huge number of European and non-European wines which likewise fill our wineglasses.

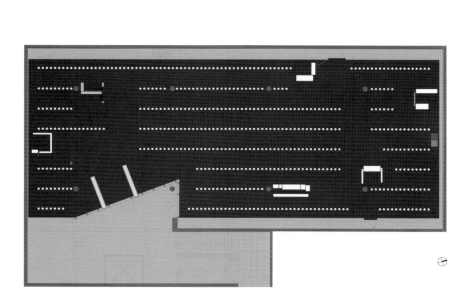

Haarwerk Munich

This high-end hair dresser shop is located in the luxury shopping centre of Munich. The designers plans to create a modern and cool place, combining with luxury and comfort. Hollin + Radoske combined a hair dresser shop with a shop of jewellery and fashion. Concrete ceiling and floor works with exotic veneer walls and tinted grey glass. The middle zone is hovering close to the floor, giving a soft indirect light out of shadow gaps. The VIP area for special treatments is connected to the shop and can be connected or separated with huge sliding doors.

Apartment S

The focus of this residence was to create a continuous open space while maintaining the connection of livable spaces through the use of materials, lighting, and ceiling elements. Once the walls were removed, the home opened itself up from one end to the other. This allowed for a functional progression and an abundance of natural light to flood the space. Piercing through the entire length of the home, a ribbed structure, doubling as a light fixture, threads each space terminating in the dropped ceiling above the fireplace/entertainment wall. A connection of the main spaces was achieved through the path that was laid in the floor by the contrasting types of wood.

MB Exhibition

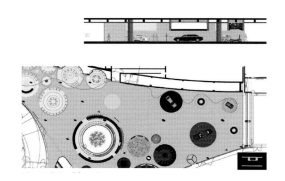

The Mercedes Car Group has been presented in the lower part of the "passage" to create a thematic connection between the Museum and the Mercedes Benz Centre. Its total area amounts to 519 square metres and it offers 56 seats. This space consists of five individual circles accentuated by the cylinders which seem to grow out of the ceiling. Each brand is represented in one circle which becomes a small world of its own. The representation of the corporate identities is limited to the inner surfaces of the cylinders. The outside is kept in neutral white. In combination with the light gleaming from the inside of the cylinders, the visitor's curiosity is stimulated and they are drawn into the circles.

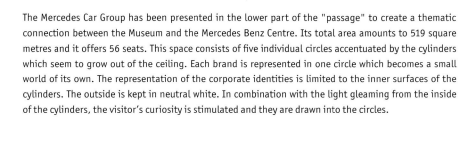

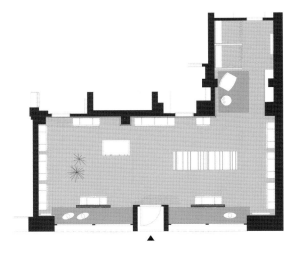

Geometry

plajer & franz studio created a whole new ambience. True to the motto "how weird can you get", geometry implicates the apartment of someone crazy but with good taste. It takes you by surprise like the first visit to your professor's home. The professor is not only obscure but also has a cultivated taste for proportions and moods. He is collecting all kind of strange items like photos of skeletons, lamps that look like jackstraws having to do with analysing. Everything refers to the symmetry (skeleton) and asymmetry (overlapping reflections of the angled bronze mirrors). Still everything is very stylish — the mud-coloured wall, the dark wooden floor and the brushed white oak furniture.

B27

The living space is distributed around two open patios which fill the interior with overhead light: one of them is surrounded by a bamboo garden and has a large hydro-massage and shower for the summertime; the other is a contemplative space, from a clearly oriental inspiration, with wood deck and gold fish pond. The central nucleus of the house is the kitchen, with a rough slate surface which extends into the dining area and dies off in the living room, bringing fluidity to all three. The guest bedroom has a separate entrance and is designed to obtain the most flexibility possible, as all the bedrooms can be connected or divided among themselves.

Steigenberger Day Spa

As Steigenberger is a traditional German hotel chain, the design shouldn't be for a boutique hotel, but still somehow timeless modern, but cosy and warm. The Spa area is located on the 4th floor of the neighbouring building — to reach by the hotel lift. At the entrance beside the leather reception desk is located the waiting area. Here the guests select the treatment. Six different treatment rooms and one exclusive double Spa suite are available. The Spa suite attracts the guests by its Jacuzzi with aroma and light therapies as well as with a huge waterbed with a solarium ceiling. The Fitness area is located on the top of it in a newly- built vitrified roof system.

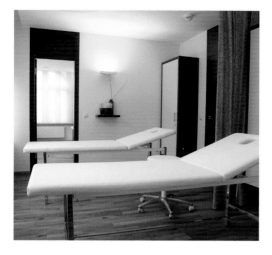

Villa Skandinavia

Villa Skandinavia is a new concept for detoxification and body cleansing. The Atrium is characteristic of the total look with a luminous stele that echoes abstract bamboo motifs and constantly changes by altering its light colour. The complete colour scheme and light atmosphere is inspired by the natural beauty of the island and its spectacularly fast changes in weather conditions, let alone its dramatic sunset. The treatments offered are wide-ranging and guests are looked after by an entire team of physicians. The centre boasts doctors' surgeries, massage rooms, colohydro- treatment rooms, an infusion room and relaxation rooms and it offers gymnastics, yoga, Kneipp treatments and fitness.

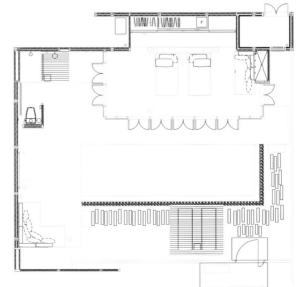

ADA 1 Office

The horizontal striped façade with its floating "eyes" celebrates the view onto this unique context. A public park in front of the building continues the design strategy of the façade into the landscape. The "eyes" in the façade and the platforms in the park form places that are to be met and contemplated. The office spaces serve both a generic spatial layout and specific moments related to the "eyes". The office building "An der Alster 1' links interior and exterior spaces to the public park in front of the building and to the city context of Hamburg, becoming a new anchor at the prestigious Aussenalster waterfront.

25hours Hotel Frankfurt by Levi's

25hours Hotel Company opens its third design hotel for young urban travellers. In close cooperation with the iconic brand Levi's®, 25hours has designed an unconventional hotel environment with the charms of a modern urban community. Levi's® is a symbol of the young lifestyle that has endured for generations. "The hotel's interior reflects the spirit that Levi's® embodies, even in the smallest details", adds Michael Strehler, CEO of Levi Strauss Germany GmbH. The guest rooms sized S, M, L and XL come in different designs and different shades of blue. The furniture, lamps, carpeting, wallpaper and fabrics used on each floor are carefully selected to evoke a different decade of the 20th century.

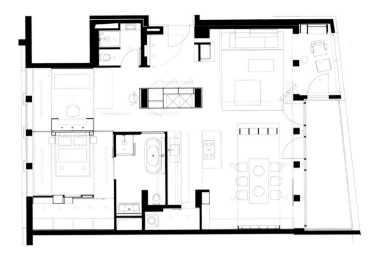

Quant 10

The concept is about creating a living environment that goes far beyond the average and approaches what living is really about: getting the most out of life. Similar to a loft space, the apartment is immediately tangible as a generous, continuous space. It can be apprehended in its entirety from certain vantage points. All functions are accommodated in freely-defined areas, which can be closed off by means of sliding doors and heavy curtains, if so desired. In this way, a whole range of new and beautifully-framed interior and exterior vistas become apparent. The bedroom and study form a common zone, defined by a circle of oak, encasing the wall, floor and ceiling.

Penthouse Schrader

Hollin + Radoske designed this apartment all in white with a few contrasts in graphite grey and grey oak. Nearly everything is hidden behind built in doors. Four dressing rooms provide specially-designed space for the clothes collection of the owner, a lady with a special interest in haute couture. The layout of the apartment is open and fluent; the whole glass façade is visible in the huge living and dining area. The designers formed the dining table as a sculpture as a concept together with the cooking block in the centre of the kitchen zone. The kitchen comes as a hanging frame integrated in the white core of the apartment.

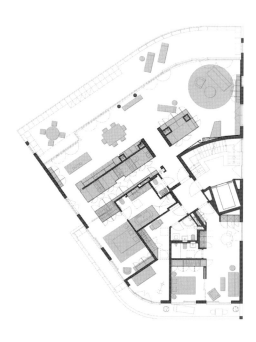

Panasonic

"Living in High Definition" was the theme of Panasonic's stand at the IFA 2007 in Berlin. ATELIER BRÜCKNER, together with media artist Marc Tamschick, translated the catchy tag line motto into a kinetic, three-dimensional platform for product display: the Blue Box World. The designers took the aspect ratio of today's high-definition flatscreens (16:9) as their point of departure, using it to structure the interior and overall proportions of the trade-fair stand and to create the basic visual element featured in the media space. The beating heart of the stand was a huge volume, 10-metre-wide and 5-metre-high, which consisted of nearly two dozen 103" Viera screens. Surrounding the public area, an enormous 5-metre-high projection surface stretched some 145 metres in length. Visual impulses from high-definition displays appeared on walls in every direction. A total of 38 synchronized SD, HD and Full HD video channels generated a media space that demonstrated the clarity of image, detailed accuracy and overall quality of Panasonic products.

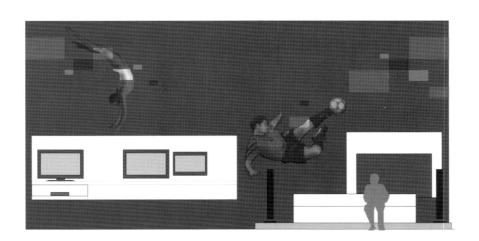

Lancôme Beauty Institute

High-quality materials and refined details like polished or reflecting elements in contrast to high-gloss white furniture create the basis for the stylish, conceptually stringent and functional design. Structured wall coverings and fabric hangings, mosaic tiles by Bisazza and warm wooden surfaces create visual and haptic contrasts, which stimulate all senses. Elements from floor to ceiling create an open frame for the exclusive LANCÔME beauty institute, a generous atmosphere, a well-being ambience, a vital calmness. A formally discreet, intelligent lighting concept emphasises the sensitive interior design of the whole arrangement. It accentuates particular areas with different emotional light atmospheres.

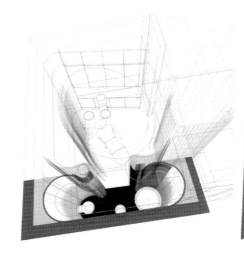

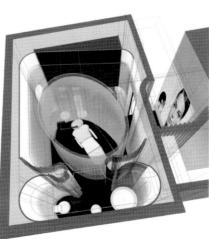

Photo: Schweiger GmbH, Hohberg-Hofweier

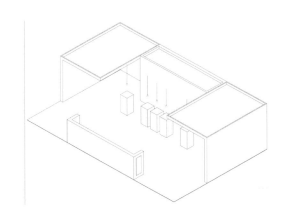

Swarovski

The Swarovski lighting & architecture project was an electrifying competition, which IDA 14 won with the idea of a completely white modular exhibition stand. The white room is the best possible setting to showcase the spectral colours of the broken light reflexes produced by the Swarovski lights. The crystalline countersunk and backlit wall (branding) as well as the individual discussion cubicals and seating are from Corian. The modular recesses allow different light collection themes and specific uses to be produced. The pile carpet and the luxurious fabric of the ceiling contrast with the cubical image. Both also serve to absorb the sound, something that is often forgotten in exhibition stands.

Dress Code

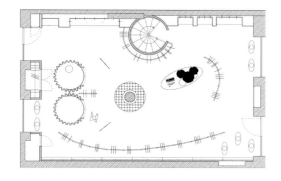

The new Irma Mahnel shop is something somewhere between exhibition, installation and shopping. The design idea is oriented towards the clients, whose female curves primarily bode a sensuality that inspired the design of a unique and powerful atmosphere. The new interior by Irma Mahnel is emotional, curvaceous and shimmering glam. People are ideally the focus of activity; the architecture is not to represent, but to caress people like a third skin while contributing to a feeling of well-being. Like apparel envelopes the body, a relationship between the body and the space is formed.

Photo: : Holger Knauf, Düsseldorf

Designstudio Regina Dahmen-Ingenhoven, Düsseldorf

Showcase "Crystal Waves"

Water, light and crystal-high-quality fittings, opulent and dreamy mosaics, are glittering bathroom worlds. Like a screenplay for "luxury bathroom meets textiles" the "Crystal Waves" showcase combined bathroom textiles with luxurious details. To provide an optimum backdrop for all the materials on show, the special area has been laid out along a precise grid, with the principal materials used being glass, quarry stone, crystals and premium-quality fabrics. The core theme was the element water. A "stream" ran through the showcase area, filled with polished mosaic tiles by Bisazza and glittering crystals by Swarovski.

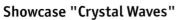

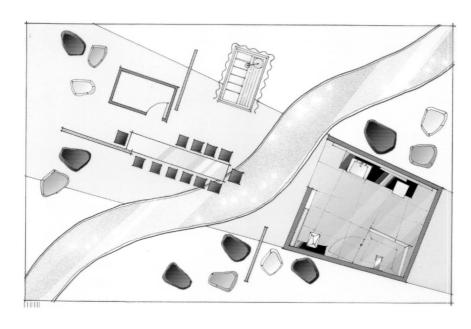

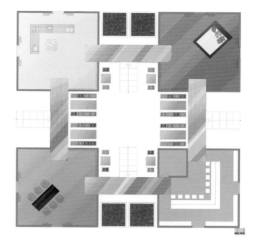

Showcase "Outside In"

Outdoor and indoor merging as interior design makes space concepts transparent "Outside In". This showcase transformed the ground plan of an urban villa with adjacent garden into a walk-on stage set with three cubes showing the situations "sleeping", "living" and "dining" and a fourth cube, featuring a bar for catering purposes. These days, the conventional way of dividing up living space is frequently ignored by architects. A mini boulevard allowed visitors to roam around the area, with small wooden walkways linking the cubes with one another and offered with its generously-sized garden a quite special meeting place.

Photo: JOI-Design

JOI-Design

Architonic Lounge

The whole lounge can be completely reused and modified for any purpose. The umbrella frame is crafted by 100% recyclable aluminum, and the light-weight stretchable membrane minimises the material usage. The lounge seats are carved from off-cuts in industrial products and can be reused for a diverse range of products, including packaging and filling material. Each lounge seat weighs 6kg, much less compared to the weight of a standard office chair and the lounge is therefore easily and environmentally friendly to transport. Umbrellas were designed to be projected with media that contributed to the atmosphere as it presented information for the visitors.

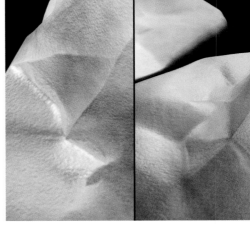

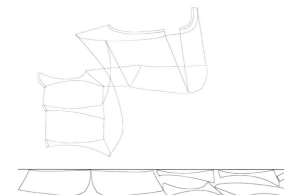

Olymp & Hades Augsburg

In the city of Augsburg, the multi-brand concept of retailer "Olymp &Hades" emerges on a sales area of 800 square metres over four offset half-level floors. Technical fixtures below the ceiling have not been covered due to the low height of the ceiling on all levels. The economised room height contributes positively to the quality of each level's spatial conception. The technical look is opposed by the glossy, sleek style of the coloured epoxy flooring and the polished glossy furniture. The ambience of the shop changes from the lowest to the highest level, starting with a colourful wall design in the downstairs floor and ending with a mainly black background upstairs.

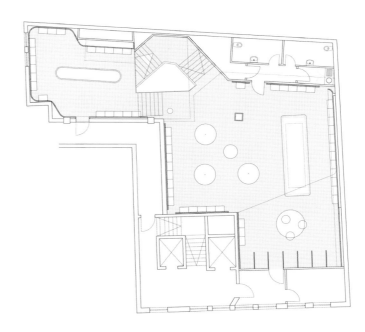

Showroom Kunert Ag

The fundamental statement of the appearance designed by plajer & franz studio is to show the revival of the traditional labels and a customised design that stands out from the crowd and competition. White is the colour of constant recurrence. Equal continuous design for the particular elements links the brands together. But every unique brand experiences an individual presentation with replaceable elements, customised wall arrangements, images and logos. The combination of different materials enhances the modern and yet intimate character. While the picture frame imparts a view out of the window of a country home, it creates depth of space.

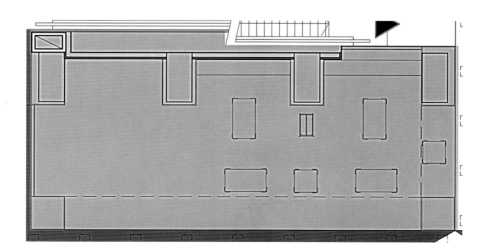

TechniKomm-Showroom Polycarbonates

In close cooperation with Bayer's advertising and events department, GOLDEN PLANET developed the idea to create a space which would link the laboratories where the materials are developed and optimised to the finished products and applications showing the possibilities of high-tech engineered polymers. The entire ceiling and parts of the walls are clad with the most well-known polycarbonate material Bayer produces: translucent Makrolon® sheets. With the light shining through these diffusing panels, and a special light choreography, the space has an almost floating, clean atmosphere.

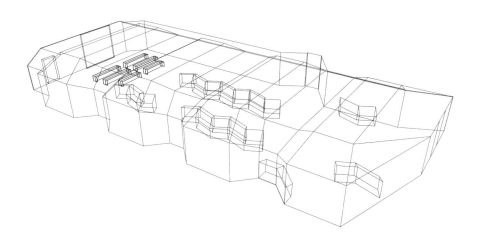

Stylepark Corridor

Corridor is a rooftop apartment in Berlin. A stretched and winding space is running through the entire apartment. It is not just a connecting space for circulation or direction by separation of individual rooms, instead it becomes the main space for this apartment. Walls and ceilings are coated with after-glowing colour. At night corridor is changed into a graphic photonic copy that fades out slowly in darkness. Architectonic strategies borrowed from safety and security are newly interpreted and extended. Textile surfaces like furniture, curtains, table cloths and selected clothing made of self-glowing fabric transform the user into a dark silhouette or negative form.

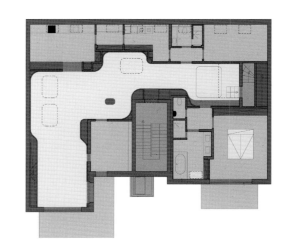

Mini Showroom

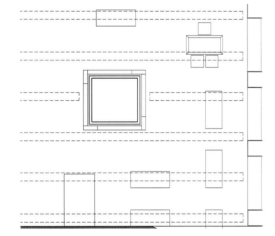

The interior is animated by the contrast between the black surfaces, colourful accents-accomplished by the Minis themselves and different moods of lighting. The designers also played with various frames to implement the new mini effect. The showroom itself is designed as a location containing enough space for presentation, helpdesk and sales of vehicles and accessories as well as a catering-concept already in planning. The ceiling as a strong visual element is constructed of metal panels and provides space for technical equipment, the sprinkler system and a flexible lighting concept which again picks up the new mini concept.

Photo: Ken Schluchtmann

Plajer & Franz Studio

Dental Lounge, Düsseldorf

The main source of inspiration is the Aesculapius Staff; the image of a snake winding around a staff is the common symbolism for the medical profession and proved to be an enticing concept. The narrow confinement of the floor plan actually helps accentuate this experience, as one is beckoned to delve further into the room, and gradually comprehends the full scope of the interior. The commonly associated cold and sterile environment yields to the lounge atmosphere; warm colours of brown, orange, and red along with the successful space sculpture are all important elements within the effect of the practice, signifying the patients' comfort and well-being.

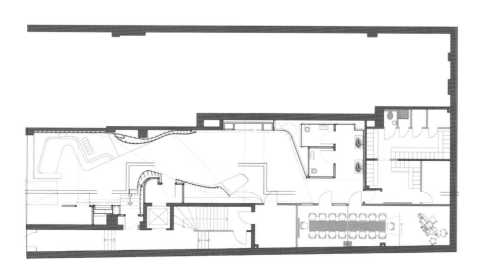

Wittlinger Hahn Stern Health Centre

The challenge in designing a suitable interior lay in uniting the necessary high degree of technical integration with a lucid functional layout. The radiology practice is characterised by a high patient turnover, long waiting time due to the complicated diagnostic procedures involved, and an apprehensive mood on the part of its patients. The waiting rooms convey a sense of security, the orientation system is designed to make finding your way around easy and the technological apparatus remains hidden to a large extent. All these serve to endow the patient with a greater sense of security and he begins to feel that he has come to the right place.

QS by s.Oliver

To express the singularity of the s.Oliver QS label, plajer & franz studio has been asked to develop an holistic design concept which transfers a clearly visible modern and up-to-date identity of the brand as an integral part of the s.Oliver portfolio. The use of more modern and urban materials generally known from the industry and other contexts is meant to appeal to the young target group. The lighting concept is based on linear black cable trays at the ceiling and light cubes of perforated metal. The shop is defined by an open anthracite ceiling. The focus is clearly marked by a large animated light wall made of stained acrylic glass.

House

Germany

Ludwigsburg

Photo: : David Franck

Juergen Mayer H., Georg Schmidthals, Thorsten Blatter, Simon
Takasaki, Andre Santer, Sebastian Finckh

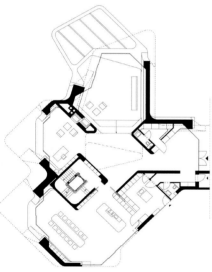

Dupli.Casa

The interior is much quieter than the outer sculptural appearance and guarantees a long lasting comfortable living based on an absolutely individual programmatic setting. The whole upper floor is rotated to generate spectacular views towards Marbach on one side, while the back of the building provides privacy and intimacy. The open ground level is according to programme individually linked to the landscape and the white stucco façade extends horizontally into the garden to manifest the anchoring of the building to its ground of origin. This creates a constructed ring around the house, followed by the lawn and by naturally growing plants and trees that blur the border of site and nature reserve.

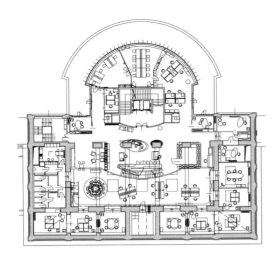

Office Accenture

Accenture's new office is located in the heart of Vienna, situated in a historical building. Different sorts of architectural implementations generate a new space perception. As a result, a new overall appearance has been created without destroying the historical substance of the building. The main hall is extended through different new views and light elements. Glass panels and mirrors reflect and expand the surrounding spaces. An "artificial landscape" expands — as a combination of mirrors and plants — the windowless offices. A highly diffuse light quality generates the perception of openness. Light ceilings and indirect light substitute for the missing daylight.

Oyler-Wu

With a deliberate contemporary design, huge SilverTravertino marble plaques and walnut oiled wood were used in the great majority of the areas. These materials along with walls' colour and texture created neutral and warm spaces ready to welcome simple and few furniture and ornamental elements. A diversity of furnishings was used to achieve original material combinations: leather, glass, wood, minerals and metals and colours generated a special harmony within the house. The vertical dividing elements of polychrome gold Cristal reflects multiple tonalities depending on light and perspective, and metal lattice is used.

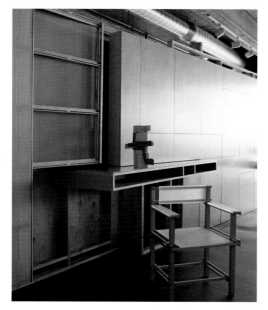

BAD Office j14

The innovative sliding-wall structures separate the main office space from the secondary office spaces like meeting room, kitchen, bathrooms, model making-shop and storage. The sliding-wall is made of foam, making out of a basic building material. The panels of the foam wall are mounted on a sliding rail to the ceiling. The whole floor is covered with orange linoleum; the ceilings in the main office area and the meeting room are covered with foam panels just as they are used in music studios, in order to approve the acoustic climate in the large office space.

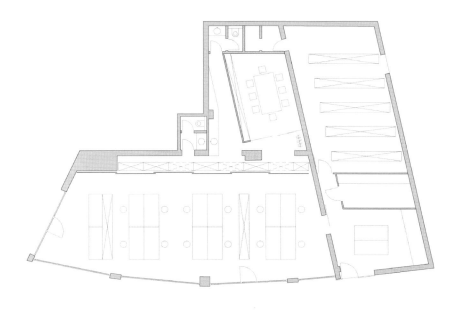

Manner Shop

The concept behind the design of the Manner Shop on St. Stephen's Place unites the century-old history of a long-established business with the freshness of a modern, dynamic corporation. The surface of little chocolate-brown tiles creates the impression of the whole area being coated in chocolate. This consistent dark colour causes the arches to lose their significance, thus allowing the products on display to stand out. Furthermore, the shiny surface of the small glass tiles creates an elegant, shimmering ambience with astonishing light reflections. In the style of the well-known Manner Schnitten, the shop interior also features a pink banderole.

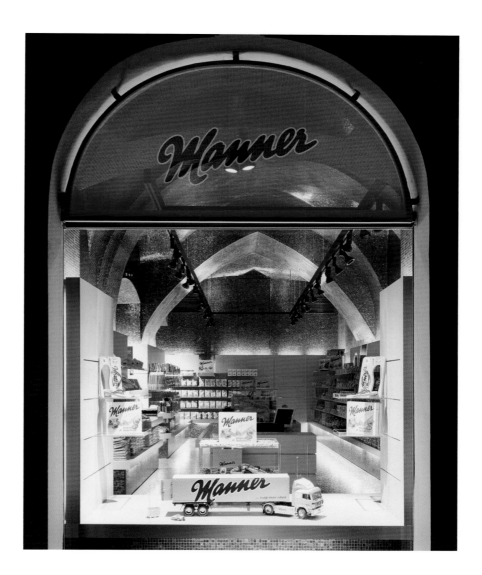

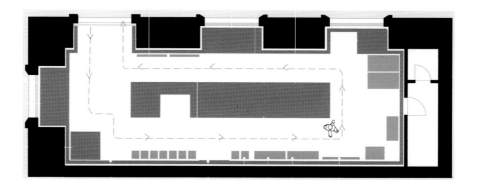

Photo: Rupert Steiner

Susanne Thomanek, Thomas Duregger, Robert Charuza

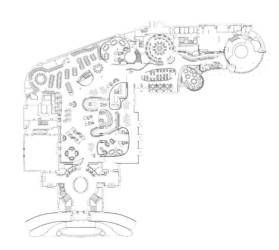

Casino Baden

Strong connections and intensive blending of the gaming and gastronomy functions wherever possible merge the different contents and differently designed, separate areas to one exciting, eventful whole, a dialogue between the past and the future. By systematically covering the existing substance in shades of deep black, the space acquires new elegance while at the same time providing a neutral backdrop for all new interventions. The colour red runs like a thread from the lobby to the dining room, where it multiplies in the many different materials, surfaces and patterns and dominates the room. An organically-shaped, 70-metre-long bar redefines the structure of the gaming room, creates a new space within the space and connects all the Casino's different-content areas like a clip.

Roche Diagnostics

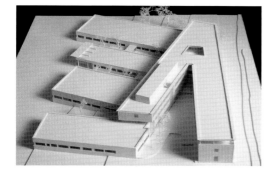

Comfortable conditioning of the office interior is provided by an innovative heating and cooling system, making active use of the concrete core, accompanied by a colour scheme that gives an atmospheric touch to the meeting rooms whilst also helping people to find their way. As is often the case with Ernst Giselbrecht, the exterior is dominated by monochrome white. A skin is built up of a single panel format, separate from the structural layer, which is also drawn over the window strips in the form of a moveable element with aluminium sheet on the outside and glass to the inside. Any individual adjustment brings it to life and alters the façade.

Photo: DI Ernst Giselbrecht

KSP Engel and Zimmermann Architects

The Levante Parliament

The original building dates back to 1908, and is a perfect example of the Modernist architecture that was initiated by the Vienna School and Bauhaus. Its main characteristics, still evident today, are an emphasis on rationalism, the elimination of ornament and the use of technological advances in materials that allow for flexibility in design. The search is also the guiding principles by which the multidisciplinary team of architects, designers and artists transformed the building into an innovative space. The glass design objects by artist Ioan Nemtoi have not only been given 4,600 square metres of prominent exhibition space, Nemtoi was also instrumental in the design of the restaurant and bar.

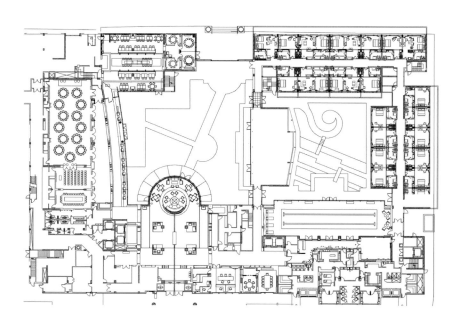

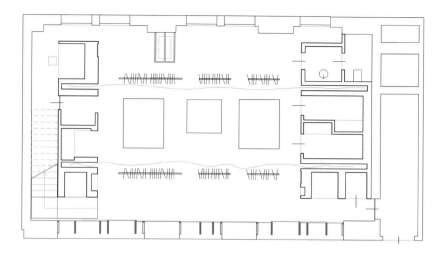

2006Feb01

BEHF is famous with its professional concept of design. These two worlds — the busy streets outside and the stillness of the garden — are the framework for the shop's "living area". The historical stone façade of the former bank building was playfully re-interpreted for its new purpose. The hardware (such as floors) will bear the typical BEHF signature: untreated, smooth cement surfaces in a pure grey. Niches, shelves, drawers and changing rooms are decorated using different luxurious materials, for example polished stainless steel or magnificent tapestry fabric. These can be varied and changed like in a puppet theatre or stage.

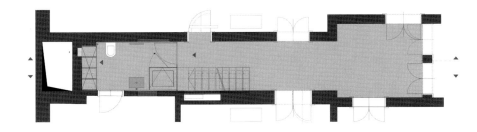

Bathroom I

In this specific project the designers were looking for a material/colour merging the different kinds of wooden floors in the anteroom. Therefore a yellow acrylic surface was used and extended into the bathroom. The bathroom was only separated with a glass front, and to maintain privacy there are sheds. The side walls of the bathroom were mirrored, in order to duplicate/triplicate/... the room. As the defined space was quite small, the designers doubled the bathroom vertically and used the height of the apartment to stack two bathrooms over each other.

Gallery Graben

In this particular project, the designers tried to create a space, which is empty, but still has all the features it needs. Therefore you will find just minimal inventions in the red floor, which is mainly used as a gallery space, for seminars and body work. The building in is approximately 300 years old, therefore all the walls are shifting and the interior has to be custom made. The green floor was used as a place for getting together and having parties. The designers liked the way how the chairs are moving, which gives the whole design a free flow. Red and green are dominating in the custom-made furniture.

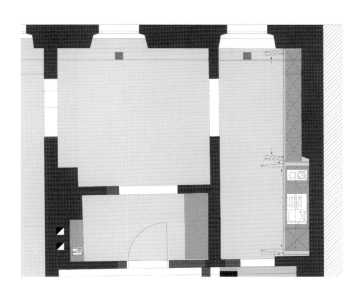

Photo: ISA Stein Studio

ISA Stein Studio/Team M

Photo: Margheritha Spiluttini and Andreas Schmitzer

A.01 architects ZT GmbH

Production Hall Schiebel for Camcopters

The building is composed of two parts: the office unit is arranged lengthwise facing the street and the production hall is located next to the airfield. The office area holds the major administrative functions of production, marketing, research and education. The meeting room is attached to a generous deck for visitors, which is used for air shows. The function of the employee's area was considered to be important and accordingly arranged with an independent terrace accessible from the lunchroom. The production area contains 2,000 square metres. The hall holds not only an area for assembly and fabrication work, but also an area for design, development and attendance.

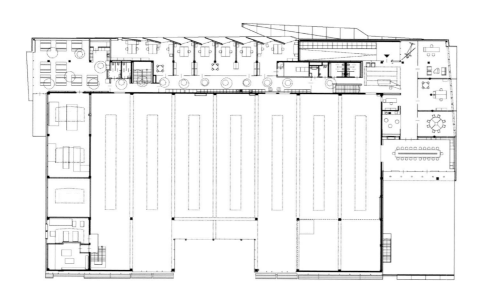

Lichtlabor

Lichtlabor, a 200-square-metre special exhibit, is located at the Igeho 06 in Basel. The images show how different lighting effects can significantly affect the atmosphere. Diffused light illuminates the room uniformly without accent. Aimed light provides illumination of the vertical plane and creates atmosphere. The luminaire remains discreetly in the background. At night, the atmosphere is completely different. Crystal ceiling fixtures, fitted with LEDs, shine like stars in the heavens. A true novelty and the world's first, this system from Swarovski lends banquettes ambience, which is enhanced by "dabs" of light from a multipurpose system by FontanaArte.

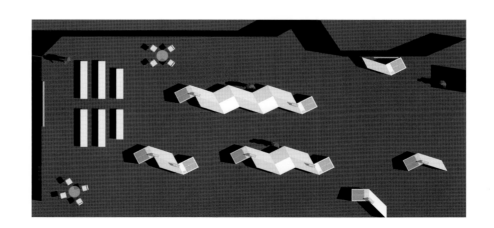

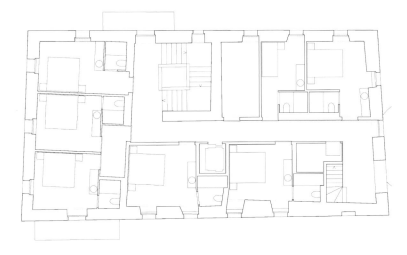

Hotel De La Poste

The project is well-integrated, reflecting the general character of its location. Historically, this site is characterised by the complementarity of the urban environment of the Rue du Bourg and the rear courtyard and garden space. The project, which highlights the redevelopment of the gardens of the adjacent city hall, extending them to the former car park just in front of the Hotel de la Poste, has given rise to the further project of constructing a pavilion in the park. The project plays on the relationship between the mineral and vegetable aspects, which has inspired a new structure seeking to complement the mid-18th-century Hotel de la Poste.

Spa Tschuggen Berg Oase

The different areas of "Berg Oase" are characterised by their interrelation and by their privileged relationship with the environment through technological trees that guarantee natural lighting and an extraordinary sight towards the landscape as well as becoming signals of the internal life at night through the artificial lighting that gives to the whole resort a magic atmosphere. The interior space is divided into four floors. The new structure is accessible through a glass walkway ("promenade architecturale"), from the existing hotel as well as (for the external visitors) from the entrance level to the hotel.

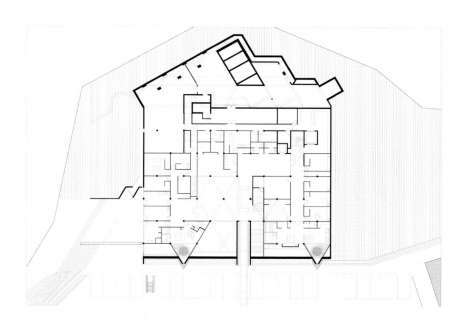

Omnia Hotel

The interior design takes its cue from the 20th century American modernism established by Europeans who settled in the United States. The design concept could be summarised as a Continental-American dialogue. The interior of the Omnia, in the true modernist tradition consists of a highly-edited and natural colour palette. While the Omnia is a hotel, the goal is to create an atmosphere where the guests would feel "at home." The interiors are meant to create a calm background to the breathtaking views of the landscape and the village of Zermatt. While the design and furniture are based on cross cultural references, the materials are very much of the Valais.

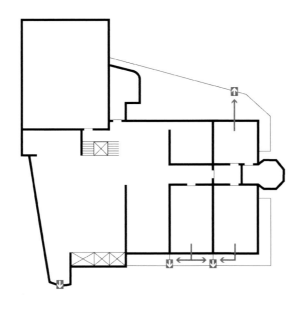

Forever Laser

The space is in two joined converted office building in downtown. Forever Laser is an institute that combines laser technology with the latest spa treatments and aesthetic pleasure. The space is designed as an ephemeral scientific white space coloured by reflections and refractions of light bouncing off shiny surfaces. The application of coloured plexiglass makes the space colourful, fresh and warm. Small gardens inserted inside the walls and made of real plants chemically treated to last forever, together with plants turned into furniture complete a setting that is both conceptual and sensual.

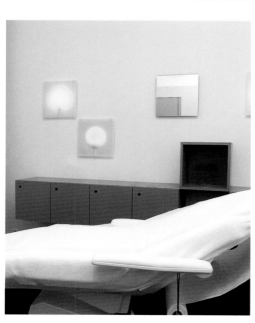

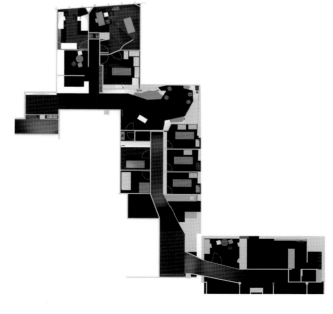

Wellness Stoos

The goal was to enable the guest to sense and experience the beauty and uniqueness of this mountain region in the setting of a decidedly modern and warm interior design. With exclusive and locally-sourced materials and poetic details, the designer showcases the themes of water and the Alps, without a single stereotyped romantic Alpine picture. The wave-like shingle cover in the bio-sauna and rest room embodies an element of Alpine architecture while also creating an element of distortion. The designer set the scene selectively, poetically bringing together this and many more Alpine references.

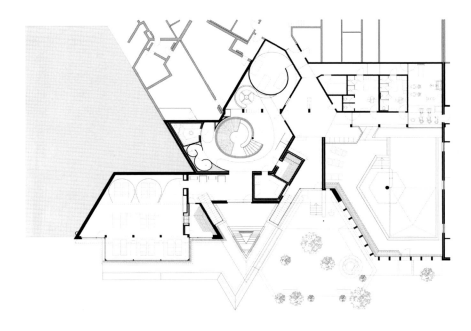

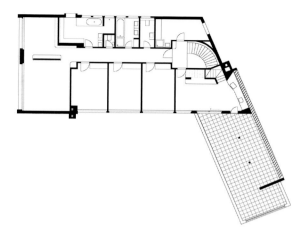

Conversion House Grieder Swarovski

The aim of the conversion was to not merely restore the original character of the house, but to amplify and even accentuate the rudimentary remanents of the original architecture in order to heighten their contemporary relevance and to anchor the architecture in the present day. Particularly the encrustations on elements such as the curved staircase or the concrete slats, which once denoted the somewhat more liberated architectural language of Brazilian Modernism, were peeled away to reveal the hidden qualities in their original lustre. The former wash room with its adjacent terrace for hanging the laundry was transformed into a particularly attractive kitchen.

Photo: Valentin Jeck

Andreas Fuhrimann, Gabrielle Hächler Architects Eth/Bsa

New Google Microkitchen

The diversity of the communal areas provides a great choice of distinctive emotional and visual experiences and activities. These ensure that there is a suitably relaxing or inspiring environment for the individual needs of the more than 50 nationalities represented in the Zurich office. To allow speedy movement with fun between floors, "quick connections" comprising fire poles to slide down, link some of the communal areas with the floor above — making sure the Zooglers can reach their coffee that bit faster. For the really hungry Zooglers, a steep and fast slide spirals down from the offices on the first floor directly into the centre of the Milliways cafeteria on the ground floor.

Niederglatt High School

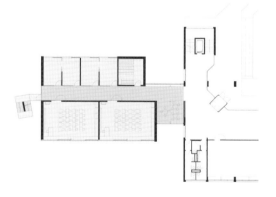

The courtyard of the school house was amplified in an urbanistic way. In contrast to a rawer plasterwork, the GRP façade has a structure in itself, but both materials react very strongly to lighting conditions. The classroom has a wonderful glass façade, and the opposite wall is painted into bright orange, creating a vivid atmosphere and contrasts with the concrete ceiling and floor. The solid glass parts of the sliding windows are without frames, the additionally attached outer frame of the slider is fixed when open takes over the function of a safety rail, and also gives the effect that the window is open when actually closed and vice versa.

Noble Bank

The inspiration behind the project was based on old English interior bank design. The reception area, conference room, and corridor wall facings and shining veneer plate, are in dark, chocolate colours, and the ceilings, in which recessed lighting was used, are made of upholstered dark brown textile panels. Each room of four private offices is in a different colour, but they create a flowing unity defined by colours like warm beige, cream, gold, and sky blue. All rooms are equipped with round black glossy tables and four armchairs covered with sky-blue suede. "Murasuede" wallpaper on the walls is a unique design. The same design is replicated on the glass wall divider between reception area and conference room.

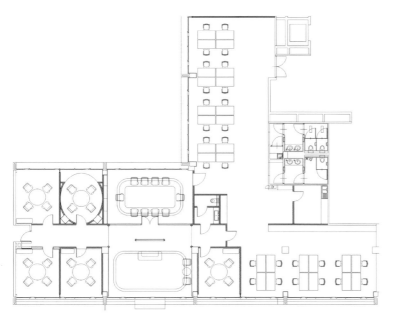

Andel's Krakow

The design develops the core principles established by the previous Andel's style and comfort, with respect for the specific requirements of the traveller in this part of the world. The design and detail make reference to the locality, using the best locally sourced materials. Warm, textured, riven stone lines the rear of the reception, contrasting with burnished metallic shells enclosing the restaurant. The shells interlock to locate and define zones, establishing set routes and views through the building, while allowing space to flow freely. The bars are lined with locally sourced stained glass in saturated colours with warm stained timber.

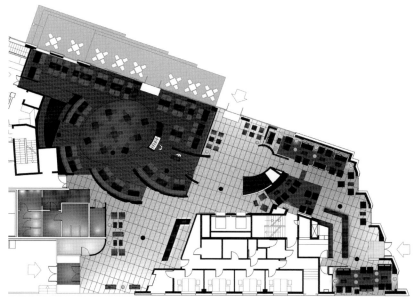

Photos: Illés Attila , Juhász Tamás

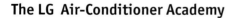

The LG Air-Conditioner Academy

Opposite the front door, a reception desk made of brick and wood panel welcomes the visitor. Above the reception desk there is a special lamp, but the desk is lighted from below with spot lamps built into the floor. Next to the reception there is an exhibition room. In the exhibition room, there are LG lamp and air conditioners around the wall and on the metal podium and on the ceiling. The training room has space for up to 33 people. The floor and the desks are covered with beech-patterned laminated wood. On the walls of the dining room a plasma TV, collection of pictures, and photos can be seen.

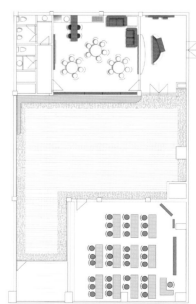

Illés Attila, Sotkó Anikó

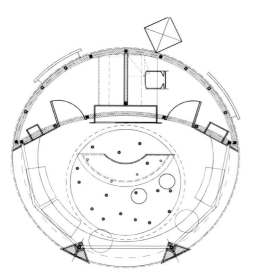

Frey Wille Jewerelly Shop

The shop's floor space is 22 square metres. This small place includes an office, a tea kitchen, vitrines and a counter. This shop has got the company's characteristic colours: blue, white and gold and the elegant, noble colour scheme. In the middle there is the counter painted in blue, with a glass showcase. Behind the counter there is the office and the tea kitchen. Above the counter there is a white suspended ceiling with many little spot light. In the glass display cases and above there is indirect lighting. Near the entrance there are two white cylinder mobile storages on the left and on the right.

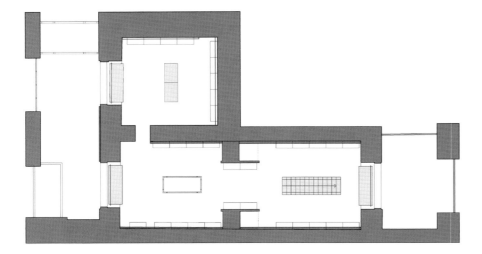

Shop Red Plaza

Located in the centre of Moscow at the red place, this luxury shop reflects the historic building in the shape of its rooms. Huge arcades, an old shop façade in timber wood and heavy stone walls are set in a contrast to the designers' cool concept with black walls and ceilings, backlit glass walls and patinated brass panels. For the merchandising tables and the cash desk the designers have chosen white marble and stainless steel. A gallery had to be built in the huge main room to provide additional space for the men's collection. An impressive stair made of patinated brass and illuminated glass steps invites the guest to step up to the men's level.

Teaspoon

SHH created a bold and striking new design concept for Russian tearoom operator Teaspoon, with the first outlet now open in the new-build O'Key shopping mall in southern St Petersburg. The Teaspoon offer is based around a range of specialty teas, along with savoury and sweet pancakes. Each pancake is made to order and so the client briefly asked to underline the theatricality of the preparation process, whilst customers await their order. The designers use different colour and style to decorate the wall of the whole space. Especially, bright orange is adopted all over the room (even the light is designed in orange) and also, the chairs are designed in comfortable and fashionable style.

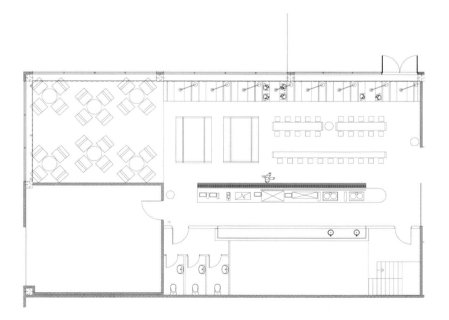

Globe Restaurant and Lounge Bar

Globe Restaurant and Lounge Bar is located on the top floor of Coin Department Store Building in the heart of Milan. The renovation of the restaurant has been held at the same time of the entire building. Globe Restaurant has a unique and privileged location in Milan: on the 8th floor of a commercial building. As Milan is a very flat city and has a very few emerging buildings, even going up on the top floor and enjoying the look to the city below is an exciting experience. The recent renovation project emphasised this aspect related to the position by opening new glass façades and conceiving the space as open and continuous to see the city outside even from the most inner area of the restaurant.

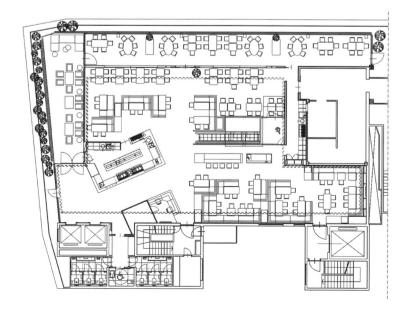

Romano

Romano is a shoe shop located in the historical centre of Florence. The idea of the project was born from the tartan textile design. All the walls were created as the weaving pattern of tartan design. The base of the wall was made of stucco to give a general effect of a warm and organic feeling all in different shades of white and grey. From the horizontal lines of the textile design, were born the three dimensional shelves and seating benches. The idea becomes more evident at the back of the space where the design is printed on metal panels and covers the whole space of the small resting area.

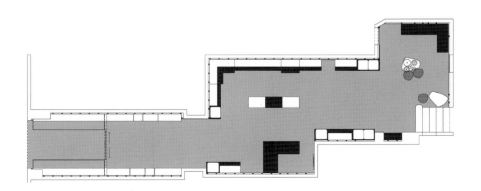

La Saliere

Federico focused on an interior design and centred on a novel conceptuality of space and layout. This was essential in order to provide functionality and adaptability. The architect created a new lounge area, developing an alternative use of space thanks to sliding separators. The restaurant's various spaces become modular, easily divided and adaptable to differing needs, without sacrificing La Salière's characterising elegance, function and formal discreetness. Covered in soundproof "Eraclit" panels, the ecological pale walls encompass mostly Wengé wood furniture items. Light is trimmed or narrowed producing an alteration of shadows and bright geometric forms.

Gonzalo Mardones Viviani Architects Studio

The soul of the design was simpe and natural. The L-shape plan was not orthogonal in order to tense the circulations and the space. The designers work with one material and one colour: all the walls and roofs here white. The floor was furnished with light grey ceramic and the designers separate the spaces with transparent crystals. The furniture was white too and also there are no elements that compete with the white.

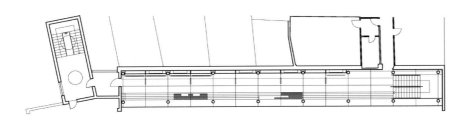

"Olivarte" Cultural Centre

"Olivart" is a cultural center for the promotion of Tuscan olive oil. Located near the city of Arezzo, the centre is subdivided into areas for seminar and meetings, a demonstration kitchen and a restaurant. The exterior of the building is characterised by a wood trellis running along the entire façade and by a semicircular bench surrounding a lawn with a large olive tree. All the furnishing elements are custom-designed: the floating copper lamp in the restaurant hall, the dining tables, the movable wood shelves and the copper radiators for space heating.

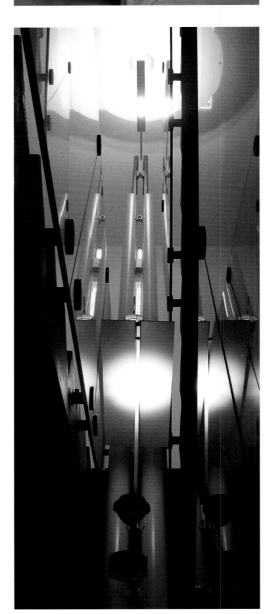

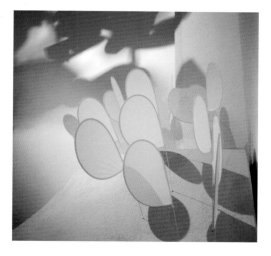

The Secret Garden

The suggestive installation "The Secret Garden" shows an impressive and artificial flowered hill, which covers the façade of the Lyceum and acts as the main entrance. The designer chose to colour the hills in a sunny yellow and dressed them with white kite-petals, which move in the wind like beautiful field flowers. Inside the pavilion, the central area turns into a big green lawn with little yellow hills on which people can sit and rest like in an unexpected park. The kite-petals are discomposed and re-arranged in vaporous white clouds which move freely in the sky-ceiling like blown-out dandelions.

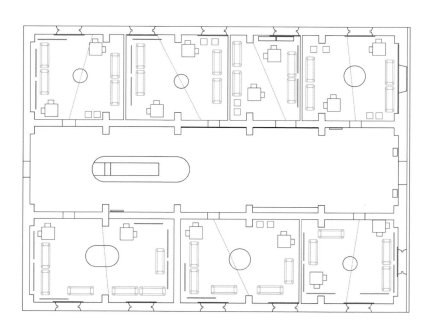

Exhibition

Italy

Florence

Photo: Ilaria Marelli

Ilaria Marelli

417

Exhibit: "Leonardo Genius and Cartographer"

The exhibit "Leonardo Genius and Cartographer" was housed on the ground floor of a 15th century Renaissance building within the historic centre of Arezzo. Important documents, maps and astronomical instruments of the Renaissance were housed in specifically designed display cases lit through a system of optical fibers. The last two rooms were dedicated to the display of 5 original maps drawn by Leonardo da Vinci, property of the Windsor Collection. The original drawings were located on easel stands to indicate their painting-like quality.

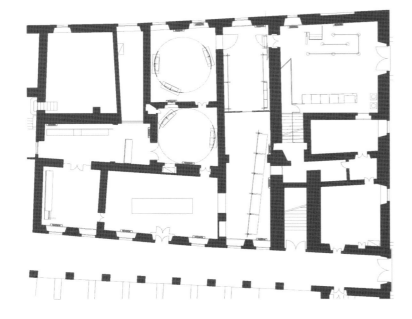

Hotel Santa Rosa & Serenity Spa, Amalfi Coast Italy

A small luxury hotel within a 17th century convent already conjures up precisely the aura of this property; moreover, the location is both beautiful and breathtaking, located high above the calm deep blue sea, a refreshing mix of fragrances formed by the local flora, lemon trees and sea fills the senses. Hotel Santa Rosa is only one hour from the original Spa at Pompeii, with gorgeous views both up and down the Amalfi Coast — this will be an exceptional Spa and Hotel.

Cave

"Cave" installation at Pitti fashion show takes inspiration from geological caves: dark spaces, beams of sunlight entering through crevices, amazing shapes of minerals and precious stones, intense natural colours. Ilaria Marelli has given all these elements an abstract look in order to create a fascinating, masculine scene. Shape and surface of the entrance façade are jagged like natural deposits of basalt. Just behind the entrance door, visitors go through a curtain of transparent strings hanging from the ceiling. Inside the pavilion, further coloured light-cascades cut the dark spaces and reflect on vertical mirrored panels, offering other surprising views.

Vaulted House

In a long central hall and modulated in plan on three squares of six metres wide, the heart of the design is formed. The flooring in travertine and a covering of Venetian stucco spread on the ample side developed lengthways, create, via a chromatic homogeneity, a continuous ribbon which, enveloping the observer, offers a sort of blank page on which to write his or her own experience. At the same time, the light, coming from the sides of the room, has the possibility to interpret the space. On the south side the position of the windows welcomes the winter sun and, through a thick wide cement "lunette", screens the sun in summer.

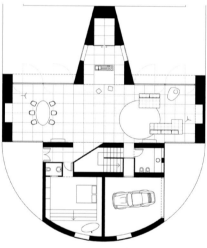

Sabine Schweigert

"CORTE" installation by Ilaria Marelli, the fifth exhibit design for Pitti Immagine, creates the relaxing atmosphere of Mediterranean houses, courtyards and squares by featuring their typical tones of white and blue, architectural and decorative elements and the characteristic painted ceramics and tiles called "azulejos". A wide staircase, featuring a vaulted ceiling, leads the visitors to the elliptical central space with its walls entirely covered with figurative decorations, a reproduction of Lisbon "azulejos", the traditional ceramics painted with rural scenes and mythological figures. Further characteristic elements are placed in the middle of every room, emphasising the courtyard mood.

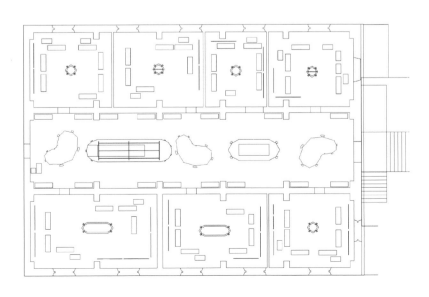

Azimut Rehabilitation Centre

It was built in a prime structure of an historic industrial building. The regular pattern blends with new forms. In the central space 5 metres in height bathrooms and small rooms are for medical visits. Surrounding the central body, a ring-like path leads visitors to the centre's service areas. Two colours have been chosen for the building. Grey optically lowers the vertical perception of space, adding a pleasant perspective to the space. Beyond the grey wall and on the upper portions, white adds airiness and luminosity. Lighting was given special emphasis with the intent of reinstating the warmth of natural light while giving a sense of openness.

Photo: Federico Delrosso

Federico Delrosso

Pall Italia Headquarters

Thanks to the combined experience of specialists and complementary professionals, according to the principle of "integrated design", the team led by Architect Massimo Roj was able to design a building with lower management cost and simultaneously superior standards of functionality, usability and efficiency. Moreover, being aware of the environmental awareness of the Customer, Progetto CMR proposed to Pall the creation of a green building, a high energy-saving project which allowed the designers to implement the extensive research carried out over the years on the subject of environmental sustainability, energy control and low noxiousness.

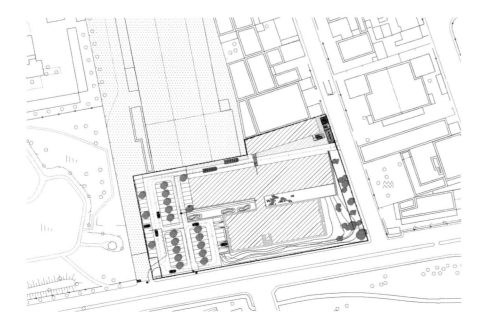

Bruschi Bolzano

Located in the old town centre of Bolzano, the shop expands on 4 floors and can be accessed through one of the characteristic arcades of the town. The main concept of renovation philosophy was to differentiate four interiors of the shop by using different kinds of material, expositive typology and lighting system on each floor and to keep at the same time a harmonious atmosphere and style. A sound diffusion system, which is integrated with lighting (created ad hoc), drives customers through a sensorial experience among floors of the shop. Ground floor — the real window of the shop — is completely covered with Brazilian green marble slabs.

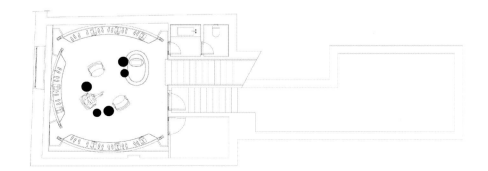

Photo: Arch. Alessandro Bartolini

Arch. Alessandro Bartolini

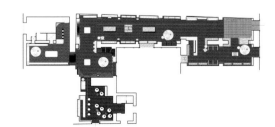

Energie Boutique

"Energie" brand was established in Italy twenty years ago as a line of young men's wear. Today "Energie" shops are to be opened up all over the world with a new concept. The rational clean and minimal characteristics of this architecture were perceived by the architects as masculine and therefore suitable for the "Energie" as men' wear brand. The references to the 1950s were suggested by the client and sparked a profound research made by the architects. The aim was to reconstruct a space that evokes the past but is, at the same time, made of up-to-date materials and style. The architects believed that only in this way would it be possible to create a design that is beyond a fashionable statement.

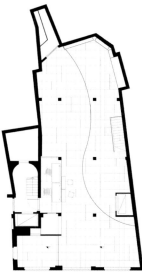

Malino Shop

The "Corian®" Design — Milano Store" applies several materials and products by DuPont in its design and decor. Among these, Zodiaq® (cut in large size tiles) for the showroom floor; Corian®, for a large, backlit and curved panel (about 21 metres long by 1 metre high with surface decoration via sublimation and carving), mounted at a height of about 2.5 metres, as decorative and display covering for some walls and built-in furniture and for the three internal and external store window frames; laminated safety glass SentryGlas® Plus for the three shop windows; decorative safety glass SentryGlas® Expressions™ for an interior glass wall.

Photo: Lorenz Kaz Studio

Lorenz Kaz Studio

S.P.Acqua

Water is the source of life. This exhibition design has "water" as a starting point and inspiration. Each display unit consists of three supporting elements realised with big bottle racks usually used for water transportation, on which are welded metal profiles connected by a central joint providing balance to the structure. The same metal profile is' also holding the photographs that are protected by a thin Perspex sheet. The exhibit design gives a sense of lightness, transparency and simplicity. The weight of the water, becomes an essential element, without which the structure would loose its balance. The displays were also designed to be easily dismantled, moved to a different location and re-installed.

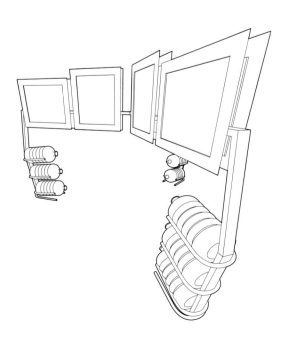

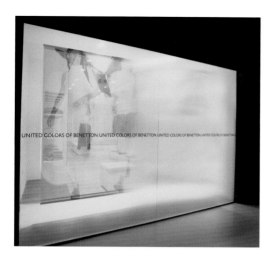

Benetton Concept Shop

Interior design for the United Colours of Benetton showroom shop in which displays the brand's latest fashion lines and products to their worldwide clients. In response to the colorful nature of the merchandise, the interior is a composition of pale-hued surfaces and components. The main one, being the curvaceous translucent modular wall system peels down from the suspended ceiling and runs throughout the shop, which ultimately defines the atmosphere and shape of the space. This "floating" component creates a series of intriguing perspectives, light and shadow conditions and a soft partitioning of the internal spaces.

Photo: Yael Pincus

Miss Sixty Milano

Here you can find a glamorous world of fantastic scenery and an imaginary reality. An organic space designed with curved walls, sculptured counters, soft and cozy surfaces with bright colours, is to create a reality bigger than life. A space gives you the freedom to be whoever you want to be, the freedom to be yourself. In the heart of fashionable Milan, giant flowers are lit up; precious materials such as ceramic tiles and luscious moquette cover walls and ceiling. References to Andie Warhole pop art and the 1970s' elements become a giant 3-D flower that lights up.

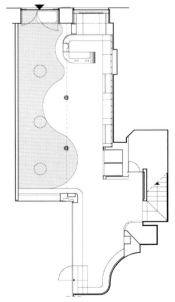

Siemens

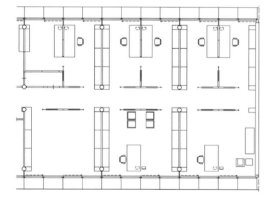

In today's fast-paced, global marketplace, workers are constantly on the move, but always necessarily connected. The work environment revolves around them and everything becomes minimalist, immediately accessible and easily movable, beyond all real and virtual boundaries: the office becomes flexible. Here a former industrial building was transformed into a functional, comfortable and attractive environment, complete with a series of differentiated support areas for a whole range of work activities: on-demand workstations, mobile archives, private meeting rooms, enclosed areas for increased privacy, and a "club area" exclusively reserved to flexible workers.

Photo: Sabine Schweigert

Progetto CMR - Massimo Roj Architects

Rosato Florence

The concept for the Rosato Florence derives from the brand's slogan: Gold is Glam. The designer wanted the space to resemble a gold mine, a very luxurious, glamorous gold mine. The white ceramic walls have an organic form as if handmade. On their surface are organic shaped "holes" carved out to form the display window. The rest of the walls and ceiling are made of gold leaves, the floor is covered with off-white colour moquette, the lighting is very soft and elegant, all lighting fixtures are hidden. All the materials used are precious materials that reflect the use of gold, silver and diamonds in the jewelry. The space is very clean and glamorous.

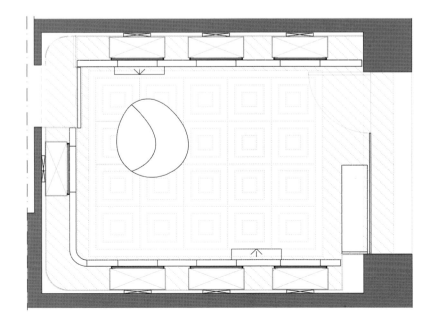

Private Spa

A wall completely covered by grey mirrors, extends the length of the room with interplay of reflections which endlessly multiply the space. The resin floor is the perfect surface to work out with the fitness equipment that with its chromed finish camouflages perfectly with the wall covering. The sliding doors are made with frosted extra white glass. The wellness area consists of a tepidarium, a rainfall shower, a swimming pool and a whirlpool zone. Floor, walls and seats of the tepidarium are heated to provide a relaxing and regenerating effect. The shower is recessed into the ceiling.

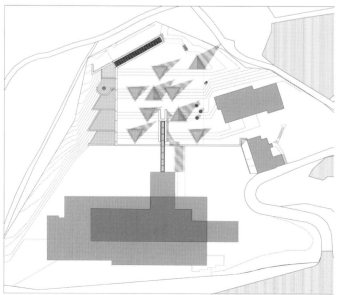

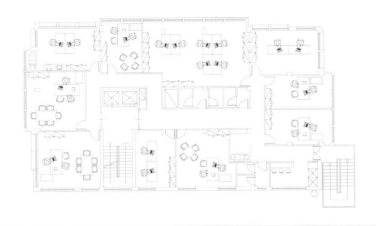

Finmeccanica

To create a new look for Finmeccanica, Progetto CMR carried out an interior restyling based on the characteristic use of colour to redefine spaces while simultaneously reinforcing the corporate identity: bright red (the corporate colour) is used for common areas such as the reception and corridors, while floors are painted in different shades of grey. The offices, closed cells arranged according to a classic distributional scheme, are designed with a view to ensuring maximum flexibility and functionality. On each floor are meeting rooms and break areas, with larger meeting rooms on the top floor and common services located in the basement.

Photo: Beppe Raso

Progetto CMR

Fila and Ciesse Piumini

The project's concept is inspired by the new corporate mission, "art in sport": the workspaces reflect a new, young and flexible company that opens to positive changes. On the ground floor, the reception distributes access to the two companies in the group — Fila and Ciesse Piumini, each with their own spatial identities and corporate colours: red and white for Fila, yellow and blue for Ciesse. The two brands share the spaces in the building while maintaining a clearly distinct image: the Fila brand is associated with the theme of sport performance idealised in great sports champions, while Ciesse is linked to traditional sports activities and free time.

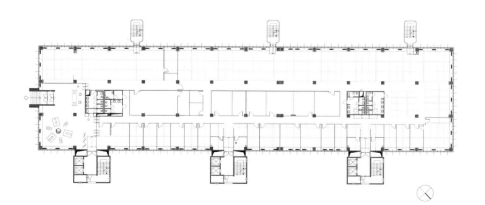

Photo: Beppe Raso

Progetto CMR

Office

Italy

Milan

Photo: Architect Giulio Ripamonti

Architect Carlo Bartoli, Architect Giulio Ripamonti, Collaborator
Maria Rosa Corazza

BCC Bank Directional Centre

The spaces led to the design of a huge lighting vault, which covers the whole width of the open-space main hall. This artificial skylight is made of rectangular and separated polycarbonate panels, which seem to float under the "nocturnal" black painted ceiling, that hides the electric and air conditioning systems. The floor plan is subdivided by vertical screens made of different materials; a concrete-and-glass wall divides the meeting room from the open space, while maple multi-striped soundabsorbing panels partially cover walls and pilasters. Red or pomegranate orange walls with "clouded" effect, stand out against dark backgrounds, as for the ceiling.

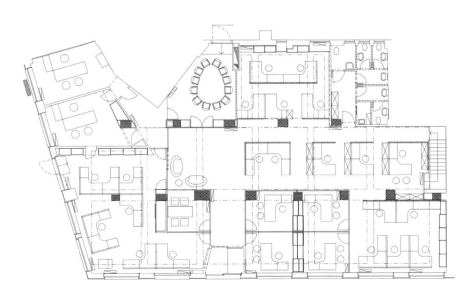

SSB

The corporate blue colour in the reception area is a leitmotif of the design, clearly visible in both of the control room wall (behind the main desk) and the waiting area, marked by a luminous strip running across the floor, up the walls and over the ceiling. The corporate blue colour perfectly unifies the offices with the custom-designed glass dividing walls that have partitioned the whole space into various premises. There are also soundproof panels placed between the open space work stations. The lift entrances are fitted with information panels also in corporate colours, and the entrance to the office area is secured through controlled-access glass sliding doors.

Loft BA

A highly interesting composition, it is formed of two square pavilions with high-hip roofs and a lower parapet along the two boundary sides. The internal façades overlooking the patio are completely glazed with large sliding panels that permit the maximum visibility of the space and leave the dimensions and unique proportions unaltered whether the panels are open or shut, in summer or winter. White is the dominant colour that characterises the walls, ceilings and most of the furnishings, whilst the floor materials vary according to level; polished concrete is used for all of the upper ground floor and large wood planks for the upper floor.

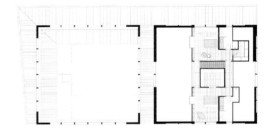

Biasa Boutique

Realised in 2007, in Jakarta, in the Kemang district, the project of the Biasa Showroom is grafted onto a confined and long lot and it is developed on four floors. The first two floors are Boutique while the upper two floors are for the Art Gallery. The main expressive point is the reinforced concrete staircase in the heart of the boutique. It is realized with a series of elements. These elements are profiles with a rectangular section folding up following a G shape. They have been realised on-site in reinforced concrete in different heights following the height of the steps. The upper part of the G profile is the step of the staircase, while the lower one becomes the exhibition of the shop.

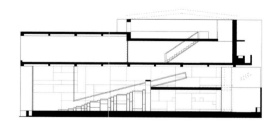

Inflatable House

The structure, entirely transparent and aligned with a traditional house style, is based on the principle of modulation. In fact, it is composed of three inflatable elements measuring 2.50 metre in length, 2.30 metre in height and 1.5 metre in thickness. Modules, anchored on the ground by a system made of steel platforms, are assembled together through zip closings, and set in such a way as to prevent water flowing into the walls. Once the length of the house has been determined, each module is concluded in non-inflatable plugging panels that can contain a door or window as needed. These last elements themselves, which allow for the ventilation of the internal space, are characterised by a side zip closing system.

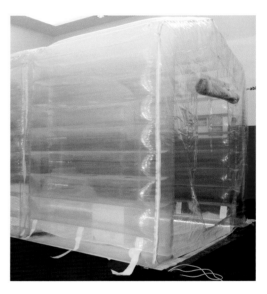

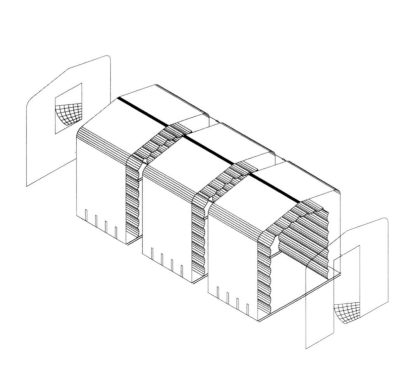

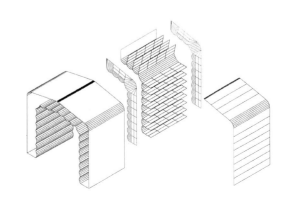

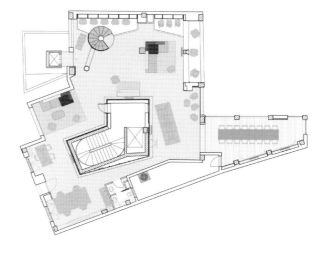

Fritz Hansen

A major challenge to Stefano Tagliacarne was to overcome the spatial irregularity of the showroom, composed by three levels of different size and shape. Tagliacarne links these three levels by the means of a big red column and a wood clad wall, both developing from the bottom of the basement to the top of the first floor. The wooden wall itself, set up in a spectacular and attractive way with "Series 7" chairs designed by Arne Jacobsen in 1955, becomes an extra exhibition area and a visual guideline from the entrance throughout the whole space and levels. The entrance at the ground floor connects to the first floor by a concrete spiral staircase, dedicated to the staircase at Copenhagen Radisson SAS Hotel.

Photo: Tom Vack, www.tomvack.com

Arch. Stefano Tagliacarne

L'Oreal

On every floor is a large open space divided up by glazed screens creating rooms able to accommodate four to six people. Only on the executive level are closed offices. Along the corridor, lined by glass walls, are located the meeting rooms, copy areas and break areas. The originality of the design is not only in the use of colours — gold, green, blue — to delimitate space, but also in the use of specific iconic elements to identify the various brands, with a view to reinforcing the ideas of marketing and communication. Every brand has its own meeting room and projection room where workers are trained. They are located in the basement near the company and VIP restaurants.

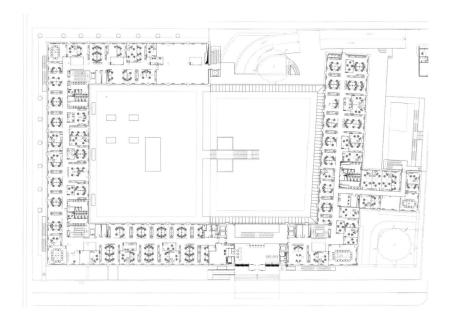

Linea Banche Popolari

The building had a very peculiar shape, made up of three long and narrow elements converging into a central support area for stairs and lift. Progetto CMR's team thoroughly revolutionised the existing internal structure, achieving maximum flexibility with structured open spaces, also for managers, and very few closed offices. The metamorphosis of the company's headquarters was not only structural but also chromatic: Progetto CMR's architects created a young, vibrant space through the use of colour and glass, in marked contrast with the rigour of the structure. The result is a dynamic path that breaks the linearity of the corridors, reflecting the company's vitality.

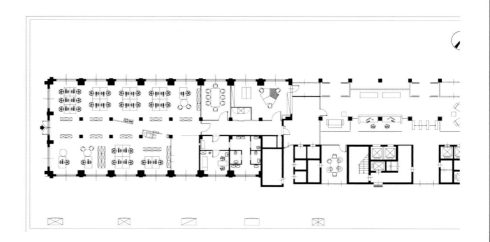

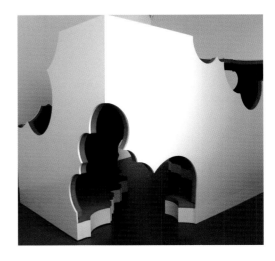

Super Neen

Super Neen was an exhibition of Neen works at Galleria Pack in Milan. The designers' contribution was to convert the space into a "Neen World" environment. They treated the gallery as an apartment and converted the pavilions into furniture for that apartment. Simple interior design and exquisite art works of Neen were in sharp contrast. The design gives prominence to the artistic atmosphere, and at the same time provides visitors with a profound understanding and impression to Super Neen's works.

Pergola Residence

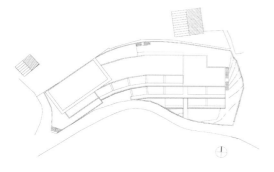

The Pergola is a masterpiece of site-sensitivity, blending seamlessly with the surrounding vineyards and hills. Built on a slope above the Adige Valley (of which there are magnificent views from all 12 studio rooms), the hotel, which extends up the hill in four steps or terraces, is made of unvarnished larchwood treated in different ways for different visual effects and textures. The bathrooms are in delicate, cream stone, more wood and minimalist chrome. Designed to allow guests to self-cater if they want to, each studio has a fully-equipped kitchen, an ample dining-sitting room and a large, decked terrace shaded by vines.

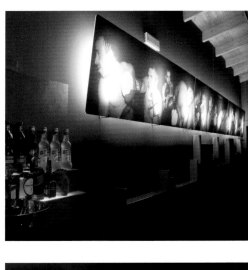

Hurricane Pub

Young people, male and female, feel a particular attraction in front of body care, as evidence of strength and privilege youthfulness, so this pub concept is based on or born like a sort of "light fight club" or a gymnasium: basic forms and poor materials, basic furniture, low level illumination, hot and dark colours, with a box ring in the middle of the pub. The best side of the "noble art" is given by the images of a young and winning Cassius Clay and Robin "Hurricane" Cartre characterised by Denzel Washington in a famous movie.

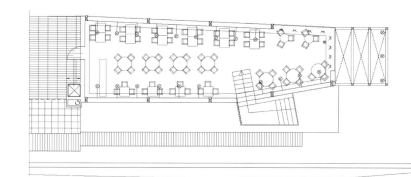

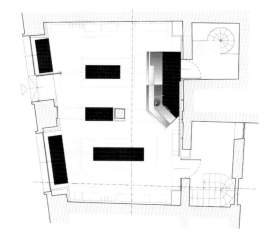

Bialetti

A peaceful moment amongst objects and images evokes old memories. The shops are made with carefully selected colours, forms and materials where past and future meet to create a contrast of shades and shapes. The dialogue between the bleached oak wood and the warm dark oak of the walls, the stainless steel of the counter and other elements that ironically follow the form of the famous coffee maker, create a fascinating warm atmosphere.

Ellipse 1501 House

The original compositional set-up is reinterpreted by means of a cross-sectional system, rotated in plan relative to the largest axes of the ellipse. It coordinates several stereo metric spaces including the guest bedroom on the ground floor and the open plan bedroom on the first floor. Over the course of days, nights and seasons the thick reveals of the windows register the changing colours of the celestial hemisphere. Thus the light of the sky makes a mutable architecture articulating the passing of time, so the light colours the space and changes with itself. In supporting these changes, the fabric remains in its original essence: colourless or tending to be grey.

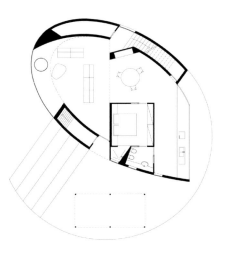

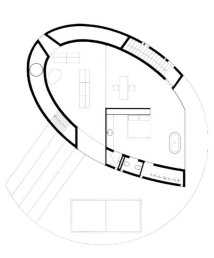

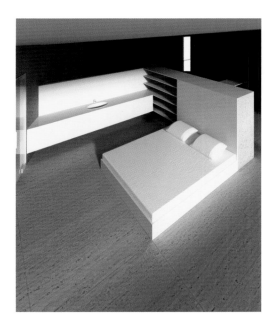

Merano Thermal Baths

Merano Thermal Baths are located at the heart of the old South Tyrolean resort on the banks of the River Passer. The architect's aim in Merano is "to create a natural oasis in the heart of the town" and "to employ shapes and materials to evoke memories of the primeval strength of water". Recreation, harmony and relaxation are among the main aims in the Merano Thermal Baths, featuring a total of 25 pools and a refined sauna area. Cosy warmth and a unique flair are provided by a first-class sauna area. Among the state-of-the-art facilities are a Finnish sauna, two steam baths, a sanarium, a hay bath, a caldarium and an outdoor log cabin sauna.

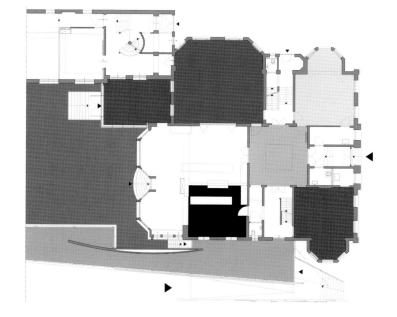

Caffe Bar In

The main bar counter is all in wood, made from a different kind of wood and painted in two colours. Some parts of a counter surface are made of tiles in two colours —grey and beige. Rear side of bar is made of plaster board with spaces for bottles and cups. The working part of the all bar counters is made of stainless. Floors are made of two kinds of materials — tiles and parquet. Bigger accent is on tiles, but parquet also gives some kind of warmness to space. Tiles are in bright grey and beige colour. Parquet is more in red colour. Walls are painted in beige, smooth green and brown colour.

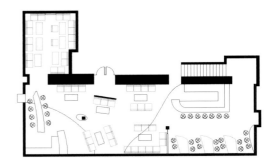

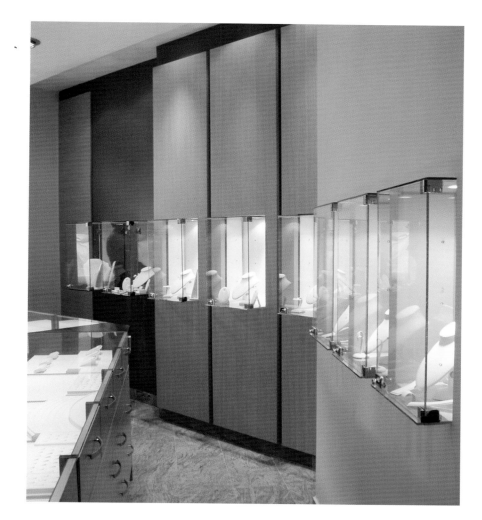

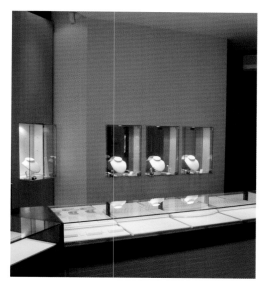

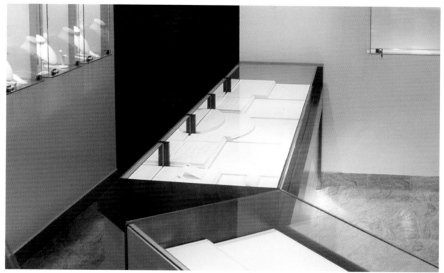

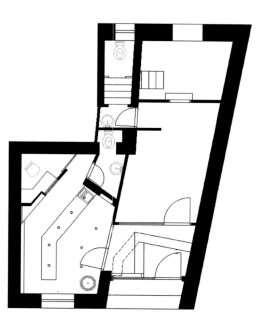

Jewellery Kuqi

The designer follows the old line of concrete walls with some parts of plaster board, which is quite interesting in space, because all furniture is based on the line of this wall. As follows, the wall behind the counter is painted in dark grey, with some parts in wood, and the rest filled with glass boxes, needed for jewellery. Boxes are all in glass, fixed with special hooks on the wall. Ceiling is of two different heights, because of lighting. Behind an official room, the designers added some rooms for toilette, and a room for repairing jewellery.

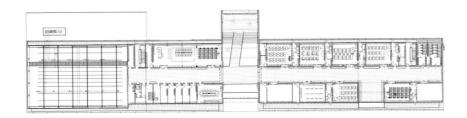

Elementary School Sesvetska Sela

The school building is an elongated two-storey building containing a sports hall that rests on the lower ground. The linear scheme and a specific cross section have provided for the subsequent differentiation of the interior, so that the rooms on the first floor facing the north have higher ceilings and can, as such, accommodate a library and art classrooms. The corridor on the ground floor of the school becomes a gallery of the gym. In an attempt to blend the serving and the served spaces, all the corridors are lined with a continuous blackboard and fitted with benches.

Panoramic Garden of CCIS

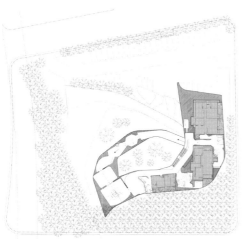

The large summer banquet terrace is to be glazed and extends into the current VIP room. Thus the designers formed an interior winter garden, where a spatial ribbon carries the troughs and baskets with lush tropical greenery, wherefrom one can enjoy a magnificent view of the city centre. It may be characterised as a new type of the business and club room that is intended for events such as ceremonial receptions, award-granting ceremonies, banquet luncheons as well as for meetings of extended management team. The green ribbon also enables the partition of the space into several micro-ambiences that may be used according to the type of event and the number of participants.

Termalija Wellness Centre

The goal was to stimulate one's senses as much as possible. Rooms are in vivid colours with walls decorated in stylised graphic impressions from nature (eyesight) and equipped with different atmospheric sounds (hearing) and distinctive aromas (smell) to stimulate visitors' senses even more. The new design winds by the edge of the site and addresses the passing road. Throughout the day, the object blends with surroundings not aggressively but like a fence, though in the evening and throughout the night when neighbouring elements are no more present changes face completely. It becomes very vivid and glows as a billboard in many colours of "inner nature".

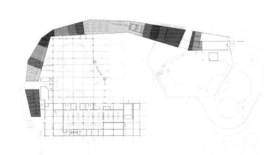

Lasko Wellness Park

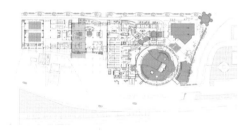

Wellness Park Lasko, a part of the well-known and established Health Resort is extended with the wellness hotel with 104 rooms, a restaurant, a café and a revamped spa centre. In addition, the current capacities are being expanded with a hotel with 100 rooms, a congress centre, a night club, and a wedding hall. The whole project is expected to be finished in 2010. The concept was to create lively, atmospheric and invigorating environments that would inspire wellness and well-being. The complex is split into several parts: the spa and wellness areas. Each area carries a specific story embedded in the use of the materials and the colour codes.

Photo: Bogdan Zupan, Tomaz Gregoric

Borut Rebolj, Studio Rebeka d.o.o.

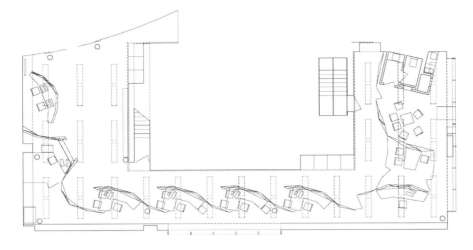

NKBM Bank Branch

The interior design project for the NKBM Bank branch utilises a territorialising system that was developed as a set of basic functional elements. They regulate the spatial ratio between customer and employee areas and provide private spaces for banking discussion. The conventional vertical screen was mutated into a deformed glass shell of a complex geometry in order to provide optimal spatial ergonomics in a limited amount of space. Glass triangles are locally assembled with steel clips, which enables angle adjustments for individual fixation. Glass shells are a self-supporting system that does not require additional structure.

Cyclos C Club

The most important Circle and Hub of exclusive activities in Mykonos and the Cyclades, Cyclos is a multi-functional club with exclusive members. The Outdoor terrace has a unique design, with landscape walls mixed with tropical nature and white Mykonos typical walls. Cyclos C Club is also a media centre connected to the world and directs events transmissions. The indoor space is a multi-functional club with private bars. There is a large projection screen in the club. Contemporary design furniture adds simplicity to the white interior and exterior.

Life Gallery Athens

The hotel has a contemporary style touched by elegant Asian elements: Bamboo wall coverings, traditional Indonesian furniture and typical Asian agave plants greet visitors in the lobby. Encircling the building, the expansive landscaped gardens are dotted with mature pines and cedar trees and blend in harmoniously with their suburban surroundings. Two sundecks and swimming pools set in the greenery of the grounds offer guests a continuation of tranquility within their rooms. Orange light recessed into panels on the threshold to the modern bathrooms sets a warm tone for the simple and functional Gervasoni bed with a black stained bamboo surrounded.

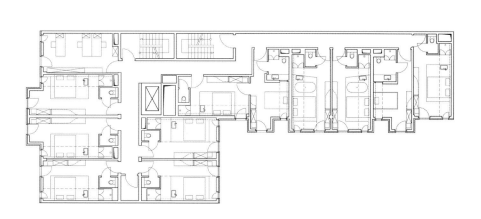

The Belvedere Hotel-Greece

Inspired by the Aegean Sea, the project is a three-level space. The materials and design elements used echo those that are native to the sea. Guests enter on the top level, where is a bar composed of a live edge wood bar top supported by a marble bar face. Hand-carved marble stones on stainless steel standoffs cover the bar face and are backlit to create the appearance that they are floating. In the Standard Rooms, the Junior Suites and the Belvedere Suites, the designer used classic Mykonian materials of marble and plaster, mixed with a twist on other luxurious natural materials. Hues of whites, warm tans and greens reflect the Mykonian and Aegean land and seascapes outside.

Hotel

Greece

Mykonos

Photo: The Late Aris Constantinides

The Late Aris Constantinides Yiannis Tsimas,
Angelos Angelopoulos

Mykonos Theoxenia

The designers didn't stray far from the late Kostantinides' master plan, opting to revamp the 1960s' glam interiors while bringing the hotel up to the most modern design standards. Stone-clad walls, orange and turquoise hessian fabrics and sweeping minimal surfaces all create a backdrop for Patricia Urquiola's deep blue bar stools and sofas for Moroso. Interior designer Ron Adler developed the white chairs in the pool & Breeze Out bar area, which is also surrounded by curtained four-poster beds and makes a tempting alternative to the beach. Angelos Angelopoulos have added accents in bright lime, orange and red to Greek standards of white and blue to the hotel's 52 rooms.

Family House

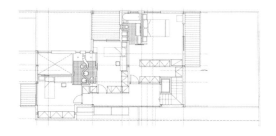

The ground floor comprises the living and dining area in contact with the kitchen, a study and a bathroom. The first floor accommodates two bedrooms with two small bathrooms, a master bedroom with dressing room and en suite bathroom. Connection is achieved via a linear corridor and lighted by a rectangular window. Large openings on the two main façades create interesting views. The pitch roof contributes to the linearity of the house's volume. The cantilevered balconies partly extend the first floor plates to the exterior. The smooth plastered surfaces and colours painted are fit to the Mediterranean context and climate.

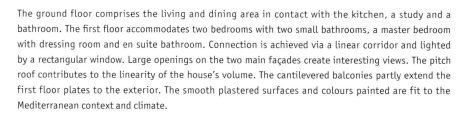

Seydap Showroom Seydap

The design concept was based on the element of water considered both as moving wave-form and as still, calm reflecting surface. The first inspired the major design structures of the interior and exterior space. The second inspired the logotype and the advertising imagery. The logotype is designed as a mere reflection of the name of the company in black and orange background. The orange colour was proposed to escape the strict exclusiveness of water, and also allude to heating, an area on which the company also specialises in its other branches.

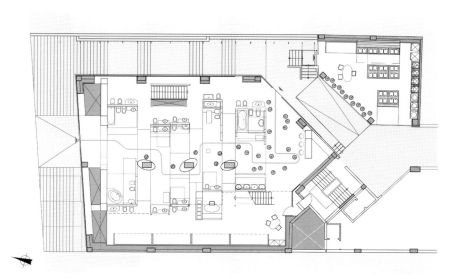

Meandros House

The project consists of a group of 5 houses of different sizes and features. The design protects the independence of each house through the use of careful urban planning, whilst at the same time ensuring the homogeneity of the scheme by using one architectural language for the whole project. The volume breaks with a desire of symmetry by the creation of an elevated courtyard separated in four properties. The meander sets a second level of perspective and vanishing points unifying the horizontal surfaces of the balconies with the use of vertical elements.

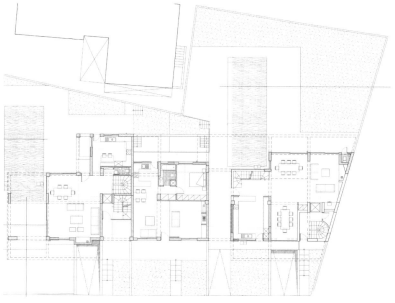

House

Greece

Athens

Photo: Babis Loizidis

KLAB Architects

463

Vogue Jewellery Shop

The aim was to create a luxurious atmosphere, and enhance the emotional value of the jewels sold. The representation of each product was thought as a glittering gem in an extravagant yet gorgeous garden. The new shopping experience was achieved by creating a garden jewellery display system such as abstract plant pot window display, and interior display cases that were designed for special items or gold and silver watches. This is how the Vogue shop became known as the "Glam Garden", a place where spirituality is exposed to the outside, a place of secrets that will be revealed only to those who deserve it.

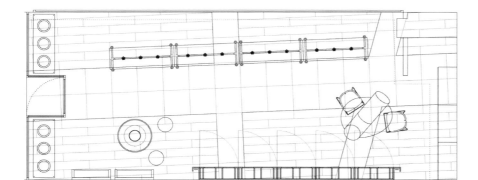

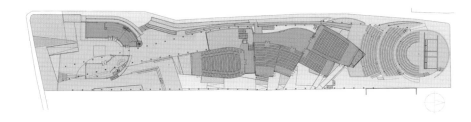

Cinema Complex

The key design concept was to create a characteristic outdoor element linking the various spaces, guiding visitors through the complex. A series of green, metallic triangular structures were designed. The concept of the exterior walls was that there were no openings; there were three horizontal zones of varying materials. They are solid zinc (upper), perforated zinc (central) and the inner plaster (lower) covered concrete wall. In the interiors materials were used to continue directed movement, guiding the visitor through the space and connecting spaces. In the main lobby RGB lighting was used, changing colour over time-based regular intervals, hence transforming space in relation to the movement of time, reminiscent of the moving image of cinema.

Photo: Anamorphosis Architects

Anamorphosis Architects

Sovereign Insurance Headquarters

The Sovereign building is an integrated base building/workplace designed by a single client, design team and contractor, providing an innovative and culture changing workplace. The building is comprised of three low-rise floor plates surrounding an open central atrium crossed by bridges and linked by stairs. The building structure is largely fabricated off-site using pre-cast concrete elements to create highly flexible clear spans of up to 18 metres. The project is serviced by a central plant facility which achieves economies of scale — both finance and energy. A new bus interchange is being constructed on-site to serve the development and commuters transferring into Auckland CBD.

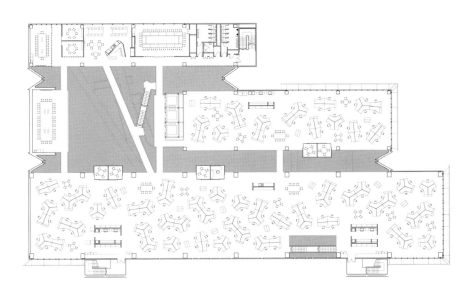

Sackville Hotel

A building with an internal courtyard begins to breathe. It takes on a new dimension that surprises and activates. The methodology initially, is based on planning and sectional explorations. The three dimensional aspect of the form and plan is explored in depth with 3D modelling software. In this way the plan can be built with complex spatial understanding. The architects designed all the furniture, acoustic linings and collaborated with lighting designers for a unique light fitting. All structural frames for benches and tables were uniquely designed to work with the language of steel flat plate and set up a grammar of steel detailing linked to steel window and door frames and steel furniture frames, etc.

Photo: Murray Fredericks

Indyk Architects Pty Ltd

Carriageworks

The new forms stand free of the rows of original cast iron columns, creating circulation routes in the interstitial spaces with views through the building. The foyer spans the entire width of the building. The linear entry structures to each of the theatre spaces are like "ghosts" of the carriages that once moved through the space. The front of house is divided by glass doors from the back of house activities, which are located adjacent to the railway tracks. The new elevated roof echoes the rhythm of the original roof monitors.

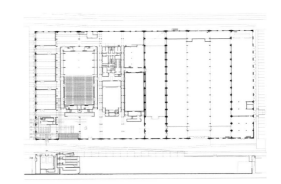

Arianne

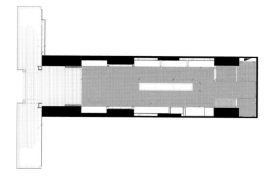

Design Clarity's concept for this small site was perfect to create an intimate and luxurious shopping experience for this decadent product. The finishes palette is restrained with white decorative timber panelling to the walls and joinery creating a subtle and sophisticated backdrop on which to display the merchandise. The original structural archway has been retained and worked into the design in response to the heritage architecture. However the standout feature of the design is the treatment of the generous shopfront windows flanking the shop entry. Design Clarity has created a boudoir themed display complete with a theatrical sweeping staircase for the lingerie models to climb and drape themselves upon at leisure.

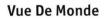

Vue De Monde

The design for Vue de Monde, a contemporary Melbourne restaurant highly regarded for its fine French dining experience, sat to juxtapose the functionality of a hardworking restaurant with the luxury of sampling fine food and wine. Highly patterned stone bench tops and timber floors provide texture to the stark white walls while the large globe light fittings create illuminated highlighters dotted through the space. In contrast, the gleaming stainless kitchen equipment is evident providing a working insight into a functioning kitchen during service. Ceiling-mounted mirrors above the preparation benches divide the kitchen and dining spaces.

Maroubra Bay Hotel

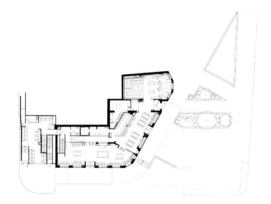

The location of the Hotel, in the opposite of a rather exposed and beautiful Sydney beach led the design team to look for "local" inspiration. The Besser "block breezeway" walls seen as fences and garage walls along the seaside suburbs became the main "screen" element within the hotel. Designers decided to use striped canvas in a new form as large glowing light boxes, and in the "internal tent" concept, within the lounge. The striped colours are brought to life, when lit from behind or within. The concrete floor finish was the same concrete boardwalk aggregate mix that one finds on almost all un-renovated beach promenades. The grey timber boards lining the bar fronts, was a gesture to the seaside timber sheds.

Gingerboy

The Gingerboy dining concept draws on traditional Asian materials featuring a robust bamboo long-bar where clientele can sample Asian influenced cocktails and tapas, while viewing the activity and animation of the open kitchen during service. Central to the dining experience is the installation of a random array of dark bamboo poles with hundreds of point lights inter-woven, creating an atmosphere of airy night markets and open night sky. A grand, low hung, "lantern" style light fitting, expressly designed for the space, is centred over the more casual dining area creating an intimacy akin to the Shanghai tea rooms of the 1950s. The place has energy, rigour and buckets of informal style.

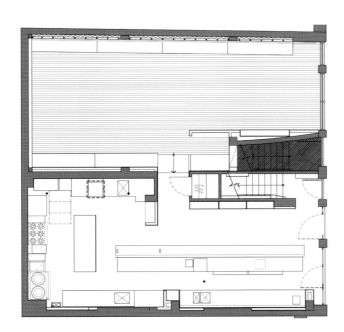

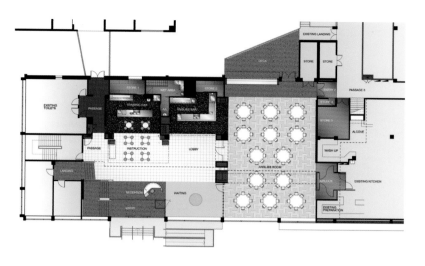

Angliss Restaurant

This commercially functioning restaurant, combined with educational spaces, delivers new outcomes in contemporary interior design. The front areas of the Training Bar and Angliss Bar have been designed and developed to reflect the most up to date industry requirements. This will enable students to become familiar during their skills development, with both the operational and functional requirements of restaurant and bar service areas. The layout and design of the spaces have also been developed through liaison with local authorities to reflect up-to-date food and beverage services and the latest staff and hygiene requirements.

Photo: Peter Clarke, Latitude

Gray Puksand

Calibre Chadstone

The inspiration for this shop came from the richly-textured tones of European bespoke glamour. French inspired parquet flooring rubbed with a grey brown stain and finished with a matt lacquer evokes a masculine Parisian apartment atmosphere. The treatment of the stain allows the subtle pattern of the timber to provide an interesting graphic within the shop. The bold warm orange tones of the crocodile leather created a luxurious counters and custom designed feature mirror. Green Chinese Onyx marble is used both in the window display and counter tops acknowledging Calibre's interest in high-quality unique materials. The chrome trim to the joinery contrasts alongside the leather and stone.

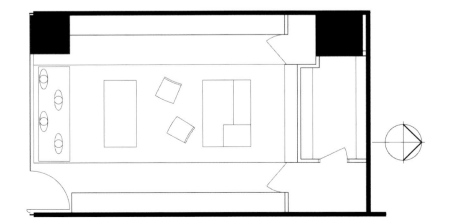

Calibre Collins Street

Calibre Collins Street combines a new element of boutique shopping at its best. Large change rooms, signature chrome rack, hand-woven sea grass wall panels and custom terrazzo flooring are a few of the high-quality features. With layers of subtle textures, discreet detailing and gracious space planning, homage was played to the integrity of the Calibre range. The large windows overlooking Collins Street will of course display the artistic and imaginative visuals and clothes that Calibre are renowned for. The shop within will be somewhat more intimate, providing the shopper a relaxed and easy environment layered with personal items like the original moulded fibreglass chaise designed by Eames.

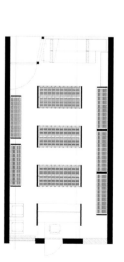

Calibre Chapel Street

Between the ceiling and floor suspended polished chrome hanging racks to defy gravity and they are painfully detailed and constructed. The terrazzo flooring, specially formulated and tinted to match the "Chinchilla White" paint colour, Aubergine carpet, and a timber paneled ceiling evoke the sense of a 1950s' bachelor pad tailor shop, inviting customers to relax on a Mies van Der Rohe day bed upholstered in tan leather imported from Italy. To continue the 50s' theme, a combination of wall in "Chinchilla White" was used to give a degree of difference while maintaining the single tone.

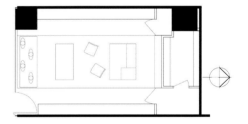

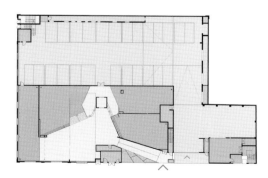

PYD

The revitalisation comprises the interior design of a retail centre selling products exclusive to the Sydney market — 16 retail outlets, a café and a flexible atrium space to be used for design lectures, awards ceremonies and exhibitions. The design intervention within the warehouse has involved a removal of complete sections of the first floor to create a large 3-storey, naturally ventilated atrium space. An addition of a mezzanine level allows additional space for the retail tenancies, and a modification of the existing roof allows for greater sunlight to both atrium and shops. According to the brief, the focal point was the atrium and the staircase, which naturally leads to the upper floors.

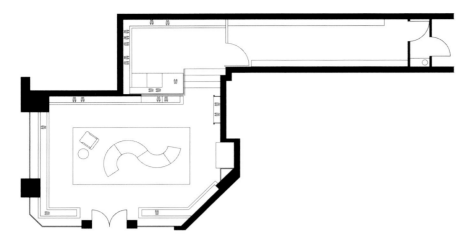

Tino Lanzi

The soft, feminine ladies' shoes shop was designed to be like a modern summer garden gazebo. The walls are lined in a champagne paint finish and bronze floral wallpaper with little summer wrens and delicate ribbon stripes. The joinery is set in stark contrast using white (ANTIQUE WHITE USA) polyurethane with sharp lines creating a lattice like effect. The green carpet creates a grassy floor finish; the oak chevron floor with earthy and organic decorative motifs gives formality. A huge Lily chandelier and sconces literally grow from the surfaces.

Aquabmps

The east wall of the gallery is minimalist, with smooth, white surfaces and perfectly spaced artworks. It will showcase Aquabumps' highly sought after acrylic pieces, which use a special technique to create a shiny surface on the artwork that mimics the slippery sheen of the water captured in the photography. On the west side, in dramatic contrast, the space is raw and rough, with exposed bricks and a massive iron girdle acting as a stock shelf. Here, artworks are unevenly displayed, challenging the buyer and causing them to pause and reflect on each piece. The west wall will feature "Typical Bondi"— a collection of images that capture the essence of a suburb that has captured the international imagination.

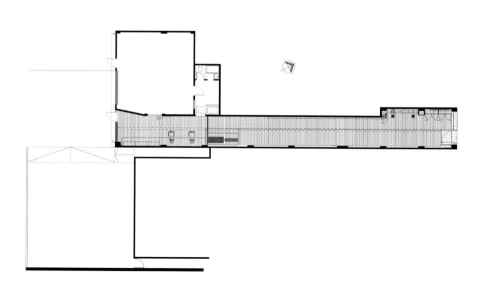

Photo: Steffen Burggraaf

The World is round Pty Ltd

Crest

The internal colours, materials and furnishings were carefully selected to enhance the corporate image. The client's brief was to create an international headquarters, showroom and distribution warehouse that would be used to build the company's international reputation. The mix of open plan and enclosed offices was directly related to the functions of the department. The office culture of encouraging communication between departments was facilitated through locating various meeting rooms and spaces throughout the office. The large number of staff in the warehouse and office required a large staff lunch area and atrium space for social gatherings.

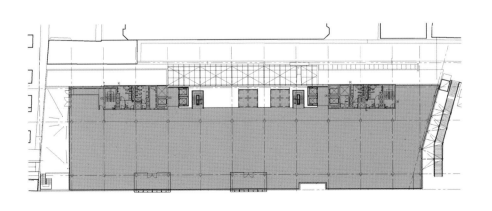

Santos Centre

The brief was met by working closely with the Santos team to understand their business, culture and future direction as well as their physical accommodation needs. Santos recognised that their previous accommodation no longer supported their values and business model. The business was separated over multiple branches and the staff were located in a mixture of offices and the leadership team was isolated from the business. The new headquarters needed to reflect the progressive approach Santos had as a business and employer and to create a physical environment that inspired and included its people and supported its business objectives.

The Santos Centre is a tangible expression of the character and culture of Santos as an organisation - from the front door to the detail of each floor's theme. This project is a holistic solution that builds on and extends leading thinking in workplace design and has seen the best in sustainable design, engineering, information technology and change management come together to deliver a unique space for the people of Santos.

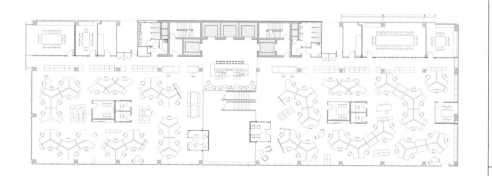

Office

Australia

Adelaide

Photo: John Gollings

BVN Architecture

481

Toga Group Head Office

The project is located within a heritage wool shop building that has been adapted to office space. Bates Smart refurbished the base building, removing intrusive additions such as plasterboard ceilings, column claddings and walls, to reveal the original timber ceilings, beams and joists. The lobby was fully refurbished, with all materials and finishes removed to expose the original construction. Concrete floors were exposed and polished and glass was used as balustrades and walls to maintain visibility of the original fabric. The Toga Group's brief called for an environment that encouraged integration, visibility, collaboration and team work.

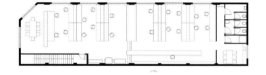

Cooper Street

All the furniture has been specifically designed for the room. The desks and storage units are created from recycled carcasses from a second-hand office warehouse and bespoke steel frames which have then been dressed with form ply. This has created seating facilities for 8 groups of 4-6 people, with a central storage unit that could be converted into further desks if required. There is also room for expansion, backing onto the conference room and the utilities at either ends of the main space. The desks have removable sections in the middle creating easy access to all the CAT5, telephone and power cabling, and all the cabling leads back to a large server in the utilities area.

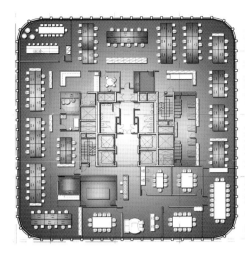

BCS Office

BCS is the brand of household furniture, of the Shanghai Ever Rich Furniture Manufacturing Company Ltd., which is a member of Hongkong Novel Enterprise Limited. BCS concepts design reflects the perfect combination of modern design with European and American classical styles. It is luxurious, yet simple, unique and full of elegance. Combining outstanding design talent, superior craftsmanship, a desire for perfection and years of experience in furniture making, BCS Concepts aims to create furniture that meet the principle of the highest personalisation of your demands. BCS Concepts keeps the same pace as European and American furniture companies.

Sanofi Aventis Workplace

In 2004 two prominent pharmaceutical companies, Sanofi Synthelabo and Aventis Pharmaceuticals, merged into one of the largest pharmaceutical organisations worldwide. With a mandate from Head Office to co-locate within 12 months of their merger, Sanofi Aventis engaged Sydney firm, PCG, to implement their move, including tenant advocacy, interior architecture and project management. The new workplace planned over 8,500 square metres, delivers a functional and creative environment that stimulates communication and interaction between the two merged cultures. The communal space on the ground/entry floor, invites all employees to create their own bustling work & social space.

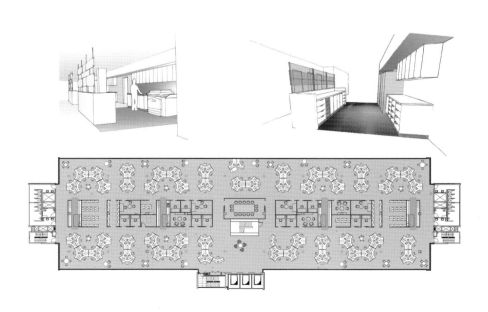

Db Rreef

Soft studio and 3-D community represents the future for Db Rreef in a new workspace for their George Street offices. The approach is to embrace technology in a holistic manner, integrating high-tech aesthetics and heritage architecture into a unified design. Stimulating social spaces and flexible work zones along with environmentally sustainable development, it will increase productivity and realise a totally resolved, quality environment. The soft studio approach is based around providing a combination of architectural edge with gentle lines and seamless transitions between spaces. The design does not rely on fashion to achieve an effect.

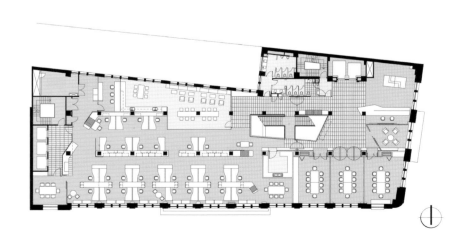

Washington H Soul Pattinson

Washington H Soul Pattinson appointed PCG to manage the refurbishment of their corporate headquarters at 160 Pitt Street Mall, Sydney. In recognition of the building's significant contribution to the local heritage, it is registered on the NSW Register of Historical Buildings. The refurbishment and upgrade of the building's existing engineering services enabled the project team to focus on unusual aspects of the building's original architecture. The introduction of a single passenger lift and a new enclosed atrium space at the rear of the building significantly improves the quality of the working environment for Soul Pattinson's staff.

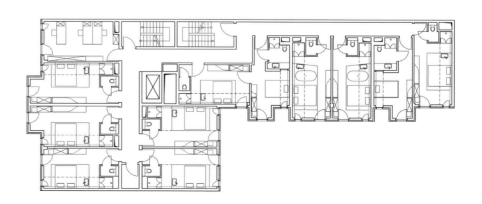

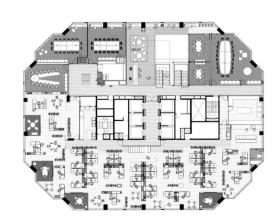

Stockland Head Office Sydney

Locating the new head office in this building was seen as an extraordinary opportunity to demonstrate that the building could be "turned around" to create a contemporary, engaging and sustainable new workplace. A vertical street underpins the new workplace. This street is in the form of a void (8.5m x 5.5m) that winds its way up the building's eastern side. The void contains stairs that spiral through the 8 floors from level 22 to 29, staggered in its vertical location to maximise the views between floors and provide a greater sense of connection. The void and stair not only provides a greater sense of physical connection, but becomes the symbolic connection of "one Stockland".

Five Dock Library

Minale Tattersfield wanted to create a memorable, yet state-of-the-art library facility for the new Five Dock Library fitout. From the cosmopolitan café/bookshop to the busy street life of Five Dock village, a feeling of Avant Garde was devised to complement the library's urban surroundings. Essentially two distinct schemes overlap each other to create a dramatic, vibrant and enticing composition. Brightly sculptured walls make an exciting basis for the library fitout with colours defining various sections of the library. Dividing walls are lined with translucent acrylic and lit from above with bright blue lighting.

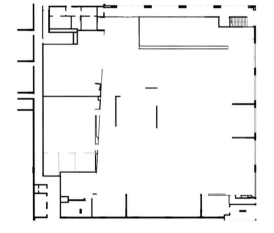

Photo: Greg Bartlett and BHA

Minale Tattersfield

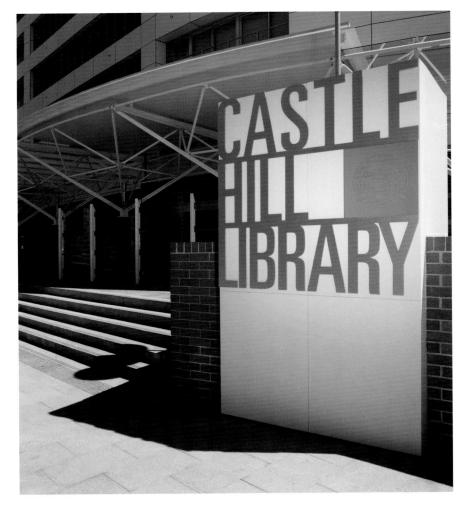

Castle Hill Library

The new library includes a large "bookshop style" lending library, a café, a fully equipped research oriented reference library and digital research facility as well as a large children's and youth library. Environmental graphics have been used extensively to create an exciting internal atmosphere; the internal fitout is designed to evoke the feeling of an upscale bookshop. The graphics form an integral part of interior elements such as dividing walls between sections of the library and feature walls. Each section of the library had to be identified by a distinct graphic, composed of an edited visual, overlaid with a background graphic and the name of the section.

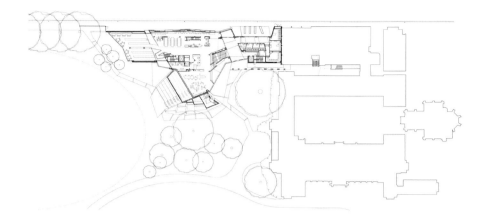

Melbourne Grammar School

The brief for the building is to create a new campus entry, consolidate the school's library facilities and provide supporting lecture theatre and seminar room to forge a new campus heart focused on learning. The main active body of the library comprises a series of giant oversized steel framed windows of varying shapes with a series of overlaid patterns to glass within. The patterning alludes to the random ashlar block work of the historic buildings on site, while from the interior, the various windows frame differing views to the greenery of the historic gardens beyond. The book stack pavilion stores the main book collection and is clad in a burnished healer brick.

Hardwick Turnbull Beach House

This original 1960s' home was already in great condition but needed updating. The designers reworked the original 1960s' style with Mid Century Modern iconic furniture of the likes of Eames and Jacobsen. These were mixed with modern furniture from Minotti and new custom-made carpets. The colour palette was inspired by the houses. Being by the ocean, the designers chose to use materials that referred to the sand, water, timbers and fauna of the local Palm Beach area. Timbers, blue upholstery and paint finishes, yellow textured fabric and natural stone mimic the outdoors. The room is walled in by the use of bamboo and the floor is paved in natural local sandstone.

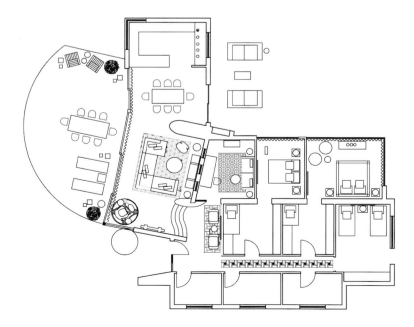

Spring Hill House

Passive climatic design was integral ensuring adequate natural light, shading and ventilation throughout the house. The roof form of the bedroom wing incorporates the dual ideas of a lower-pitched verandah roof and window hoods. This results in a pitched roof with a distinctive off centre ridge and overhang that acts as sun and weather protection on the north facing wall and windows. Window seats have been incorporated to provide sun shading, privacy and to frame the city views. The bedroom wing has been positioned to encourage natural light and ventilation into the main living areas of the house while still maintaining outlook and privacy. The covered outdoor living spaces provide a connection with the landscape, and take advantage of the subtropical climate and city views.

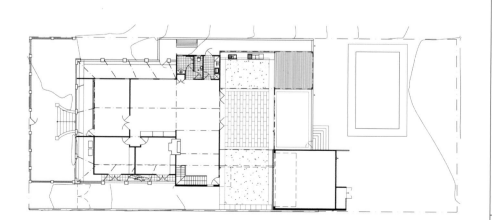

Photo: Taylormade Digital Images

8i Architecture Pty Ltd

Windsor Loft

The design is a reflection on architectural strategies — spatial intervention/differentiation in a fluid continuity; visual/subliminal permeation between the private and public domain in contemporary domestic spaces in urban fabric. A cruciform column stands in the middle of the first floor living areas. Traversing floor tiles and recessed ceiling lighting tracks radiate from its four edges, virtually dividing the open plan into entertaining, dining, sitting and circulation area. With its wall-lined high gloss white joinery and north orientation to the internal courtyard, the kitchen blurs into an inconspicuous whitewash in daylight. At night it becomes an annex to the house.

East Coast Trucks Showroom Office

The new layout is an evolution of east coast commercials' corporate identity and a departure from a traditional truck sales yard. External colours and materials were carefully selected to reflect the updated corporate image of the company and served as a backdrop for the building's signage. The new office included a reception and customer waiting area, open plan office area, partitioned offices, kitchenette and lunch room and refurbishment of existing amenities. A simple three-colour palette was used to create a modern interior. White was used as a base colour which was accentuated by red bulkheads and green walls. The patterned charcoal carpet and ceramic tiles reflected a sophisticated corporate image.

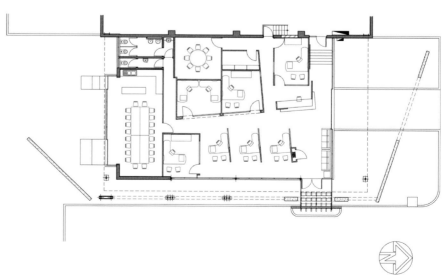

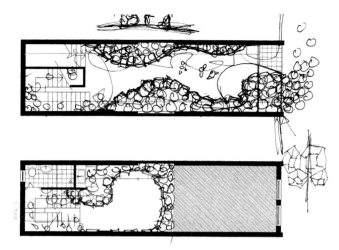

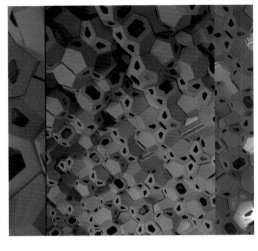

Digital Origami

The danger of digital creations is the virtual worlds they depend on, or rather the lack of constraints in the virtual if compared to the physical world. Most of the time digital creations end in just being crazy flythrough computer renderings. With the Digital origami, the designers wanted to realise concepts. They studied current trends in parametric modeling, digital fabrication and material-science and applied this knowledge to create a space-filling installation. The aim was to test the fitness of a particular module, copied from nature, to generate architectural space, with the assumption that the intelligence of the smallest unit dictates the intelligence of the overall system.

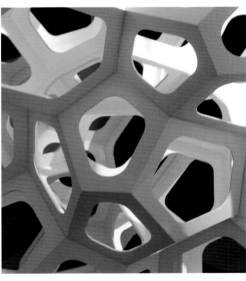

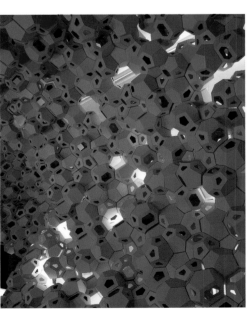

Paddington Inn

The rooms surrounding the courtyard are washed in daylight. The interior planning upholds the various rooms of the old Hotel. Most notably, the small Nook — with its "moorish" inspired stepped timber ceiling; and The Bistro/bar/lounge which is a long room — its end focus being the bar with its bronze mirror reflections. The steel post and beam construction of the courtyard is refined and strong, bracing the old structure and supporting the new. The courtyard is an outdoor urban room, highly acoustically attenuated so that the patrons can enjoy it both day and night, and the neighbourhood is not imposed upon. The stepped section of the courtyard allows for diversity of standing and seating areas.

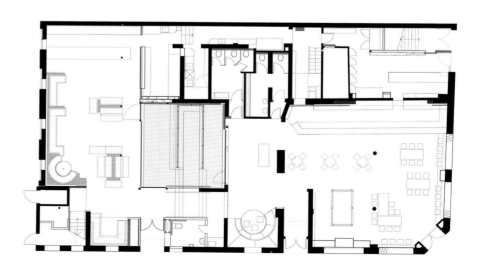

Photo: Murray Fredericks

Indyk Architects Pty Ltd

Harley Davidson, Australia Headquarters

For design inspiration, the designers looked to the bikes themselves: their emotion and efficiency. The design does not copy them; however, it suggests this movement and style. They wanted to express the elegance and aerodynamics of this movement in the lines of the space. The main showroom is the strongest feature of the design. As a triangular site, the showroom occupies the corner and forms a gateway to the project. The 3-D technology used to resolve and construct the geometry is the most innovative feature. The designers used a complex structural model to locate every element in space.

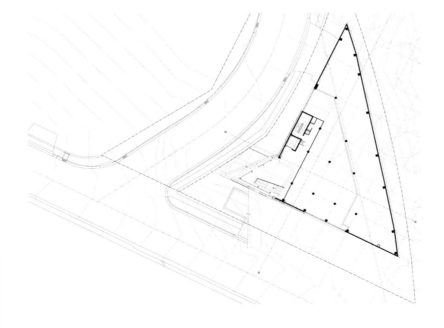

Stylecraft Showroom

Stylecraft wanted to create a dynamic and innovative space that draws customers to the showroom and encourages them to return. Geyer's design solution embodies Stylecraft's brand attributes energetic, confident, kinetic and fun. The space has been designed to evolve and change with the business, and enables a diversity of customer experiences. A highly flexible environment has been established that allows the space to constantly evolve and change to support a range of local and international brands and new product lines. Two key environments have been created, the showroom and sales work area.

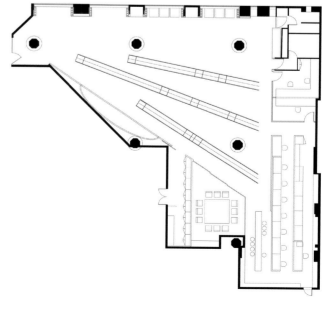

Photo: Tyrone Branigan

Geyer Pty Ltd

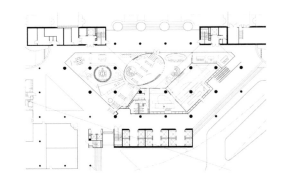

Fuji Xerox Epicentres

The vision of the centre is to offer Fuji Xerox's global customers a complete "digital print" experience. Visitors are provided with a personalised journey depending upon the reason for their visit and the level of existing knowledge of the Fuji Xerox products and services. A series of "experiential zones" are personalised for each customer, ensuring relevance of brand communication through sales conversion and customer retention experiences. From arrival the customer's experience is extraordinary. An iconic sphere, projecting welcome messages to the customer, denotes the entry point. Visitors are greeted by a roaming attendee, unrestrained by the confines of a reception desk.

Kelso House

To allow maximum sunlight to penetrate deep into the living areas, 3 linear roof lights run full width of the extension, creating an ever-changing light setting as the day progresses. There is another roof light right above the shower, so that while showering one can experience the quality of the day. Due to overlooking and west facing issues, large unobstructed glazing facing the garden is not feasible. Five vertical fin walls are designed to partially block off possible overlooking. The fin walls break up the façade into 4 openings, allowing doors to be inserted. These are also structural columns supporting the roof and the wide box gutter above.

Photo: Shannon McGrath

Architects EAT

501

Industrial + Commercial Bank of China

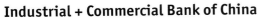

ICBC wanted the space to reflect their global position as a modern, first class financial institution, while acknowledging regional influences and creating a unique identity within the market. The ground floor retail presence is modern, fresh and distinctly Australian in appearance, distinguishing it from all domestic and foriegn banking competitors. An illuminated teller box floats visible from the street reflecting ICBC's objectives of transparency and openness. The retail space is supported by a corporate zone, housed across two levels with an inter-connecting stair, and also includes a club area for focused discussions with high-value customers.

Photo: Marcus Clinton

Geyer Pty Ltd

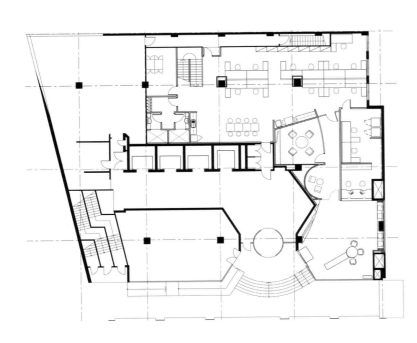

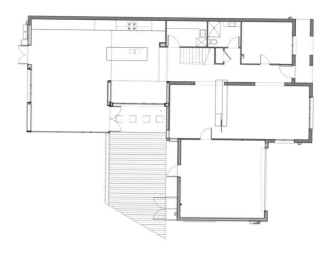

Village Park House

Alterations were made primarily to the rear ground floor plan & roof above the garage. The ground Floor - The rear of the house was redesigned to accommodate a new north-facing living area with a new roof & high ceiling. The ceiling height was raised to heighten the sense of space as well as to capture more northern light. The family room has replaced the previous living room at the front of the house. A larger master bedroom has been created above the existing garage which overlooks the courtyard & opens out to a private balcony. As each site brings along its own set of challenges & demands, this project in particular challenged the designers economically.

Photo: Shannon McGrath

Architects EAT

Maedaya Bar

This project demonstrates the possibility of using ordinary recyclable material for hospitality projects without compromising the sophistication of the food and service. Traditionally sake is bottled in wooden casks and secured with ropes. Current commercial method of bottling sake is similar to that of red or white wine. The designers' interest in sake bottling lies in the bounding of the cask using ropes. Thereafter they chose to investigate and translate their interpretation of "bounding" with the use of Manila ropes. The ropes held in tension at specific points form a shape of a house or a hut. A house, whether it be a tea house or sake house, is a sacred place in traditional Japanese times.

Photo: Derek Swalwell

Architects EAT

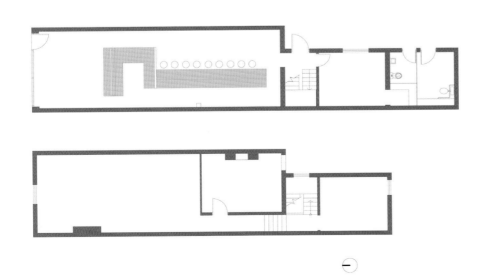

Royal Sovereign Hotel – Darlo Bar

The new works to the ground floor of the hotel, incorporates a new Bar and courtyard which is in effect, two storeys in height. Deep within the structure of the existing Hotel, this space is fully lined with acoustic perforated, lapped aluminium panels. The panels are painted in gold, silver and green colours to accentuate a "garden" room in the heart of the building. The interior of the Bar was guided by the "Retro"nature of the ground floor fitout. A collection of old steel wired and framed furniture was collected from auction houses and shops. All were painted white. The concept was simple: the courtyard Bar would have the character of a quirky outdoor garden room of the 1960s' in Sydney.

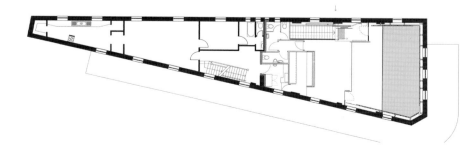

Hotel Realm

The built in flexibility of the interiors has resulted in a robust formal building structure designed to offer flexibility in response to the changing programme needs of the client. At the detail level there is an emphasis on utilisation of natural light, natural ventilation and solar access that largely determine the expression and form of the Hotel Realm. In the RAIA jury's words, "Hotel Realm is commended for considerable control of material and proportion throughout the public and private accommodation spaces, resulting in consistently formal expression of wall planes and openings to the surrounding areas. The level of control is admirable."

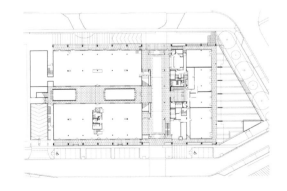

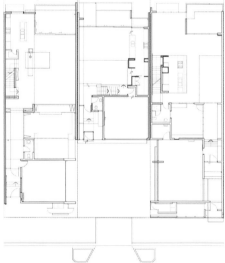

Catalina

Catalina is a town house that lies on the spectacular Teneriffe reach of the Brisbane River. The house aims to create a unique environment that addresses both the stunning river aspect and the significant urban context of Macquarie Street. The modern interior, promotes an easy living atmosphere by using simple forms and functions. The natural materials and neutral colour palette is used to enhance these elements. The large stacking glass doors and the seamless threshold at the internal/external junction, allows for fantastic indoor/outdoor living and maximises exposure to the views and river. Screening and restricted window openings were used to create a balance between sun access and street surveillance to the street side.

©2010 by Design Media Publishing Limited
This edition published in December 2010

Design Media Publishing Limited
20/F Manulife Tower
169 Electric Rd, North Point
Hong Kong
Tel: 00852-28672587
Fax: 00852-25050411
E-mail: Kevinchoy@designmediahk.com
www.designmediahk.com

Editing/Design/Layout: WU Yang
Proofreading: Maggie Wang

ISBN 978-988-19508-0-2

Printed in China